Principles and Parameters
in a VSO Language

Recent Titles in
OXFORD STUDIES IN COMPARATIVE SYNTAX
Richard Kayne, General Editor

Principles and Parameters in a VSO Language

A Case Study in Welsh

Ian G. Roberts

OXFORD

UNIVERSITY PRESS

2005

OXFORD

UNIVERSITY PRESS

Oxford   New York

Auckland   Bangkok   Buenos Aires   Cape Town   Chennai
Dar es Salaam   Delhi   Hong Kong   Istanbul   Karachi   Kolkata
Kuala Lumpur   Madrid   Melbourne   Mexico City   Mumbai   Nairobi
São Paulo   Shanghai   Taipei   Tokyo   Toronto

Published by Oxford University Press, Inc.
198 Madison Avenue, New York, New York 10016

www.oup.com

Oxford is a registered trademark of Oxford University Press

Library of Congress Cataloging-in-Publication Data
Roberts, Ian G.
Principles and parameters in a VSO language : a case study in Welsh /
Ian G. Roberts
p. cm. — (Oxford studies in comparative syntax)
Includes bibliographical references and index.
ISBN 0-19-516821-6; 0-19-516822-4 (pbk.)
1. Welsh language—Syntax. 2. Welsh language—Grammar, Generative.
I. Title. II. Series.
PB2171.R63 2004
491.6'65—dc21   2003047109

2 4 6 8 9 7 5 3 1

Printed in the United States of America
on acid-free paper

Preface

This book, like a much more groundbreaking work on Welsh, has a history. I began it in February 1996, while still at the University of Wales, Bangor. Later that year I put it aside for a temporary pause, which eventually lasted three years. I took it up again on my arrival for a sabbatical semester at the University of Siena in October 1999. Most of 2000 was taken up by a further pause, and this book was completed only after another move, this time to Cambridge in the autumn of 2000. I would like to thank the University of Wales, Bangor, and the University of Stuttgart for providing me with sabbatical leave in Spring 1996 and Winter 1999–2000, respectively, and I would like to thank the University of Siena for providing me with academic hospitality in 1999–2000.

My thanks are due to many people. My former colleagues at Bangor, particularly Bob Borsley and Anna Roussou for the initial stimulus to write this book and many helpful and insightful comments and criticisms over the years; Luigi Rizzi and Adriana Belletti for all kinds of hospitality in Siena; audiences in numerous places who have heard parts of this material, particularly the ongoing Welsh Syntax Seminar series, now held annually at the beautiful Plas Gregynog, and Cecilia Poletto and Paola Benincà at the University of Padua; my long-suffering informants Susan Clack, Mari-Eluned Williams, Emyr Davies, Bob Morris-Jones, Mair Parry, and Mari Jones (for Welsh) and Janig Stephens (for Breton); the students in my Hauptseminar on Celtic Syntax at the University of Stuttgart in Summer 1999; the members of the East Anglian Welsh Syntax Circle; three anonymous and very punctilious reviewers at Oxford University Press; and my wife, Lucia.

Last, I'd like to thank the wider community of Celtic linguists for living up to various positive ethnic stereotypes when it comes to the noble pastimes of drinking and telling tall tales. I hope that what follows is not too tall a tale for them to digest soberly.

Contents

Principles and Parameters
in a VSO Language

Introduction

The main empirical issue addressed in this book is the analysis of word order and clause structure in Welsh. Since I am assuming the theory of Principles and Parameters (P&P theory, henceforth), and since Welsh is a Verb-Subject-Object language, one central question is: which values of which parameters of Universal Grammar (UG) determine VSO order? Although I will concentrate on Welsh, I also draw data and inspiration from work on Irish by Acquaviva (1996), Carnie (1995), Carnie, Pyatt, and Harley (2000), Chung and McCloskey (1987), Cottell (1995), Doherty (1999, 2000), Duffield (1995, 1996), Guilfoyle (1990), McCloskey and Hale (1984), McCloskey (1979, 1990, 1991, 1992, 1996a, b, 2000, 2001), and Ó Siadhail (1989); work on Breton mainly by Borsley, Rivero, and Stephens (1996), Borsley and Stephens (1989), Schafer (1994), and Stephens (1982); and work on Scots Gaelic by Adger (1996, 2000). For Welsh, I rely on previous work by Awbery (1976), Borsley (1986, 1992, 1993, 1996, 1999), Borsley and R. Morris-Jones (2000), Borsley and Tallerman (1998), Clack (1993), Harlow (1989, 1992), Hendrick (1996), J. Morris-Jones (1913), R. Morris-Jones and Thomas (1977), Rouveret (1991, 1994, 1996), Sadler (1988), Sproat (1985), Tallerman (1996, 1998, 1999), Watkins (1991), and Willis (1996, 1997, 1998, 2000). Many of the essays in Carnie and Guilfoyle (2000) have also been useful sources.

Behind the basic descriptive goal of this book as given here, there lie two related theoretical questions. The first is that there are two general desiderata that we can impose on any parameter P that we introduce in order to account for a cross-linguistically variant phenomenon: P must be both *typologizable* and *learnable*.

A parameter is typologizable if it either yields new patterns of cross-linguistic variation or accounts for observed patterns of variation. A parameter is learnable if we can clearly isolate a simple, accessible aspect of the data that can plausibly be seen as trigger experience for the values the parameter has; if, in the terminology of Clark and Roberts (1993), the parameter is expressed. So we want the "VSO parameter(s)" to be typologizable and learnable.[1] Clearly the learnability criterion corresponds to Chomsky's (1964) notion of explanatory adequacy. If we take explanatory adequacy to consist in relating different states of UG in terms of proposed parameter values (i.e., relating the final state to the initial state), then the typologizability criterion falls under this heading, too, as this is a matter of relating different final states of UG to one another in terms of parameter values.

A more specific technical issue runs through almost all of what follows: the question of the status of the Extended Projection Principle (EPP). This principle, which has always been slightly mysterious, has had three major interpretations since it was first proposed by Chomsky (1982). First, it was seen as a subject requirement, simply stating that, in addition to the requirement for the realization of complements in complement positions (as enforced by the Projection Principle of Chomsky 1981), all clauses have to have a subject position. As such, we might think that it is straightforwardly satisfied in VSO languages, with the usual questions regarding the analysis of null subjects and PRO. In these languages, the issue is simply what the respective positions of the verb and the subject are. Later, in Chomsky (1995), it was formulated as the requirement that a DP must occupy a specific position, corresponding to the canonical, obligatorily filled subject position of English (SpecIP or SpecAgrSP in the theories of the first half of the 1990s). Put this way, VSO languages might challenge the EPP, as we shall see. The third conception of the EPP was as a (parametrized) requirement that a functional head F have a filled Specifier (see Chomsky 2000, 2001). As such it applies not just in IP (where its effect is to create a subject position, as in the previous conception) but also in CP, giving rise to V2 (this was first proposed, to my knowledge, in Roberts 1993; see also Laenzlinger 1998, Haegeman 1996), and possibly also in vP, giving rise to object shift (see Chomsky 2000, 2001). I will consider the nature of the EPP, particularly in chapters 4 and 5, arriving at the view that it is a parametrized property of part of the C-system and part of the I-system, for reasons that seem to be connected to the defective feature makeup of various heads.

I begin by considering the possible analyses of VSO order (chapter 1). Once this is established, we see what the "VSO parameters" are, formulated in terms of Chomsky (1995) as strong and weak feature-values associated with certain functional heads. Here we see that the second conception of the EPP mentioned earlier (a requirement for a universal, fixed subject position) cannot be maintained (McCloskey 1996b arrives at the same conclusion on the basis of Irish data). Chapter 2 is an analysis of the Case-agreement system of Welsh as it applies to both subjects and objects. We see that the EPP at the Agr-level can be reduced to principles for check-ing/valuing Agr-features (at least in "strong-agreement" languages, like Welsh and the Romance languages). I also propose a system for Nominative Case-licensing and extend it to Accusative in a general analysis of the initial-consonant mutation

(ICM) system. Chapter 3 deals with the properties of phrases headed by "verbal nouns," which I analyze as a participial construction and compare fairly systematically with Romance participles. The result of chapters 2 and 3 is a fairly comprehensive analysis of the Welsh Case-agreement system, which also accounts for the generalized head-initial typology.

The specific result regarding the "VSO" property is that this derives from the fact that Welsh has subject clitics that trigger V-incorporation of an otherwise bare V-stem. In other words, Welsh combines properties of Northern Italian dialects (the subject clitics that function as agreement markers; see, among many others, Vanelli, Renzi, and Benincà 1986, Poletto 2000, Manzini and Savoia, forthcoming) with well-known properties of the Mainland Scandinavian languages (the lack of any verbal morphology that functions as agreement-marking; see Holmberg and Platzack 1995, Vikner 1994). This idea explains a host of word-order, agreement and cliticization facts—in short, many of the core syntactic features of the language. As I show in chapter 2, this idea is integrated into a general theory of subject positions, subject clitics, and verb-movement.

Chapter 4 takes up a separate but related question: the structure of the C-system in Welsh and elsewhere in Celtic, and its connection to the generalized EPP (i.e., the third variant mentioned earlier). I show how the EPP holds at the C-level in Welsh, Breton, and Old Irish, and integrate the analysis of this with a general analysis of Germanic V2, arriving at a more abstract and general account of "V2"-type phenomena in terms of the third version of the EPP described earlier. Chapter 5 tries to state the generalizations arrived at in chapter 4 regarding the C-level EPP and some of the generalizations about Agr-systems that arise in chapter 2 in terms of the system proposed in Chomsky (2001). The result is that EPP-features are obligatorily associated with heads that are in a clear sense (which remains to be formalized) defective in feature content. I also suggest a way of incorporating head-movement into Chomsky's system.

Before I go any further, a word about the Welsh data is in order. Most of the examples in what follows are secondhand, being taken from the works cited earlier. Attributions are made as appropriate. A number of examples were elicited from native speakers, and I thank Mari Jones, Mair Parry, Mari-Eluned Williams, Emyr Davies, and Susan Clack for their invaluable assistance in this. All the examples have been checked by native speakers, and my thanks are due to Mari Jones, Mair Parry, and Bob Morris-Jones for this. The term "Modern Welsh" can refer to one of at least four registers or varieties, to a first and very rough approximation. First, there is Biblical Welsh, a somewhat archaic variety that is not at all part of colloquial usage, although it is familiar to most educated Welsh speakers. Second, there is Literary Welsh; most of the secondhand examples taken from the authors named represent this variety. Third, there is Colloquial Welsh: examples from King (1993) are supposed to represent this variety and therefore diverge somewhat from some of the others (these examples also tend to have Northern regional features). Fourth, there are the myriad dialects, which are highly divergent both among themselves and in relation to the other varieties. The dialects have hardly been studied from a generative point of view, with the notable exception of Awbery (1990). The focus of this study, like most work on "Modern Welsh," is on the second of these varieties; when other varieties are referred to, this will be made clear (e.g., reference to King 1993 implies the third variety). It may well be that a number of the generalizations to follow do not hold of Colloquial Welsh or of the dialects; to what extent this is true is of course an empirical question, but unfortunately not one that can be addressed here.

The Analysis of VSO Languages

Although R. Morris-Jones and Thomas (1977) were the first to propose a verb-movement rule for Welsh, Emonds (1980) was the first to propose that VSO orders generally are derived by verb-movement (Emonds was not, however, directly concerned with Welsh). In general terms, Emonds's idea was that the existence of VSO orders is not incompatible with the postulation of an underlying VP constituent. As long as verb-movement rules exist (see chapter 5 for a technical discussion of this point in terms of the proposals in Chomsky 2001), such a rule can move the verb out of the VP and to the left over the subject. This gives a derived VSO order from an underlying SVO or SOV order.

In Welsh, we can very clearly see that something like this is going on in VSO clauses. There is a general possibility of using periphrastic tenses, up to the possibility of what we can think of as free "*do*-insertion." Free "*do*-insertion" is available in the future and preterit tenses, as illustrated in (1). (Rouveret [1994: 71–85] argues that *gwneud*, "do," and *bod*, "be," are in fact main verbs with a particular type of complement in examples like (1b); in chapter 3, I will adopt a variant of Rouveret's proposal, but this does not alter the fact that we can treat the general availability of "do" as a kind of free *do*-insertion, even if the 'do' in question has properties distinct from those of English "do"):[1]

(1)   a.   Fe/mi **welais** i Megan.
               PRT saw   I Megan
               'I saw Megan.'

    b.   Fe/mi **wnes** i weld Megan.
          PRT   did   I see Megan
          'I saw Megan.'

(The particle *fe* is more standard and more widely used in South Welsh, while *mi* is characteristically Northern. Use of the synthetic ["short"] verb form is neutral as to register, while the periphrastic form in [1b] is more colloquial.) It seems clear that the lexical verb *welais* in (1a) is in the same position as the auxiliary verb *wnes* in (1b). Both elements appear in between the clause-initial particle *mi* and the subject *i*. Moreover, except for the possibility of infixed pronouns in Literary Welsh (which I briefly discuss and analyze in 1.2.2), the *only* thing that can appear in between the particle and the subject is a finite verb or auxiliary. It seems natural to think that this position is the position for the finite element of the clause, especially given the general possibility of periphrastic tenses (see note 1). If the verb is chosen as the finite element, it moves to that position; if an auxiliary is chosen, the main verb remains in VP (although see 3.2 for a refinement of the latter point). Example (1b) shows that the order of elements in the clause that follows the position for the finite element is SVO (and this is in line with the general head-initial typology of Welsh).[2]

Sproat (1985) gives a number of other arguments that lead to the same conclusion; in particular, he shows that non-finite verbs typically appear in SVO orders and that a non-finite verb can be fronted along with its complement, stranding the subject. The relevant facts are illustrated in (2a) and (2b), respectively:

(2)   a.   [Cyn i Siôn ladd draig], y mae rhaid iddo brynu llaeth i'r gath.
           before to John kill dragon, Prt is necessary to-him buy milk for-the cat
           'Before John kills a dragon, he has to buy milk for the cat.'
           (Sproat 1985: 205)

        b.   [Gadael y glwyd ar agor] a wnaeth y ffermwr.
           leave the gate   on open Prt did   the farmer
           'Leave the gate open, the farmer did.'
           (Rouveret 1994: 77)

I conclude with Sproat, and following the general consensus of work on Welsh (and the Celtic languages in general; see for example the introduction to Borsley and Roberts 1996), that VSO clauses involve an operation that moves the verb out of VP to the left over the subject.

The preceding considerations are straightforward and easy to motivate. However, I have not explicitly said (a) what the position that V moves to is, (b) what the position of the subject is, or (c) why either element occupies the position it does. In a theory that posits the existence of one or more functional categories above VP, a range of different options are available in this connection. Assuming a right-branching structure (presumably as a universal; see Kayne 1994), the one thing we have to ensure is that the finite verb occupies a position higher than and

In the remainder of this chapter, I consider a range of possible analyses of VSO clauses. First, in terms of the EPP of Chomsky (1982) (the subject requirement), I will show that the subject leaves VP (1.1). Second, I will show that the EPP-preserving analysis of VSO—placing the subject in SpecIP and the verb in C—cannot work (1.2). This means that we have to accept an intermediate possibility that involves a more elaborate functional structure than just CP containing IP containing VP. The full analysis of VSO clauses will be given in 2.1.

1.1   The Subject Leaves VP

On the basis of the preceding considerations, it should be clear what the simplest analysis of VSO would be. We have seen that V raises to a VP-external position and that this position is associated with finiteness. It seems very natural to identify this position as Tense. Hence we could posit that (a) Tense (T) has a strong V-feature and (b) T has a weak D-feature. In terms of the system in Chomsky (1995, chapters 3 and 4), this feature specification would give rise to a T that attracts V while at the same time preventing the subject DP from moving into its Specifier, thus giving rise to VSO order. Proposal (b) entails that the Extended Projection Principle (EPP) as formulated in Chomsky (1995, chapter 4) can be parametrized.[3] Given that Chomsky proposes that it is just the categorial features of functional heads that are subject to parametrization, this seems like a good result (see Chomsky 1995: 284). In fact, Chomsky assumes essentially this analysis for VSO clauses in Irish (see Chomsky 1995: 374–375). Moreover, McCloskey (1996b) argues on independent grounds that the EPP does not hold in Irish. These proposals yield a derived structure like the following for (1a) at Spell Out (glossing over the matter of the position of the initial particle for now; see 1.2):

(3)

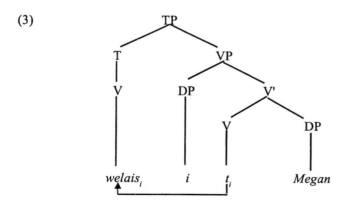

In addition to it being adopted in Chomsky (1993, 1995), Koopmann and Sportiche (1991) also consider this as a possibility. The approach is appealing from a cross-linguistic perspective in that it means that we can set up a typology of properties of T along the following lines (see also Chomsky 1993; Carnie 1995; Bobaljik and Carnie 1996):

(4)   A possible parametrization of T's features:
        Strong D, Strong V: French, an SVO language with V-to-T movement
                (Pollock 1989)
        Strong D, weak V: English, an SVO language without V-movement
        Weak D, strong V: Celtic
        Weak D, weak V: German (Haider 1997)

There are, however, a number of arguments against an analysis of the type in (3). Most of these are quite well known by now, but I go through them here to show the strength of the case against this analysis.

The first argument has to do with adjacency effects. McCloskey (1991) shows that V must be adjacent to the subject in VSO clauses in Irish:

(5)   *Dúirt sí go dtabharfadh amárach a   mac turas orm.
         said she that would-give tomorrow her son visit on-me
                V   X   S

The same observation holds for Welsh:

(6)   *Mi welith yfory   Emrys ddraig.
         PRT will-see tomorrow Emrys dragon
              V   X   S

It is widely assumed that the space between T and VP contains positions in which adverbs of various kinds can appear (see Cinque 1999 for a very detailed set of hypotheses in this connection).[4] If so, then we expect such adverbs to intervene between the raised verb and the subject if the structure of a VSO clause is (3). The fact that these orders are impossible indicates that (3) is not the correct analysis of VSO clauses.

The second argument was noticed by Koopman and Sportiche (1991) and by Rouveret (1991). In a way it's the inverse of the first argument. In modern spoken Welsh, the form of negation seems to be similar to French *ne . . . pas*, in that there are two elements, one a preverbal clitic-like element and the other a postverbal adverb-like element.[5] The relevant observation in this context is that the second element of negation follows the subject:[6]

(7)   a.   Cheisiodd Gwyn **ddim** ateb y cwestiwn bob tro.
               tried   Gwyn neg answer the question each turn
               'Gwyn didn't try to answer the question every time.

        b.   Dydy Gwyn **ddim** wedi mynd i Aberystwyth bob tro.
               is   Gwyn neg after go   to Aberystwyth each turn

'Gwyn hasn't always gone to Aberystwyth.'
(Borsley and R. Morris-Jones 2000: 27)

If we assimilate *(d)dim* to French *pas* (see notes 5 and 6), then we take it to occupy a VP-external position lower than T and higher than the position in which the subject is merged. In that case, the order *subject—ddim—VP* in (7) shows us that the subject is not in its merged (VP-internal, or vP-internal) position. Concretely, let us follow Pollock (1989) in assuming that the *pas*-type negative is in SpecNegP and that NegP intervenes between TP and VP. This situation is illustrated both for Welsh and for the comparable French sentence in (8):

(8)   *(Ni)   ddarllenodd Emrys* . . .
        Jean   ne   lut . . .

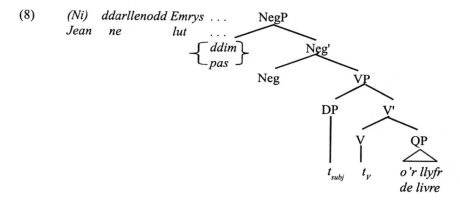

We must conclude that the subject raises from VP.

Not all the Celtic languages are like Welsh as regards the relative order of the subject and the second part of negation. The Goidelic languages just have preverbal negation (Irish *ní* [present], *níor* [past]; Scots Gaelic and Ulster Irish *cha*). However, McCloskey (1996a) shows that certain adverbs, which it is plausible to think of as attached to VP (or vP), intervene between the subject and the object in Irish VSO clauses and cannot intervene between the verb and the subject:

(9)   Níor   shaotaigh **Eoghan ariamh** pingin.
             Neg-Past earned   Owen   ever   penny
             'Owen has never earned a penny.'

This example indicates that the subject leaves VP in Irish.

Breton has a "double negation" *ne* . . . *ket*. Here, unlike Welsh, the order is *verb—ket—subject—object*, as (10) illustrates (as [10] also illustrates, the preverbal particle may delete; cf. Stephens 1982: 67):[7, 8]

(10)   (Ne) lenn **ket ar vugale** levrioù.
         Neg read   neg the children books
         'The children don't read books.'

This observation raises an interesting comparative question, which I will not explore here. For our concerns, (10) can be taken as indirect confirmation of the claim that the subject raises in Welsh. It may be that the subject remains in a VP- (or vP-) internal position in Breton (but see note 16 and later for some indications that this is not so, despite initial appearances); the comparative evidence then clearly indicates that it does not do so in Welsh.[9]

At least one dialect of Welsh appears to behave partly like Breton; this is the Pembrokeshire dialect discussed by Awbery (1990) and Rouveret (1994). In this dialect, *(d)dim* is the principal clausal negator; *ni(d)* does not appear overtly (although the initial consonant of the verb is mutated, suggesting that it is syntactically present but deleted in the phonology; see 2.3). On the one hand, pronominal subjects must precede *(d)dim*:

(11)   Chwrddes i ddim ag e.
            met   I neg with him
            'I didn't meet him.'
            (cited in Rouveret 1994: 137)

On the other hand, definite nominal subjects are able, but not required, to follow *(d)dim*:

(12)   a.   Ath **'y nhad ddim** i mâs   i ddrychid.
            went my father neg   to outside to look
            'My father didn't go outside to look.'

       b.   A   fywodd **ddim 'r 'en grwban bach**.
            and   lived   neg the old tortoise little
            'And the little old tortoise did not survive.'
            (Rouveret 1994: 137)

In an example like (12b) it appears that the subject is able to remain in a "low," possibly VP-internal, position (unless *'r 'en grwban bach* has undergone Heavy NP-Shift, a possibility pointed out by Mair Parry p.c.). I have nothing to say about the existence of variation in the position of the subject in this dialect but conclude that the (definite) subject raises from such a "low" position in other varieties of Welsh.[10]

The third argument is due to McCloskey (1996a), who makes the argument for Irish, although it carries over to Welsh. McCloskey points out that the standard A-dependencies (passive, unaccusative, and raising) are all found in Irish. These are illustrated in (13):[11]

(13)   a.   Tá sé críochnaithe againn.   (passive)
            is it finished   by-us
            'That has been finished by us.'

> b.   Neartaigh a ghlór.   (unaccusative)
>   strengthened his voice
>   'His voice strengthened.'

> c.   Ó   ráinís   tigh a cheannach ar an maile so. (raising)
>   since you-happened house to buy in the town this
>   'Since you happened to have bought a house in this village.'

Such constructions are also found in Welsh:[12]

(14)   a.   Cafodd y dyn ei ladd.   (passive)
>   got   the man his killing
>   'The man was killed.'

> b.   Diflanodd y dyn.   (unaccusative)
>   disappeared the man
>   'The man disappeared.'

> c.   Mae Gwyn yn siwr o   fod yma.   (raising)
>   is   Gwyn in sure from be here
>   'Gwyn is sure to be here.'

While there is no doubt about the existence of passive and raising verbs in Welsh, no reliable diagnostics for unaccusatives exist in the literature (although cf. Tallerman 2001 for some relevant considerations). One likely argument is based on the behavior of deverbal adjectives in *-edig*. Although they are rather unproductive, such adjectives, like adjectival passive participles in English, have the property that the nominal they modify must be an internal argument, giving the following contrast:

(15)   a.   llyfr printiedig
>   book printed
>   'a printed book'

> b.   dyn printiedig
>   man printed
>   'a printed man' (impossible in the interpretation of
>   'man who has printed something')

Unergative intransitives therefore cannot form such adjectives, while putative unaccusatives (intransitives whose single argument undergoes a change of state) can, at least marginally:

(16)   a.   *dyn canedig   (unergative)
>   man sung
>   'a sung man'

b.   ?dyn diflanedig   (simple unaccusative)
      man disappeared
      'a disappeared man'

Thus, in an example like (14b), *y dyn* appears to act as the internal argument of the verb and is therefore a good candidate for an underlying object that has raised to subject position (thanks to Mari Jones and David Willis for help with and useful discussion of these data). We can tell *y dyn* is in subject position here by making the tense compound. In that case the subject appears between the auxiliary and the verbal noun, while the object position follows the verbal noun:

(17)   a.   Mae'r dyn wedi diflanu.
             is-the man Asp disappear
             'The man has disappeared.'

       b.   *Mae wedi diflanu'r   dyn.
             is   Asp disappear-the man

I conclude that in (14b) and (17a) the single argument of *diflanu*, "disappear," has raised from the underlying object position to the surface subject position.

On minimalist assumptions, A-movement, like all movement, must be driven exclusively by the need to check (or value; see Chomsky 2001) features. Features are assumed to be checked as a result of movement to the Specifier of a functional head. It follows from these assumptions that movement to Spec,VP—a position in the checking domain of a lexical head, but not a functional one—is impossible; lexical heads do not offer the possibility of feature-checking. (Hornstein 1999 proposes that lexical heads check θ-features and that correspondingly movement to their Specifiers is allowed. He claims that such movement to θ-positions gives rise to control relations, as such it is not relevant here; see also Manzini and Roussou 2000). Now, if the subject position were VP-internal, A-dependencies would precisely involve movement to Spec,VP. Hence the derived subjects of raising, passive, and unaccusative verbs cannot be in Spec,VP. If we can show that these subjects are no different in their position in their clauses from other subjects, then we have an argument that subjects in general are not VP-internal.

We can use the considerations raised earlier to show that the derived subjects in (14) are not in a position different from that occupied by other subjects. Example (18) shows that these subjects, like others, must be adjacent to the finite verb/auxiliary; compare (6):[13]

(18)   a.   *Cafodd ddoe   y dyn ei ladd.   (passive)
             got   yesterday the man his kill

       b.   *Diflanodd ddoe   y dyn.   (unaccusative)
             disappeared yesterday the man

c.　　　*Mae yfory　　Gwyn yn siwr o　fod yma.　(raising)
　　　　is　　tomorrow Gwyn in　sure from be　here

Example (19) shows that these subjects precede *(d)dim* in negatives; compare (7):

(19)　a.　　　Chafodd y　dyn　ddim o'i　　ladd.　　　(passive)
　　　　　　got　　the man neg　of-his killing
　　　　　　'The man wasn't killed.'

　　　b.　　　Ddiflawnodd y　dyn　ddim.　　　　　(unaccusative)
　　　　　　disappeared　the man neg
　　　　　　'The man didn't disappear.'

　　　c.　　　Dydy Gwyn ddim yn siwr o　　fod yma.　(raising)
　　　　　　is　　Gwyn　neg　in sure from be　here
　　　　　　'Gwyn isn't sure to be here.'

There is thus no difference between the position occupied by the derived subjects of A-dependencies and the position occupied by other subjects. I conclude that derived subjects raise to the Specifier of a functional head and therefore not to Spec,VP, and that other subjects, since they do not appear to occupy a different position from clearly derived subjects, also raise to the specifier of a functional head.

　　　The preceding argument may be able to shed some light on the situation in Breton. We have seen that subjects follow the second element of negation *ket*—see (10)—and I suggested that perhaps subjects do not in fact raise from their merged position in this language. Of course, the order *ket—subject* does not, without further assumptions about the position of NegP, tell us that the subject has not moved at all. It simply shows that one indication of movement in Welsh is not found in Breton. In the light of the argument just made, however, we can see that if subjects are not raised in Breton, then we expect that either A-dependencies will not be found or the derived subjects of A-dependencies will be in different positions from other subjects. If neither of these expectations is fulfilled, and in particular if derived subjects of A-dependencies follow *ket*, then we must conclude that *ket* occupies a relatively "high" position in Breton—arguably higher than *(d)dim* does in Welsh and in any case higher than the position given for *(d)dim* and *pas* in (8).

　　　The basic observation is that Breton has at least one kind of A-dependency, namely passive, as illustrated in (20a). While there are, naturally enough, predicates in Breton that are plausibly thought of as unaccusatives on semantic grounds, I am unaware of any clear syntactic tests for unaccusativity in Breton, and so I will leave these aside. Moreover, it is unclear whether Breton has raising; the equivalent to "seem" is a nominal *seblan*, from whose complement raising unsurprisingly does not take place. I will thus confine my attention to passives; it is sufficient for this argument for an A-dependency to be found in just this construction. How ever, it is not immediately obvious that raising takes place here, as the subject must follow the participle (unless it is fronted into the C-system; see 4.2 and later):

(20) a.   Gwechall e oa   savet ar mogeriou gant ar vasonnerein.
            past   Prt was built the walls   by the stonemasons
            'In the old days, the walls were built by the stonemasons.'

      b.   *Gwechall e oa   ar mogeriou savet gant ar vasonnerein.
            past   Prt was the walls   built by   the stonemasons

There is, however, a possible test for subjecthood. Breton has a construction similar to the Middle and Biblical Welsh "abnormal construction" (see 4.2). In particular, in negative clauses the fronted subject agrees with the verb, breaking the usual anti-agreement pattern (on which see 2.1), as shown in (21a, b). The important point for our purposes here is that in passives the logical object triggers this agreement, implying that it is, or systemically related to, a derived subject:

(21) a.   Ar vugale a lenn   levriou.
            the children Prt read-3sg books
            'The children read books.'

      b.   Ar vugale na lennont ket levriou.
            the children Neg read-3Pl Neg books
            'The children do not read books.'

      c.   Ar mogeriou ne   oant ket savet gant ar vasonnerien gwechall.
            the walls   Neg were Neg built by   the stonemasons past
            'The walls were not built by the stonemasons in the old days.'

The paradigm in (21) establishes that *ar mogeriou* is, or is related to, a derived subject. However, its pre-particle position indicates clearly that it is in the C-system (see 4.2, for details on the Breton particle system). Most analyses of the Welsh abnormal sentence treat the pre-particle subject as linked to an empty category in the canonical subject position (usually *pro*, as in Tallerman 1996, although Willis 1998 treats the dependency as movement; see note 15 of chapter 2). Of course, we cannot tell where that position is in relation to either *ket* or the participle *savet* in (21c), and so in that sense the paradigm in (21) is inconclusive. However, if we assume that there is only one position in the clause in which a DP can agree in Breton and that that position is VP-external (both of these points will be argued for Welsh in 2.1), then we would have an argument that the empty category that corresponds to the logical object in (21c) raises to subject position, and similarly in (21b). The alternative is to assume that Breton entirely lacks A-dependencies and that the pre-particle DP in (21b, c) forms a dependency with the direct-object position, a position in which an empty category is quite exceptionally allowed to agree with the inflected verb/auxiliary.

I thus conclude that the basic difference between Breton and Welsh that is illustrated by the contrast between (7) and (10) has to do with the position of the second element of negation rather than with the fact that the subject leaves VP in one language and not the other (this does not entail that the subject is in the same position in both languages, however; there could be two differences between the languages).

A fourth argument that the subject leaves VP can be derived from Huang's (1993) work on VP-fronting and reconstruction. Huang analyzes the differences in interpretation of anaphors in fronted predicates as compared to fronted arguments that were first observed by Barss (1986), for example:

(22)   a. [Which pictures of himself] does John think that Bill would like — ?
        b. [Criticize himself], John thinks Bill never would — .

Barss's observation is that the anaphor in (22a) can be interpreted such that either *John* or *Bill* is its antecedent, while in (22b) only *Bill* can be interpreted as its antecedent. Barss proposes a mechanism that allows the complex Wh-phrase in (22a) to be "reconstructed" either into the binding domain of *John* or into the binding domain of *Bill*. Why is reconstruction into the binding domain of *John* not available for the fronted VP in (22b)? Huang's answer to this question is that the antecedent of *himself* is the VP-internal trace contained in the fronted VP. The trace must be the trace of the local subject *Bill*. In other words, the full representation of (22b), including traces and coindexing relations, is as in (23):[14]

(23) $[_{VP}$ t_i criticize himself$_i$ $]$, John thinks Bill$_i$ never would — .

Reconstruction of the fronted VP (by whatever mechanism) makes no difference to the interpretation of the anaphor since it is already contained in the binding domain of the trace, and therefore must take the antecedent of the trace as its antecedent.

It should be clear that Huang's argument depends on (a) the VP-internal subject hypothesis and (b) the idea that the subject raises from VP. Because of this, we can use sentences like (22) as a diagnostic for whether the subject is raised from VP in Welsh. As we saw in (2b), what appears to be VP-fronting stranding the subject is available in Welsh. Now, in the case where these fronted constituents contain anaphors, if the interpretative judgments are the same as for English, then this implies that there is a subject trace inside the fronted constituent, and hence that the subject has raised. If not, then we have to treat the fronting operation as fronting of a category smaller than the category containing the merged position of the subject. The relevant data are as follows:

(24)   a. [Pa luniau ohon'i hun$_{i/j}$] y mae John$_j$ yn credu y mae Bill$_i$ yn eu hoffi —?
        which pictures of-his self Prt is John Prt believe Prt is Bill Prt its like —
        'Which pictures of himself does John believe Bill likes?'

    b. [Siarad â'r hun$_{v*j}$], y   mae John$_j$ yn meddwl bod   Bill$_i$ —.
       speak with-his self, Prt is   John Prt think   that-is Bill
       'Talk to himself, John thinks Bill does.'

The judgments exactly parallel English, as described by Barss and Huang. Wh-movement of an argument category that contains an anaphor, as in (24a), allows either *John* or *Bill* to be interpreted as the antecedent. However, Wh-movement of a predicative category, as in (24b, c), only allows the lower potential antecedent—*Bill*—to be the actual antecedent. We can account for these facts exactly as Huang does, with the consequence that we must assume that the subject leaves the VP in these cases. We thus have a further argument that the subject leaves VP in Welsh.[15]

    Finally, let us briefly consider an argument that subjects leave VP that has been made on the basis of data from Northern dialects of Irish (the construction is also found in Scots Gaelic; see Adger 1996). The argument, first made by Bobaljik and Carnie (1996) (see also Carnie 1995), is based on the existence of SOV order in infinitival clauses in these varieties, as in:[16]

(25)   Ba mhaith liom   [(é)   an teach   a   thógáil].
       is good   with-me (him) a   house-ACC Prt build
       'I would like him to build the house.'

In Southern dialects, the direct object is Genitive and the order is SVO:

(26)   Ba mhaith liom   [(é)   a thógáil an tí].
       is   good with-me (him) to build   Prt house-GEN
       'I would like him to build the house.'

Bobaljik and Carnie propose that the Accusative form of the object is found when the object moves to SpecAgrOP. Therefore, the subject must have raised out of VP, because it precedes the object. The lowest available position for the subject is SpecTP. Therefore, V is higher than T. They conclude that V is in AgrS.[17]

    In conclusion, we have seen several reasons to reject an analysis of the kind given in (3). All our arguments point in the same direction: the subject is raised from its base position in Welsh (and we have seen evidence that the same can be maintained for Irish and Breton). We now know that the subject is in the specifier of a functional category, and we can be sure that the verb is in a functional head position higher than the subject. Moreover, the adjacency evidence proposed by McCloskey (1991), illustrated in (5) and (6), suggests that the subject is in the Specifier position of the functional category that is immediately subjacent to the one whose head V moves to (and that further adjunction to this category is impossible). Schematically, the situation must be as follows:

(27)

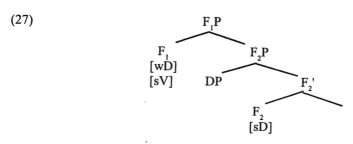

Here I have indicated—following the system of Chomsky (1995)—what the relevant weak and strong feature-values associated with F1 and F2 must be. In the next section we will consider various hypotheses as to the categorial values of F1 and F2, keeping in mind the question of the status of the EPP in relation to these categories.

1.2   Against Generalized V-to-C

The first hypothesis to consider is:

(28) $F_1 = C; F_2 = I.$

For the time being, I remain agnostic as to the precise identity of I. We could assume, following Chomsky (1995, 4.10) that there is no AgrSP (or at least that there is no AgrSP in Welsh), and so I would be T. Alternatively, I could correspond to AgrS (or to a split AgrS, as I will propose in chapter 2). The relevant point for what follows is that an analysis like (28) has V raising into the C-system (which I will also split into its component functional categories later) with the subject in the highest Specifier position in IP. If such an analysis can be maintained, then of course we can maintain that Welsh (and presumably Celtic more generally) satisfies the EPP in the sense of requiring a clausal subject, that is that SpecIP be filled.

The idea that V raises to C in Irish was proposed by Déprez and Hale (1986), Hale (1989), Stowell (1989), and Doherty (1996). However, there are three principal reasons to reject this idea for Welsh (two of which may carry over to Irish). The first concerns the lack of root-embedded asymmetries in verb-movement, as compared with the well-known situation in the Germanic languages. The second concerns the nature of the elements that can be found in the left periphery of the clause in Welsh (and in Irish). The third concerns the pecularities of the auxiliary *bod*, "be," and the distribution of certain tensed-verb forms in Welsh. I will now deal with each of these points in turn.

1.2.1   Root-embedded Asymmetries and Movement to C

If we propose that VSO involves V in C (cf. [28]), then we assimilate V-movement in Welsh VSO clauses to the verb-movement found in Germanic verb-second, whether full (as in German and the other Germanic languages aside from English; cf. den Besten 1983, Vikner 1994) or residual (as in English and French; cf. Rizzi 1996). These cases of verb-movement are illustrated in (29):[18]

(29) a.   Morgen/ wann werden sie   dieses Buch lesen?(German)
             tomorrow/when will   they this   book read (?)
             'Tomorrow they will read this book/When will they read this book?'

      b.   When will they read this book?

      c.   Quand liront-ils   ce livre?   (French)
             when will-read-they this book?
             'When will they read this book?'

The first difficulty arises when we observe that this movement is largely restricted to root clauses in the languages just mentioned. This can be seen particularly clearly in indirect questions:[19, 20]

(30) a.   *Ich frage mich, ob morgen   wird Maria dieses Buch lesen.
             I   ask   me   if tomorrow will Maria this   book read

      b.   *I wonder if will she read the book.

      c.   *Je me demande si lira-t-elle   le   livre.
             I me ask   if will-read-she the book

The simplest account of this restriction of movement to C was proposed by den Besten (1983). He proposed that the presence of material in C blocks head-movement to C ([+WH]. Cs have to be regarded as filled in cases like *I wonder who left*). Other accounts have been proposed by Kayne (1982), Rizzi and Roberts (1989), and Rizzi (1996), which I will not discuss in detail here. The important point for my purposes here is that the root-embedded asymmetry is held to be a major hallmark of verb-movement to C. In the next section I will offer a characterization of the root-embedded asymmetry in terms of Rizzi's (1997) "split-C" system.

The important observation is that VSO orders in Celtic are not restricted to root clauses (as noted by Guilfoyle 1990, McCloskey 1996b, Bobaljik and Carnie 1996):

(31) a.   Tybed   a geith hi ddiwrnod rhydd wythnos nesa? (Welsh)
             I-wonder Prt will-get she day free   week   next
             'I wonder if she'll get a free day next week.'

      b.   Goulenn a reas   hag-en oac'h   eveurus.   (Breton)
             asked   Prt did-3sg whether were-2sg happy
             'He asked whether you were happy.'

c.   Chuir sé ceist   ort   an raibh tú   sásta.   (Irish)
Asked he question to-you Prt were you content
'He asked whether you were content.'

Here the particles *a* (in [31a]), *hag-en* (in [31b]) and *an* (in [31c]) function in
a fashion precisely parallel to that of *ob*, *if*, and *si* in (30) in that they mark the embedded finite clause as an embedded question. I take it as uncontroversial that the
embedded clauses in (30) are CPs, that the head of the clause, C, is responsible for
marking clause-type (declarative, interrogative, etc.; more on this in chapter 4) and
that in (30), therefore, the particles *ob*, *if*, and *si* are in C (note that all the languages
in (30) are uncontroversially head-initial, at least at the CP level). If we apply this
reasoning to (31), we can observe that the finite embedded clauses are plausibly
regarded as CPs (there appears to be no reason not to so regard them, and in any
case, if it could be shown that they were not CPs then the basic point of this
section, that V does not raise to C in VSO clauses, would be supported since the
embedded clauses are clearly VSO here) and that the particles mark clause type. By
parity of reasoning with the standard analysis of German, English, and French,
therefore, and since the Celtic languages are clearly head-initial, these particles
can naturally be supposed to be in C. What the contrast between (30) and (31)
therefore shows is that C-elements do not block verb-movement over the subject
in Celtic, but they do in Germanic and in French.

In fact, as mentioned earlier, the only factor that conditions verb-movement in
Celtic seems to be finiteness (this will be slightly refined in 1.2.3, at least regarding
Welsh; on Breton "long" V-movement see 4.2). In this respect, verb-movement in
Celtic patterns like verb-movement in French (cf. Pollock 1989; this parallel was
first made by McCloskey 1996b). Thus, in order to maintain that V moves to C in
Celtic, we would have to stipulate that complementizers do not block V-movement
in these languages but do in Germanic and French and that the finiteness property
that triggers V-movement in French is associated with C in Celtic. Clearly it is much
simpler and more natural to conclude that V moves to I in (31) rather than to C.

The argument just given is suggestive, not conclusive. To make it more precise,
we could say something like the following: (i) in many languages embedded C is
not a position into which V can move; (ii) in many languages finiteness conditions
V-movement to I but not to C. Then we observe that V-movement in Celtic is not
sensitive to the root-embedded asymmetry but is sensitive to finiteness and, given
(i) and (ii), conclude that V moves to I but not to C in these languages. However,
this conclusion depends on the general cross-linguistic validity and theoretical
underpinnings of (i) and (ii). As we shall see in 2.3, there is good evidence that
some tense-marking is a property of the C-system in Celtic; however, the tense-
marking in question is restricted in various ways that suggest that (main) verbs do
not in fact move to C. Point (i) depends on assumptions about the C-system that
we now investigate in more depth.

Old Irish and Scots Gaelic are of some interest in our context here, since it
seems that in these languages V-movement to C is morphologically marked.
However, the root-embedded asymmetry persists, which implies that the inability

of embedded C to host incorporation is due to the presence of embedded complementizers, along the lines of den Besten's original insight.

Carnie, Pyatt, and Harley (2000) argue that Old Irish has a "filled-C" requirement, although it is not verb second (see also Doherty 1999, 2000; Doherty in fact argues that Old Irish is a residual V2 language). Old Irish, then, may be a genuine case of a language with just one part of the verb-second constraint, the part that relates to C (Ferraresi 1997 and Longobardi 1994 argue that Gothic also has a "filled-C" requirement, but only in embedded clauses). The element in C is therefore in absolute first position. Various kinds of material can satisfy this constraint in a root clause: "conjunct particles" (negation, question markers, complementizers), preverbs and the verb itself (we will discuss and analyze these data in more detail in 4.2). Most interestingly, when the verb itself occupies C, it takes on a specific morphological form, traditionally known as the independent form (the non-initial form is known as the dependent form). This alternation is illustrated in (32):

(32) a.   Beirid   in fer   in claideb.
             carries (independent) the man the sword

      b.   Ní beir/   *beirid   in fer in claideb
             Neg carries (dependent)/*(independent) the man the sword
             (Carnie, Pyatt, and Harley 2000: 45)

As Carnie, Pyatt, and Harley suggest, the alternation in form can be interpreted as a morphological reflex of the features that attract the verb to C.[21]

Scots Gaelic retains the Old Irish distinction between independent and dependent verb forms. The distinction remains productive in the future tense, where we observe examples like the following:

(33) a.   òlaidh mi   — independent present/future tense
             drink I

      b.   òl mi   — dependent present/future tense
             drink I
             (Calder 1990: 223)

The dependent forms occur when there is a particle in C (e.g., *gun*, "that"; see chapter 4 for more discussion of the C-particles in Celtic). The independent forms appear when there is no particle (see Calder 1990: 202f.).

Modern Irish retains the distinction with a handful of verbs. The dependent forms are found after a C-particle (except for the leniting particle *aL*; see McCloskey 2001); the independent forms are found after *aL* and in absolute initial position:

(34) a.   Creidim go bhfaca mé do nighean.
             I-believe that saw-dep I your daughter
             'I believe that I saw your daughter.'

b.   an bean a chonaic tú
        the woman aL saw-indep you
        'the woman that saw you'

c.   Chonaic tú í.
        saw-indep you her
        'You saw her.'

It is unlikely that these forms are synchronically associated with V-movement to C; I am aware of no independent evidence for this, and Doherty (2000: 28–31) argues that the correlation between independent morphology and initial position (i.e., C) was weakening as early as Classical Old Irish (ninth century A.D.).

In this section, we have seen the evidence that there is no root-embedded asymmetry in verb-movement in the Celtic languages. This suggests that without further refinements regarding the nature of complementizer systems (see next section), we should conclude that V does not raise to C in these languages. However, the argument is not conclusive as it stands. In the next section, I first look at some other data and then return to the question of the root-embedded asymmetry. In the process, I adopt and adapt a much more articulated conception of the structure of complementizer systems, following Rizzi (1997).

1.2.2   Adverbs, Particles, and the Structure of Comp

The second problem for the idea that V moves to C comes from the position of adverbs. On the basis of the relative positions of sentential adverbs and complementizers, McCloskey (1996a) argues that C lowers to I in Irish. The argument is based on the observation that in general across languages sentential adverbs don't adjoin to CP:

(35)   a.   In general, he understands what's going on.
        b.   It's probable that in general he understands what's going on.
        c.   *It's probable [_CP in general [_CP that he understands what's going on]].
        d.   *[In general [that he understands what's going on]] is surprising.

In (35c, d) the bracketing is meant to indicate that the adverb should be interpreted as modifying the *that*-clause. These readings are impossible in English. McCloskey calls this general ban on the adjunction of adverbs to CP the Adjunction Prohibition.

Irish shows the opposite distribution of adverbs in relation to CPs:

(36)   a.   Is doíche [faoi cheann   cúpla lá [go bhféadfaí imeacht]].
                is probable at-the-end-of couple day that could   leave
                             Adv   C   I

        b.   *Chreid siad go roimh i bhfad rachadh   na cuairteoirí 'na bhaile.
                believed they that before long would-go the visitors home

McCloskey also shows that we cannot maintain that Irish simply lacks the Adjunction Prohibition (however exactly this idea might be formulated). The evidence against this idea is that the order *adverb—Wh-phrase* is bad:

(37)   *Ní bhfuair siad amach ariamh an bhliain sin cé a bhí ag goid a gcuid móna.

          Neg found they out   ever   the year   that who Prt was stealing their turf

McCloskey proposes (i) that sentential adverbs adjoin to IP in Irish just as in English (and other languages) and (ii) that Irish has a rule that lowers C to I. The C-to-I lowering rule derives orders like that in (36a) and, since it is obligatory, explains the ungrammaticality of (37). Schematically, the relevant parts of (36a) have the following structure:

(38)   t   [$_{IP}$ Adv   [$_{IP}$ C+I . . .

McCloskey's general conclusion is that the distribution of sentential adverbs in relation to complementizers is such that we cannot claim that V moves to the C position. Before going on to look at the situation in this respect in Welsh, I'd like to propose a way of handling McCloskey's data without having recourse to a C-to-I lowering operation. This in turn will lead to a suggestion regarding Germanic root-embedded asymmetries. McCloskey's conclusion is retained under the analysis to be proposed.

The basic idea is to capitalize on the overall similarity between the structure of McCloskey's argument and the structure of Pollock's (1989) arguments for V-to-I raising in French and I-to-V lowering in English. Pollock observed, inter alia, the following contrast between French and English:

(39)   a.   *French:*   V+Infl   Adv   direct object
                as in: Jean   embrasse souvent Marie   (=[39b])

          b.   *English:*   Adv   V+Infl   direct object
                as in: John   often   kisses   Mary

Pollock concluded that V raises to Infl in French but that Infl lowers to V in English.

The Irish-English contrast that we saw in (35) versus (36) can be handled in the same way. Here what we have is the following (note that this pattern only shows up clearly in embedded contexts):

(40)   a.   Irish: Adv   C   IP
          b.   English: C   Adv   IP

So the possibility emerges of saying that Irish complementizers do not move (overtly, at least) while English ones do. We can make this idea concrete if we adopt the recent proposals for a "split-Comp" system that have been developed by Rizzi (1997). Rizzi argues that at the left periphery of the clause, above IP, there are at least three separate projections: ForceP, FocusP, and FiniteP—in that order—interspersed with possibly recursive TopPs. The categories we are interested in here are Fin and Force: Fin marks the clause as finite or not (and, since non-finite clauses usually designate unrealized events, may really be a variety of MoodP; see Cinque 1999). Force is the position associated with clausal typing and illocutionary force.

Now, as Rizzi points out, complementizers like English *that* and Irish *go* mark two things: that the clause they introduce is declarative and that it is finite. In this respect, they are each associated with features of two heads, Force and Fin, just as a finite verb is associated with properties of V (thematic structure) and T (tense). So we might expect that cross-linguistically, some complementizers are overtly realized in Force and others in Fin. Looking again at (40), we can see that in these terms, *that* can be analyzed as appearing in Force and *go* as appearing in Fin. We can in fact conclude (with Rizzi (1997: 313), although Rizzi's implementation of the idea is somewhat different) that English Force overtly attracts Fin in embedded contexts (this will be slightly qualified later), while in Irish this is not the case. We need only add that sentential adverbs either appear in a TopP in between Force and Fin or occupy Specifier positions reserved for them (along the lines proposed in Cinque 1999), and we derive the different distributions of adverbs and complementizers without recourse to a lowering rule. The structure in (41) summarizes the proposal:

(41) $[_{\text{ForceP}} [_{\text{Force}}$ *that* $] \ldots [_{\text{TopP}}$ Adv $\ldots [_{\text{FinP}} [_{\text{Fin}}$ *go* $]$ IP $]]]$

Example (41) transparently encodes the fact that English shows the order *that—Adv—IP* (as in [35b]) and not *Adv—Adv—that—Adv–IP* (see [35c, d]), while Irish allows precisely the latter (see [36a]) and not the opposite (see [36b]). We are thus able to retain the essential point of McCloskey's analysis—that V does not raise to C in Irish—without recourse to an ad hoc and problematic lowering rule. The analytic devices that effectively replace C-to-I lowering in the analyses proposed here are the split-C structure and upward head-movement of *that*. The postulation of head-movement is quite uncontroversial (but see Chomsky 2001 and chapter 5); the former is motivated by Müller and Sternefeld (1993) and Rizzi (1997), as well as numerous subsequent studies. The proposals regarding the positions of Celtic complementizers are more fully motivated and integrated into the overall comparative picture later and in chapter 4. The fact that sentential adverbs cannot precede Wh-phrases in Irish, illustrated in (37), can be accounted for if we assume that Wh-phrases in Irish move to a Specifier position higher than TopP; Rizzi argues that Italian interrogative Wh-phrases occupy Spec,FocP (FocP is situated in between ForceP and TopP). In that case, we can account straightforwardly for (34).[22]

McCloskey argues that C-to-I lowering takes place at PF on the basis of the distribution of negative-polarity items (NPIs). Assuming standardly that NPIs must be c-commanded by a negative element that licenses them at S-structure, McCloskey points out that Irish NPIs can be fronted by a process known as Narrative Fronting to a position that does not appear to be c-commanded by a negative element (the elements in question must be NPIs, since Irish lacks negative quantifiers of all kinds; see Acquaviva 1996):

(42)   Neach ar bith dínn ní bheidh beo
        being any   of-us neg will-be alive
        'Not one of us will be alive.'

McCloskey reconciles this fact with the general condition on NPIs by assuming that the NPI is c-commanded by *ní* at S-structure, with lowering of *ní* in PF.

To fully deal with this point would take us quite far afield, into a detailed consideration of how NPIs are licensed. However, I would like to briefly sketch an alternative approach to these data. The requirement that NPIs be licensed by a c-commanding negation is motivated by data such as the following (see Ladusaw 1979, Laka 1990, Zanuttini 1991, and the references given there):

(43)   a.   He didn't speak to anybody.
        b.   *Anybody didn't speak to him.
        c.   Didn't anybody speak to him?

Example (43b) shows that NPIs in subject position are bad unless the negation is raised to C (reverting momentarily to a unitary-C approach). In English, NPIs are systematically bad in SpecCP, as McCloskey observes (his [109], p. 43):

(44)   a.   *Ever haven't I seen such a sight.
        b.   *Under any circumstances wouldn't I do that.

Suppose that the c-command condition derives from the fact that the Neg head must license NPIs. In English, the Neg head is found either in the position of the finite auxiliary where there is no inversion or in C—more precisely in Foc, according to Rizzi (1997). The subject cannot form a chain whose head is the Neg-element in the non-inverted auxiliary position but can if the Neg-element is in the Foc position. Features of a complement are c-commanded by the auxiliary position. In this way, the data in (43) and (44) can be accounted for.

But what of the Irish example in (42)? Here the crucial observation is that the Irish negative elements are part of the C-system. Suppose, then, that in line with my analysis of *go*, *ní* occupies Fin in (42) and raises covertly to Force. We must regard the condition on NPIs as an LF condition, since one of the tenets of minimalism is that independent S-structure well-formedness conditions do not exist. Hence at LF *ní* will be in a position that c-commands the fronted constituent. (I am assuming that the fronted negative constituent in [42] is in SpecFoc or SpecTop).[23] The essential difference between Irish and English lies (a) in the fact that Force does not overtly attract Fin in Irish as we see from apparent violations of the Adjunction Prohibition like (36a) and (b) in the fact that Fin is inherently able to contain negative material—that is, the simple observation that Irish has negative complementizers.[24] An important feature of this analysis is that the negative head in English cannot be supposed to raise into the C-system covertly[25] and when it does raise to Foc, as in the well-formed counterparts of (41), it does not raise further to Force.

More generally, the proposals just made for the difference between English and Irish complementizers point the way to an account of Germanic-style root-embedded asymmetries in verb-movement. Following Rizzi and Roberts (1989), I assume that the generalization has to do with selection. Let us suppose, then, that a selected Force position has features in virtue precisely of being selected by a higher predicate. The fact that typical complementizers like English *that* raise from Fin to Force must then be attributed to the fact that selected Force triggers overt Fin-movement (presumably because it requires PF-realization). Let us suppose that the verb-movement part of V2 is a reflex of the fact that Fin requires a PF-realization; following the notation introduced in Roberts (2001: 99–103), we indicate a functional feature F that requires a PF-realization as F*, so in this case we have Fin*.[26] In these terms, we can see that complementizers are able to satisfy this requirement in embedded clauses, even if they subsequently raise to Force. So all the Germanic languages, including English, have Fin-to-Force movement where Force is selected (i.e., in embedded clauses). This blocks V-movement to Fin in embedded clauses as a general case of Merge pre-empting Move; exploiting the presence of complementizers in C as a way of blocking V2 is an idea that goes back to den Besten (1983).

Consistent with the idea that all the Germanic V2 languages have Fin* and that this is a significant component of the V2 phenomenon, we can observe that all these languages differ from English in requiring the presence of a complementizer in finite embedded declaratives (with the notable exception of German; see later). German diverges somewhat from the general pattern in that it requires embedded V2 exactly where the complementizer is missing:

(45)   Ich glaube, **gestern   hat** Maria dieses Buch gelesen.
        I   believe yesterday has Maria this   book read
        'I believe Mary read this book yesterday.'

But of course this is consistent with the general proposal for Fin*.

A further refinement is required in order to account for the presence of *that* in "CP-recursion" contexts in English like (46) (and the comparable situation in the Scandinavian languages; see Vikner 1994):

(46)   a.   I said that never in my life had I seen a place like Bangor.

        b.   Vi ved   at   denne bog har Bo ikke læst.   (Danish)
              we know that this   book has Bo neg read
              'We know that Bo has not read this book.'
              (Vikner 1994: 67)

Assuming V is in Foc and the negative constituent in SpecFocP in (46a), *that* cannot have raised to Force from Fin. To account for this, we assume that *that* is merged in Force in the complements to bridge verbs, again presumably to satisfy the requirement that embedded Force have a lexical realization. In these cases in V2 languages, as for example in (46b), Fin* is satisfied by V-movement (Fin* is satisfied by V-movement passing through it in [46a]). The ability to directly select a complementizer in Force is a property of bridge verbs in the languages in question (this is presumably connected to the observation that these embedded clauses have assertive illocutionary force; cf. Hooper and Thompson 1973); German presumably does not allow this but instead selects the subjunctive in examples like (45) (see also Penner and Bader 1995 on further properties of this construction). Non-bridge verbs (canonically factives like *regret*, etc.) are unable to directly select a complementizer in this position.[27]

In Wh-complements where no overt complementizer is present something more must be said. Here we can capitalize on an observation by Stowell (1981: 422) to the effect that selection for [+WH] neutralizes selection for Fin. This can be illustrated by paradigms such as the following:

(47)   a.   I explained how to fix the sink.   [+WH, -Fin]
        b.   I explained how we should fix the sink.   [+WH, +Fin]
        c.   I explained that we should fix the sink.   [−WH, +Fin]
        d.   *I explained to fix the sink.   [−WH, −Fin]

In Rizzi's system, this is straightforwardly accounted for by the local nature of selection (see Chomsky 1965) and the fact that both Force and Foc are structurally higher than Fin. In that case, it follows that selection for Force as Interrogative and/ or for Foc as +WH[28] blocks selection for a feature of Fin. Hence the requirement for a finite complement (i.e., selection for Fin), violated in (47d), is inoperative where a feature of Foc is selected, as in (47a, b). The crucial assumption here is that local selection can take place "across" a head that lacks features relevant for selection; in other words, (48a) and (48b) are possible selection configurations but not (48c) (where ". . . " contains no heads and each head asymmetrically c-commands the next from left to right):

(48)   a. A[+F] . . . B[+F]   — local selection
        b. A[+F] . . . B . . . C[+F]   — non-local selection across an inert head
        c. A[+F] . . . B[+F] . . . C[+F]— impossible for A to directly select C

The parallels between selection so construed and the Agree relation of Chomsky (2001), as well as certain versions of relativized minimality, are clear, but I will not pursue them here (for a formulation in terms of relativized minimality, see 2.2.2).

What we observe in (47), then, are the following selection relations (and non-relations):

(47a, b): V selects Force[+Q]; Force [+Q] selects Foc[+WH]; Foc[+WH] **does not** select any property of Fin;

(47c): V directly selects finite Fin, Force and Foc being inert (see [48b]), this requirement is violated in (47d) (assuming *explain* requires finite Fin where it is structurally able to select a property of Fin).

In matrix clauses, we observe essentially the same situation. Force[+Q] can select a [+WH] Foc, in which case Fin is not selected for. However, if Foc is inactive (i.e. [−WH]), then Fin must be finite. These facts are illustrated by the following paradigm:

(49) a. What to do?   Force[+Q], Foc[+WH], Fin not selected.
      b. What should we do?   Force[+Q], Foc[+WH], Fin not selected.
      c. Should we leave?   Force[+Q] selects finite Fin where Foc is inactive.
      d. *Whether/if to leave?   Violation of selection property of Force[+Q].

If Fin is active, it is Fin*; as (49) shows, where Foc is [+WH], Fin may be either active or not, but where Foc is inactive, Fin* is selected by Force[+Q] and must be active.[29]

What about Fin in (47)? Why does it not trigger movement in V2 languages if it is not selected? Clearly the reason is that this is not an inherently declarative Fin. Suppose then that Fin (and therefore the clause it heads) is interpreted as declarative just when no higher position in the C-system is active. This is very natural, since it amounts to saying that [+finite] Fin is interpreted as declarative when it is in a clear intuitive sense the head of CP. It also entails that Force is inactive in (root) declarative clauses, and so declarative is the unmarked clause type. So, non-selected declarative Fin is equivalent to root, finite Fin. Non-selected declarative Fin is in principle distinct from selected, declarative Fin; the former is a kind of default, while the latter is a selected C-head, entering into selection relations like other heads. Selected, non-declarative Fin is different again. We thus arrive at the following general picture of the varieties of Fin (here '*' means that the relevant type of Fin needs a PF-realization in the language in question, not that it is ungrammatical):

(50) a.   +selected, +declarative   * in Germanic
      b.   −selected, +declarative   * in Germanic, not in English (full V2)
      c.   +selected, −declarative   * in Germanic, * in English (residual V2)
      d.   −selected, −declarative   not found, as declarative is a default

The preceding sketch of the C-system and the root-embedded asymmetry in Germanic clearly shows that Fin-to-Force movement is available in these languages. In Irish, however, Force does not overtly attract Fin, as McCloskey's evidence shows. Given this, we might conclude that the absence of root-embedded asymmetries in verb-movement in Celtic is not an argument against a V-to-C analysis of VSO; V could be analyzed as moving to Fin, just as suggested earlier for Yiddish and Icelandic. However, we have clear evidence that V does not raise to Fin in Irish. We have seen that *go* is in Fin at Spell Out, and if we follow Kayne (1994) in assuming that all head-adjunction must be to the left of the target, then the simple fact that we find *go—Verb* and not *Verb—go* tells us that V does not raise to Fin. In this respect, Irish differs from Yiddish and Icelandic, in that in those languages it is reasonable to postulate that complementizers appear in Force (see note 28). Thus, by a roundabout route, I endorse McCloskey's conclusion that the facts of adverb placement argue against V-raising into the C-system in Irish. (However, note that I have restricted my attention to the Irish complementizer *go*; according to McCloskey 2001, this item is typical of Irish C-elements, but at least the Wh-particle *aL* shows a different "morphosyntactic profile" to use McCloskey's term.) Let us now turn to Welsh and see what the preceding considerations tell us about the position of V in VSO clauses in this language. In fact, Welsh is very interesting in this respect. In terms of the schema for the difference between English and Irish given in (40), we can observe that Welsh has the order *C—Adv—C*. In other words, adverbs can appear after certain complementizers but not others, as shown in Tallerman (1996). They cannot intervene between the particle *y*, which introduces finite clauses, and the verb:

(51)   *Dywedodd ef y   yfory   bydd   yn gadael.
        said   he Prt tomorrow he-will-be Asp leave

By parity of reasoning with what I said about Irish *go*, we could take (46) as evidence that *y* is in Fin. However, adverbs cannot precede *y* (and have lower scope), either (see also Tallerman 1996: 122):

(52)   Dywedodd ef yfory   y   bydd   yn gadael.
        said   he tomorrow Prt he-will-be Asp leave
        'He said tomorrow that he'll leave.'

Here the adverb *yfory* must be interpreted as having matrix scope, giving an anomalous temporal interpretation for this clause, as in the English translation. So *y* behaves like English *for* (see note 23) and doesn't tell us very much about the structure of C or the position of the finite verb.

In Welsh there are particles that introduce affirmative main clauses (under certain conditions—see next section). These are *fe* and *mi*, the variation being dialectal as I mentioned earlier (cf. [1]). The particles have three properties: (i) they trigger soft mutation on the initial consonant of V (see 2.2); (ii) they host infixed pronouns, for example, *fe/mi'ch gwelais i*, "I saw you(pl)" (I take these pronouns to be in the syntax Romance-style proclitics on the finite verb that are moved with the finite verb; however, they are PF-enclitic to the particle, and so the otherwise available particle-deletion operation—see note 1 of chapter 4—cannot apply when these elements are present); and (iii) they are adjacent to the finite verb, the only possible intervening element being the "infixed pronouns" just mentioned. The last of these properties is most relevant here. As (53) shows, adverbs can occur before these particles but not in between them and the verb:

(53)   a.   Bore   'ma, fe/mi glywes i'r newyddion ar y radio.

morning this, Prt   heard   I the news   on the radio
'This morning, I heard the news on the radio.'

b.   *Fe/mi bore   'ma glywes i 'r   newyddion ar y   radio.
        Prt   morning this heard I   the news   on the radio

Again we can apply the analysis of McCloskey's Irish data and take it that *fe/mi* are in Fin. Support for this comes in connection with property (i) earlier, the fact that *fe/ mi* trigger ICM on V. In 2.3.1, I show that ICM takes place under syntactic conditions that correspond to the GB notion of head-government; if *fe/mi* are in Fin and the verb in the highest head position in IP, then this configuration is met by the particle-V relation. This analysis assures the adjacency of *fe/mi* and the finite verb, as long as IP-adjunction is ruled out (which I assume it is in general, following Rizzi 1997) and the infixed pronouns are analyzed as proclitics on the finite verb, as sketched earlier.

Welsh has a general focusing strategy (traditionally called the "mixed construction") which allows exactly one XP to be fronted over the verb, followed by *a* or *y* and the rest of the clause. The choice of *a* or *y* depends on the nature of the fronted XP: *a* is associated with subjects, direct objects, and VPs, *y* with all other XPs (it is possible that *a* is associated with movement and *y* with a resumption strategy; see Awbery 1976, Sadler 1988, McCloskey 1979, 1990, Rouveret 1994, and note 3 of chapter 4). Some examples from Tallerman (1996: 100, 103) are given in (54):

(54)   a.   Y   dynion a   werthodd y   ci.
                the men   Prt sold   the dog
                'It's the men who have sold the dog.'

        b.   Ym Mangor y   siaradais i llynedd.
                in Bangor Prt spoke   I last-year
                'It was in Bangor I spoke last year.'

These particles have the same properties as *fe/mi* (they trigger mutation on V, and they must be adjacent with only an infixed pronoun able to intervene). Moreover, they are in complementary distribution with *fe/mi*. Clauses with a fronted focused XP like those in (54) can be preceded by one of a special class of complementizers, as in (55) (examples again from Tallerman 1996: 108, 117, 119):

(55)   a.   Dywedais i **mai** ['r dynion **a**   fuasai'n   gwerthu'r ci].
                said   I MAI the men   Prt would-Asp sell-the   dog
                'I said that it's the men who would sell the dog.'

        b.   **Ai** [ceffyl **a**   fuasai hi'n   gwerthu]?
                AI   horse Prt   would she-Asp sell?
                'Is it the horse that she'd sell?'

c.   **Nid** [y   dyn   **a**   ddaeth].
NEG the man Prt came
'It wasn't the man who came.'

Rouveret (1994) and Tallerman (1996) both treat these structures as involving "CP-recursion." Now, the interesting observation, due to Tallerman, is that adverbs can appear between *mai* and the focused constituent but not—with embedded scope—before *mai*:

(56)   a. Dywedais i mai fel arfer y   dynion a   fuasai'n   gwerthu'r ci.
         said   I MAI as usual the men   Prt would-Asp sell-the   dog
         'I said that it's as usual the men who would sell the dog.'

        b. *Dywedais i fel arfer mai 'r   dynion a   fuasai'n   gwerthu'r ci.
         said   I as usual MAI the men   Prt would-Asp sell-the   dog

However, it is also possible to separate a focused constituent from the focus particle with an adverb, as (57) shows:

(57)   Dywedais i mai'r   dynion fel arfer a   fuasai'n   gwerthu'r ci.
        said   I MAI the men   as usual Prt would-Asp sell-the   dog
        'I said that it's the men as usual who will sell the dog.'

Thus the natural position for *a* is in Fin. It seems reasonable to situate the focused XP in SpecFoc; this implies that the adverb in (57) occupies a position in between Foc and Fin (possibly SpecFinP or a special position for adverbial specifiers). I consider *mai* and the other elements that introduce "CP-recursion" illustrated in (55) to be in Force, like their English counterparts in the complements to bridge verbs. Hence the intervening adverb in (56a) can be thought of as occupying a specifier position in between Force and FocP.

This analysis is preferable to one that relies on CP-recursion of the kind proposed by Tallerman (1996) in that it directly captures the fact, observed by Cardinaletti and Roberts (1991), that "the two C-positions have different properties" (Tallerman 1996: 109). This is because, on this analysis, they are distinct categories. Moreover, since it is possible to have *mai—Adv*—XP—Prt* where exactly the last XP before the particle is interpreted as focused (cf. Tallerman 1996: 114), this falls directly under Rizzi's (1997) proposal that between Force and Foc there is a possibly recursive TopP. Third, we can account for the order in (57), where an adverb intervenes between the focused constituent and the focus particle, as here the focused constituent is SpecFocP, the adverb is either in a lower SpecTopP or in SpecFinP, and particle is in Fin, as shown in (58):

(58)   Dywedais i [$_{ForceP}$ **mai** [$_{FocP}$ 'r dynion [$_{TopP/FinP}$ fel arfer [$_{Fin}$ **a**] fuasai'n gwerthu y ci]]].

In order to account for these data, Tallerman must either assume that focused constituents can be adjoined, losing the generalization that there can only be one such constituent in the left periphery of the clause, or weaken the Adjunction Prohibition to allow adverbs like *fel arfer* to adjoin to C' (the latter solution is adopted in Willis 1998).

The preceding analysis implies that the verb is not raised into any part of the C-system. In particular, we can see that *a* has not raised to Foc in (58), and so the fact that this particle precedes the verb, combined with the fact that no adverb can intervene between it and the verb, indicates that the verb remains in a position lower than Fin. I continue to assume, following Kayne (1994) and *pace* Willis (1998), that the verb can't be right-adjoined to Fin.

So the analysis of the C-system of Welsh (and Irish) indicates that finite V do not move there. In turn, this means that the analysis of VSO cannot be as in (28). And this in turn indicates that these languages do not have an English- or French-style EPP as subject requirement (where the subject position is taken to be the highest Specifier position in IP).

1.2.3   The Nature of *Bod*

A further argument that V does not raise to Fin in Welsh comes from the evidence that there is one verb with peculiar morphological and distributional properties that can be neatly accounted for if we assume that this particular verb—unlike all others—is able to raise to Fin. The verb in question is the auxiliary *bod*, "be". If the peculiarities of *bod* are accounted for by its ability to move into Fin, then the fact that other verbs do not show any of these peculiarities shows that they do not raise to Fin. There is further evidence for this from a peculiar restriction on embedded finite verbs most recently discussed and analyzed in Tallerman (1998). *Bod* is the only auxiliary in Welsh, since as I mentioned in note 1 there is no equivalent of *have* (see 3.3 for a proposal regarding this).[30] The idea that auxiliaries have greater movement privileges than other verbs is of course not new: compare Pollock (1989) for discussion of the evidence that this is true in both English and French and Rizzi (1982, chapter 3) for comparable evidence from Italian.[31]

The morphological peculiarity of *bod* lies in the fact that it has tense forms that other verbs lack. As shown in note 1, all verbs have synthetic present/future, conditional and preterit forms, but all the other tenses are periphrastic (literary Welsh also has pluperfect and subjunctive forms but these are not part of the colloquial language). *Bod*, however, has synthetic present (distinct from the present/future) and imperfect forms (distinct from the conditional). This verb also has distinct paradigms in the present and imperfect according to the clause type. Here I give the Northern colloquial forms (from King 1993: 146f.):

(59)   *Present tense:*

	Affirmative	Interrogative	Negative
	dw i	ydw i	(dy)dw i
	ti	wyt i	dwyt ti
	mae o/hi	ydy o/hi	dydy o/hi

dan ni	ydan ni	(dy)dan ni
dach chi	(y)dach chi	(dy)dach chi
maen nhw	ydyn nhw	dydyn nhw
'I am' etc.	'Am I?' etc.	'I am not' etc.

(60)   *Imperfect tense:*

Affirmative	Interrogative	Negative
roeddwn i	oeddwn i	doeddwn
roeddet ti	oeddet ti	doeddet ti
roedd o/hi	oedd o/hi	doedd o/hi
roedden ni	oedden ni	doedden ni
roeddech chi	oeddech chi	doeddech chi
roedden nhw	oedden nhw	doedden nhw
'I was' etc.	'Was I?' etc.	'I was not' etc.

These forms can to some extent be decomposed, particularly in the imperfect (although third-person sg/pl present tense *mae(n)* is clearly a suppletive form; see Hendrick 1996 for an analysis). Here we see that the alternation *r-/Ø/d-* indicates clause type. The prefix *r-* is the phonologically conditioned variant of *y*, a particle that occurs with these tenses of *bod* in declaratives in the literary language (the literary 3sg present is *y mae*; the 1sg present is *yr ydwyf*). This particle is in complementary distribution with *fe/mi*, which occur with other verbs and with *bod* in other tenses.[32] The prefix *d-* is the relic of the older/literary preverbal negation *ni(d)* (see note 5). Synchronically, though, it is arguable that in the variety illustrated in (59) and (60) the prefixes *r-* and *d-* are lexically part of *bod*, given that they do not occur with other verbs.

The natural analysis of this situation is to treat *bod* as able to raise to Fin and to suppose that the Tense-features associated with present and imperfect are only licensed there. In this way, we can explain the extra forms of *bod* in terms of extra movement possibilities. In interrogatives, *bod* may raise further to Foc (see later). This analysis implies that verbs that lack the present and imperfect tenses (i.e., all verbs except *bod*) do not raise to Fin. Perhaps because of this, such verbs also lack the declarative *r-* and negative *d-* prefixes.

Support for this analysis comes from the fact, alluded to earlier, that *bod* is in complementary distribution with many preverbal particles. As mentioned previously, it is in complementary distribution with *fe/mi* (see also note 32). I regard the *r-* prefix on the imperfect as part of *bod* rather than as a separate head in the contemporary colloquial language. Also, *bod* is in complementary distribution with the focus particles *a/y*,[33] as can be seen if we change the synthetic verb forms in (54) and (55) into periphrastic tenses with the relevant form of *bod* (*sydd* in [61a] is a further suppletive form of bod that appears when the local subject has been extracted; see Hendrick 1996):

(61)   a.   Y   dynion **sydd**   wedi gwerthu'r   ci.
            the men   SYDD Asp sell   the dog
            'It's the men who have sold the dog.'

b. (?)Ym Mangor **dw** i wedi siarad iddo fo.
    in   Bangor am I Asp speak to-3sg him
    'It's in Bangor I have spoken to him.'

c. Ai [ceffyl **mae** wedi gwerthu]?[34]
    AI horse is   Asp sell?
    'Is it a horse that she's sold?'

I propose that *bod* raises to Fin, and so its syntax corresponds in an important
respect to what I proposed earlier for *a* and *y*.

Further evidence that *bod* raises into the C-system in certain contexts comes
from Rouveret's (1996) analysis of copular clauses. Rouveret argues that
identificational clauses like those in (62) are V2 clauses in the sense that in his
terms the precopular XP is in SpecCP and the copula in C:

(62) a. Y brenin **ydy** Arthur.
          the king   is   Arthur.
          'Arthur is the king.'

      b. Arthur **ydy**'r brenin.
          Arthur is the king
          'It is Arthur who is the king.'

      c. *Ydy Arthur y   brenin.
          is Arthur the king

In addition to pointing out the complementary distribution between *bod* and
particles,[35] Rouveret gives two further arguments for his analysis. First, he observes
that an indefinite predicative nominal may appear in initial position unlike what we
find in English:

(63) a. Arwr ydy Siôn.
          hero is   John
          'John is a hero.'

      b. *A hero is John.

Rouveret suggests that the definite predicate nominal occupies SpecAgrSP in inverse
predicational sentences in English such as *The king is Arthur*, a position from which
indefinite predicate nominals are excluded. This suggests that the indefinite predicate
nominal *arwr* in (63a) is not in this position but instead presumably in a higher
position.[36]

Second, fronted predicate nominals can contain an anaphor bound by the
postcopular DP:

(64)   Ei elyn pennaf ei hun **ydy** Siôn.
               his enemy chief   his self is   John
               'John is his own worst enemy.'

The fronted DP that contains the anaphor must be reconstructed in order for the anaphoric relation to be wellformed. Since reconstruction is standardly assumed to be a property of A'-dependencies (but cf. Burzio 1986), this implies that the fronted DP is in an A'-position, that is, Spec,CP according to Rouveret.

Adapting Rouveret's conclusion to the split-C system being assumed here, I conclude that in predicative sentences *bod* raises into the C-system with the fronted XP occupying the Specifier of the head occupied by *bod*. Since the fronted predicate has a focused interpretation, it is natural to suppose that this head position is Foc (see also note 36). So Rouveret's conclusion supports the general claim about the syntax of *bod* being made here.

My final piece of motivation for the idea that *bod* raises to Fin comes from embedded clauses. Since *bod* is able to syncretize with Fin-material such as *a/y*, we expect not to find any root-embedded asymmetry that involves *bod* if it is attracted to Fin in the manner described. This is true, but only up to a point. First, the fact that the full range of forms of *bod* is found in relatives and in embedded questions—both embedded contexts par excellence—indicates that the prediction is correct in a straightforward way:

(65)   a.   Dw i ddim yn siwr beth **mae** hi 'n   moyn wneud.
               am I Neg Pred sure what is   she Asp want do
               'I'm not sure what she wants to do.'
               (King 1993: 310)

        b.   Dw i 'n nabod rhywun **sy**   'n   medru siarad Hen Saesneg.
               am I Asp know someone SYDD Asp can   speak Old English
               'I know someone who can speak Old English.'
               (King 1993: 301)

Thus far, my account is straightforwardly supported. In terms of the account of root-embedded asymmetries sketched in the previous section, the difference between Welsh and the Germanic languages lies in the absence of Force-Fin relation in embedded clauses. The complementizers that appear in Force (*mai* and the other elements shown in [55]) do not attract Fin; since they must be followed by a focussed constituent, it appears that they select for properties of Foc. In fact, *mai*-type particles act exactly like Wh-complements in Germanic—since they activate Foc, they cannot affect Fin. However, since embedded Fin is in general not required to move to Force in Welsh, this does not have the consequence that Fin is unable to trigger movement, and so *bod* moves to Fin.

However, there is a class of embedded positive declaratives with extremely interesting properties. Exactly where the embedded clause contains one of the tenses of *bod* that is specific to this verb (the present or the imperfect), the non-finite form *bod* appears instead of the finite form:

(66) a.   Mae'n deud **bod** nhw fan hyn.
             is Asp say BOD they place this
             'He says that they're here.'
             (King 1993: 304)

      b.   Dywedodd hi **bod** y trên yn hwyr.
             said   she BOD the train in late
             'She said that the train was late.'
             (King 1993: 304)

Since the non-finite form of *bod* is the verbal noun, it can, like other verbal nouns, be associated with a preceding pronoun in a historically possessive form, be mutated, and be followed by an echo pronoun (see Roberts and Shlonsky 1996 and 2.1 and 3.1.3 on Welsh pronouns):

(67)   Mae o 'n deud **fy mod i** 'n dwp.
             is he Asp say my BOD I Asp idiot
             'He says I am an idiot.'

With standard verbal nouns in periphrastic tenses, pronominal objects are marked by a preceding historically genitive pronoun (and can be followed by an echo pronoun; see 3.2):

(68)   Mae Megan wedi ei weld (o).
             is Megan Asp his see (he)
             'Megan has seen him.'

In 3.2, I present an analysis of verbal nouns that has the consequence that non-finite clauses "headed" by verbal nouns are PrtPs, so (68) shows a kind of "participle agreement," as analyzed in Kayne (1989), without movement of the non-finite verb (see 3.2 for details). If this analysis of (68) is correct, then the same pronoun in (67) should be in an agreement position. Assuming that *dweud* always selects a finite CP, the only likely candidate is AgrS. If that is true, then *bod* is no higher than AgrS. Let us suppose that it is in T, with the non-enclitic agreement marker *(fy)* in AgrS.[37] In that case, we have a root-embedded asymmetry that involves *bod*: it fails to raise to Fin in these examples. The clauses are nevertheless interpreted as present or imperfect as the relevant features are present in the empty Fin that here is *not* targeted by *bod*. We can account for this root-embedded asymmetry in a manner consistent with our account for the Germanic asymmetries if we say that in precisely this case Force is selected by the matrix verb and selects the Tense-features of Fin (naturally, the relevant Tense-features are optionally selected, in that these clauses do not have to be present or imperfect). In terms of the table given in (50), present/imperfect Fin, if [−selected], [+declarative], attracts V. Only *bod* can raise to Fin, because only *bod* has the relevant morphological features. Where present/imperfect Fin is [+selected] and [+declarative], it has no PF-realization property and therefore blocks the raising of *bod*. In this sense, Welsh is a V2 system just with this auxiliary and just in these tenses (cf. Rouveret 1996 for a very similar conclusion). Where Fin cannot attract *bod*, *bod* stays in T and cannot bear present or imperfect morphology because these morphosyntactic features are inherently associated with Fin. In this case, *bod* defaults to its citation form and AgrS is manifested as a proclitic (see 3.2.4, for the idea that the proclitics are the default manifestation of Agr in Welsh). This analysis shows that the Germanic root-embedded asymmetry in interrogatives cannot be attributed to the nature of the Q-feature, because in Welsh *bod*-clauses we have the same situation but with entirely different features. So we see that just where *bod* shows peculiar behavior we can plausibly say that it does not raise to Fin. This is consistent with the idea that where *bod* does not show such peculiar behavior it does move to Fin, and therefore indirectly supports the proposal that verbs other than *bod*, which entirely lack *bod*'s peculiarities, do not raise to Fin.

Other verbs and the other tenses of *bod* are associated with the complementizer *y* in these contexts (examples from King 1993: 306):

(69)   a.   Dw i 'n   meddwl **y** dylech chi ddeud wrtho fo.
              am I Asp think   Prt ought you say   to-3sg he
              'I think you ought to tell him.'

        b.   Mae'n   sicr   **y** byddai hynny'n   beryglus dros ben.
              is Asp certain Prt would-be that   Pred dangerous extremely
              'It's certain that that would be extremely dangerous.'

Since *bod* does not raise to Fin in the conditional, it is unaffected by being in an embedded clause. The same is true for other verbs.

As I have already mentioned, *y* is probably in Fin. It is important to note that this element is absent in *bod*-clauses of the type in (66) and (67); it seems that the realization of Fin under declarative, selected Force is *y* in all tenses except the present and imperfect, and zero in the present and imperfect. In root declaratives, where Force is not selected, Fin is realized as *fe/mi* in all tenses except the present and imperfect, where it is realized by the relevant form of *bod* (see chapter 4 for an analysis of this that relates it to V2; Rouveret 1996 also suggests that Welsh shows V2 effects just with *bod*). Focused clauses, both root and embedded, require Fin to be realized by particles, as here it is Foc that determines the form of Fin, depending on the status of the focussed XP.

We see the behavior illustrated in (66) and (67) only in positive declarative embedded clauses. If the clause is negative, there are two options. One possibility, characteristic of the spoken language, is to negate the *bod*-clause with *(d)dim*:

(70)   Dan ni 'n   gobeithio **bod** chi ddim yn   siomedig.
               are we Asp hope   BOD you Neg Pred disappointed
               'We hope that you're not disappointed.'
               (King 1993: 305)

The other possibility is to introduce the complement clause with a special negative morpheme *nad*, followed by the interrogative/focus form of *bod*:

(71)   Dan ni 'n   gobeithio **nad** ydach chi   yn   siomedig.
            are we Asp hope   NAD are   you Pred disappointed
            'We hope that you're not disappointed.'
            (King 1993: 305)

The natural analysis of this construction is to treat *nad* as being in Force, in other words to assimilate it to the *mai*-like elements, with *bod* in Fin. Support for this analysis comes from the fact that *nad* can introduce a negative embedded focused clause:

(72)   Mi wn   i **nad**   y   dyn a   ddaeth.
            Prt know I NAD   the man Prt came
            'I know that it wasn't the man who came.'
            (Tallerman 1996)

Here we see the pattern of a *mai*-clause, with *nad* in Force and *a* in Fin, parallel to examples like (55).

Further support for both the idea that some Tense-features are selected on Fin by a higher predicate and the idea that V (other than *bod*) do not raise to Fin comes from a restriction on embedded past-tense lexical verbs (in the literary variety, and even there there appears to be some variation among speakers regarding the judgements; see Tallerman 1998: 71–73 for discussion). Past-tense lexical verbs are not allowed in the complements of verbs that take a finite complement, although other tenses are allowed (recall that verbs other than *bod* do not have present or imperfect forms):

(73)   a.   *Meddyliodd Aled [yr aeth Mair adre'].
              thought   Aled that went Mair home

        b.   Meddyliodd Aled [y byddai   Mair yn   mynd adre'].
              thought   Aled that would-be Mair Asp go   home
              'Aled thought that Mair would go home.'

The ban on past-tense lexical verbs is a root-embedded asymmetry, as (74) shows:

(74)   Aeth Mair adre'.
            went Mair home
            'Mair went home.'

We can account for this if we say that selected Fin bears the [past] feature; that is, some Tense-features show up on Fin (as we saw earlier, [present] and [imperfect] do as well, although these are in any case restricted to *bod*). But V cannot move to

Fin and hence cannot be licensed as past (in main clauses and generally in varieties where the restriction in [73a] does not hold, [past] is presumably realized on T). This correctly predicts that preterit *bod* can show up in contexts like (73a) (Maggie Tallerman p.c.).

Instead of (73a), we have what appears to be an infinitive, marked with *i,* "for/to" (here I follow the presentation in Tallerman; however, some native speakers reject [75] and [76] in favor of a *bod* complement to *meddwl,* "think": *Meddyliod Aled bod Mair wedi mynd adre'*, thought Aled that Mair Asp go home, 'Aled thought Mair had gone home'):

(75)   Meddyliodd Aled [i Mair fynd adre'].
        thought   Aled to Mair go   home
        'Aled thought Mair had gone home.'

However, Tallerman (1998) (following Harlow 1992) shows that these clauses are in fact finite, because (i) they are in complementary distribution with past-tense verbs, as we have seen; (ii) they have a past-tense interpretation; (iii) they coordinate with finite clauses; and (iv) they form a binding domain exactly in the way finite clauses generally do and thus unlike non-finite clauses. Properties (iii) and (iv) are illustrated here:

(76)   Meddyliodd Aled [i Alys fynd adre'] ac [y byddai Mair yn mynd yn fuan].
        thought   Aled to Alys go   home and that would-be Mary Asp go soon
        'Aled thought that Alys had gone home and that Mair would be going soon.'
        (Tallerman 1998: 8)

(77)   a.   Dywedodd Aledi [iddo fo$_{i/j}$ fynd].
              said   Aled to-3sg he go
              'Aled said that he'd gone.'

        b.   *Dywedodd Aled [iddo ei hun   fynd].
              said   Aled to-3sg himself go
              'Aled said that himself had gone.'

Presumably, *i* represents a default form of Fin here (normally it marks infinitives and as such corresponds to either English *to* or *for;* see Tallerman 1998 for extensive discussion). Note the agreement that shows up on this element, as on many "prepositional" elements in Welsh (see 2.1.2). The agreement morpheme could be in AgrS, giving the structure $[_{Fin}$ *i* $]$ $[_{AgrS}$ *-ddo* $]$. See the discussion of AgrS as a syntactic affix in 2.1.[38]

In this section, we have seen two more arguments that (main) verbs do not move to Fin (i.e., into the C-system) in main clauses. The first was based on a number of distributional and morphological peculiarities of *bod*, all of which can be accounted for by assuming that *bod* moves to Fin in the present and imperfect in matrix clauses. The second was the fact that verbs cannot be past in form in embedded finite clauses.

An important assumption behind these arguments is that Welsh Fin has tense features associated with it. In fact, it appears that Welsh differs from English (and many other familiar languages) in that some parts of its tense system are realized on Fin and some parts on T. Because only *bod* can raise to Fin, only *bod* can be associated with the tenses that are realized exclusively there, that is, [present] and [imperfect]. [Past] is realized on Fin in embedded clauses, and this blocks its realization on T. Future and conditional are realized on T consistently.[39] Other Celtic languages show similar phenomena: Irish complementizers show tense distinctions (e.g. *go* [non-past]/*gur* [past] 'that'; *an* [non-past]/*ar* [past] 'Q', etc.) and, as mentioned in 2.1, independent forms of certain verbs in Irish and Scots Gaelic are in complementary distribution with certain complementizers. Most interestingly, as observed by both Cottell (1995) and McCloskey (2001), the complementizers in question are exactly the ones that can show tense-marking (so, for example, the Wh-particle *aL* does not show tense-marking and is not in complementary distribution with independent verb forms; see [34]). In a system like Rizzi's, which explicitly allows for two positions in the clause where temporal information can appear, languages where the tense systems are split across the two positions are to be expected.

1.2.4   Conclusion

In this section, I have investigated the possibility that V raises into the C-system with the subject remaining the highest specifier in IP. We have seen a number of arguments against this analysis: the interaction of adverbs, particles, and finite verbs, the behavior of *bod*, and the restriction on embedded past-tense verbs. In the process, I have adopted Rizzi's (1997) split-C system. Here is a summary of some of the claims made about the structure of the left periphery in Welsh, English, Irish, and Germanic using Rizzi's system:

(78)

	Force	**Spec,Foc**	**Foc**	**Fin**
WELSH:	*mai/ai/nad*	fronted XP	(Adv)	*a/y/fe/mi/bod*
IRISH:		NPI(?)	(Adv)	*go*
ENGLISH:	*that*$_{bridge\ V}$	WH		*that*$_{non\text{-}bridge}$
GERMAN:	*daß*			$t_{daß}$

In addition, both Welsh and Irish have tense/agreement forms that can only be realized on Fin, while Germanic languages do not have this (although Fin attracts the finite verb in unselected contexts in these languages, giving rise to the V-movement part of V2; see 4.3). I also suggested an account of the root-embedded asymmetry, which made it possible to see how this asymmetry applies to *bod* in certain contexts, in addition to having some generality for Germanic.

1.3   Conclusion

From the arguments given in 1.2 I conclude that V does not raise into the C-system in Welsh (or in Modern Irish), and so an analysis of the kind in (28) is to be rejected. Since we have seen that V and the subject leave VP (1.1), the only alternative is that both elements occupy functional positions in between C and V. Let us look again at the schema in (27):

(27)

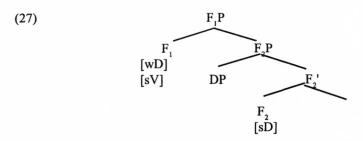

Adopting the clause structure proposed in Chomsky (1993, 1995—except for 4.10), the most likely hypothesis is:

(79) $F_1 = AgrS; F_2 = T.$

An alternative possibility might be:

(80) $F_1 = T; F_2 = H$ lower than T, e.g., AgrO or v

We can dismiss (80) immediately on two grounds. First, we know that there is very little structural "space" between the position of the particles in Fin, the position of the verb, and the position of the subject. The only things that can intervene anywhere in this complex are infixed pronouns (see 2.2). Placing the verb as low as T thus seems implausible—one would expect to find at least temporal adverbs in between particles and V. Second, if SpecvP is the position subjects are merged in, as Chomsky proposes and as I will assume in 2.3, and the arguments that we gave in 1.1 to the effect that the subject leaves its base position are valid, then this idea cannot be maintained.

So I have eliminated all plausible analyses of VSO clauses except for (79). My analysis of simple VSO sentences like those in (1a) in Welsh is thus as in (81):

(81)

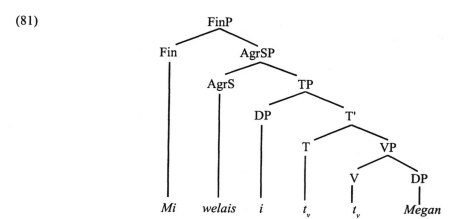

The structure of (1b) would be:[40]

(82)

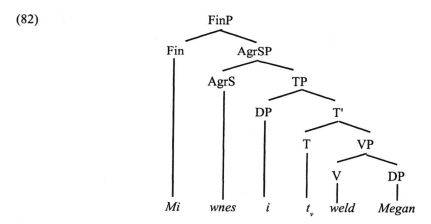

Adopting (79) entails in terms of the checking theory of Chomsky (1995, chapter 4) that AgrS has a weak D-feature and a strong V-feature. These are the parameter settings that give rise to VSO order: strong D-features in AgrS would give a French-like system (see Pollock 1989); weak V-features would presumably give an SVO system in which AgrS is completely "deactivated" (this may be the situation in German, although the question of OV vs. VO underlying order is complex; cf. Haider 1997). One could think that the subject raises to SpecTP purely to satisfy the Extended Projection Principle, which therefore applies in Celtic languages, *pace* Chomsky (1995) and McCloskey (1996b) (but see 2.1 and later). If the Extended Projection Principle is to be reduced to a strong D-feature of T, as Chomsky (1995) proposes, then we are led to propose the following feature-values for functional heads in the Welsh I-system (and presumably the same holds at least for Irish):

(83)   a.   AgrS has weak D-features.

b.   AgrS has strong V-features.

c.   T has strong D-features.

However, these proposals are problematic, despite the fact that they clearly account for the data seen in this chapter. First, AgrS is a rather peculiar agreement head in Welsh (and in Celtic VSO languages generally), owing to the anti-agreement effect. This term designates the fact that the subject fails to agree with the verb under various conditions, a phenomenon also found in Breton (Stephens 1982), Irish (McCloskey and Hale 1984), and Classical Arabic (Mohammad 1988); see also Roberts and Shlonsky (1996). The standard anti-agreement effect is illustrated by examples like (84) for Welsh:

(84) a.   Canon
            sing-3pl
            'They sang'

      b.   Canodd
            sing-3sg
            'He/she sang.'

      c.   Canodd y plant.
            sang-3sg the children (pl)
            'The children sang.'

      d.   *Canon y plant.
            sang-3pl the children (pl)

The generalization is that a plural (third-person) subject always appears with a singular verb—that is, (number) agreement systematically fails. The plural form is ungrammatical with an overt subject, as (84d) shows. However, with a null subject the plural form is allowed and indeed required for the plural interpretation, as (84a) shows. In Irish, a default form is used in some tenses and persons with an overt postverbal subject (see McCloskey and Hale 1984 for detailed discussion and analysis); an overt subject is impossible with a non-default form:

(85) a.   Chuirfeadh   Eoghan/na léachtóiri isteach ar an phost sin.
            would-put-3sg Owen/ the teachers in   for the job   that
            'Owen/the teachers would apply for that job.'

      b.   Chuirfinn (*mé) isteach ar an phost sin.
            would-put-1sg I in   for the job   that
            'I would apply for that job.'

Clearly this striking property of many VSO systems (including all the Celtic ones) needs to be accounted for. At first sight, it is not obvious how the idea that the verb raises to an agreement position can account for this.

Second, the natural way to account for the apparently obligatory movement of the subject to SpecTP is in terms of the EPP, as I just mentioned. However, there are two constructions in Welsh that provide clear evidence that the EPP does not apply (at least in anything like the standard sense). These are impersonal passives and existential constructions:[41]

(86)   a.   Gwelwyd plant.
                see-PASS children
                'Children were seen.'

        b.   ?Mae yn yr ardd   blant.
                is   in the garden children
                'There are children in the garden.'

In these constructions, there is no subject in the Specifier immediately subjacent to the position occupied by the finite verb. One might think that *plant* in (86a) is in subject position, but it can be shown that this is not so. *Plant* can be cliticized by an infixed pronoun, a possibility restricted to non-subjects, and the impersonal passive can appear in a periphrastic tense where the single argument follows the verbal noun and so must be the direct object. These phenomena are illustrated in (87a) and (87b) respectively:[42]

(87)   a.   Fe 'i   gwelwyd.
                PRT -him see-PASS
                'He was seen.'

        b.   Yr ydys   yn gweld plant.
                PRT is-PASS Asp see   children
                'Someone is seeing children.' (= There is been seeing children)
                (Harlow 1989: 310)

We will look more closely at passives like (87a) as part of the overall account of case-licensing in Welsh in chapter 2, where I will draw a rather different conclusion regarding the status of infixed *i* (see in particular 2.3.4.2). However, the point that the subject position is unfilled in (86a) holds.

Examples like (86b) alternate with the following:

(88)   a.   Mae('r) plant   yn yr ardd.
                Is (the) children in the garden
                '(The) children are in the garden.'

        b.   Mae yna blant   yn yr ardd.
                Is   there children in the garden
                'There are children in the garden.'

In (88a), *plant* appears to occupy the subject position and there is no definiteness effect. In (88b), *yna* ('there') occupies subject position and there is a definiteness effect, as (89) illustrates:

(89)   *Mae yna'r   blant   yn yr ardd.
              Is   there the children in the garden
              'There's the children in the garden.'

See Rouveret (1996) and 2.3.4.4 for more discussion. The relevant point for present purposes is that there is no absolute requirement for a subject to appear in SpecTP. Of course, one could always propose that SpecTP is occupied by expletive *pro* in these cases. However, this seems undesirable in the context of a theory where elements can only be licensed at the interfaces. Expletive *pro* has no PF property, since it is an empty category, and it has no LF property, since it is an expletive. Therefore it has no interface property, and its postulation should be avoided; see Borer (1986) and Alexiadou and Anagnostopoulou (1998) for a proposal for constructions formerly regarded as containing this element in null-subject languages like Italian and Modern Greek.

There is also an empirical argument that expletive *pro* is not present in impersonal passives like (86a). As we will see in detail in 2.3, soft mutation applies in Welsh wherever a category is immediately preceded by an XP that c-commands it (cf. rsley and Tallerman 1998, Borsley 1999). The direct object in (86a) is not mutated, which indicates that there is no immediately c-commanding XP, and so no expletive *pro* in subject position. In this respect, (86a) contrasts with sentences with an argumental null subject. In such sentences, DOM is triggered:

(90)   Mi welais *pro* **blant**.
              Prt saw-1sg   children
              'I saw children.'

2

Case, Agreement, and Mutation

In this chapter, I start from the conclusion that VSO orders in Welsh are associated with the structure in (81) of chapter 1, with the problems noted there for the assumption that F_1 is AgrS and F_2 is T. The movements that take place here are presumably a consequence of the parameter values in (83) of chapter 1. The goal here is twofold: (a) to provide at least a partial answer to the questions noted at the end of chapter 1: this will entail in part a comparison of Welsh with Northern Italian dialects; and (b) to examine more closely what it means to say that these are the values of the D-features and the V-features, with a view to establishing both what the independent corollaries of these feature values might be and what the trigger experience for setting these parameter values might be. We shall see that interesting corollaries can be found and the trigger for VSO in Welsh can be taken to be rather simple. Moreover, it will emerge that the "corollary" of the parameter values can be taken to *be* the parameter values, implying that the notions of "strong feature" and "weak feature" play no role in the account of VSO. It will also emerge that the EPP, whether seen as a condition that requires subjects or as a feature that triggers movement to a Specifier position, is not required in the account of VSO (although we return to this point in 5.2).

I begin in section 2.1 by considering the V-feature, that is, the trigger for V-movement, and then move to the D-feature, that is, the trigger for subject-movement. Full consideration of the triggering of subject-movement and verb-movement entails an analysis of agreement and anti-agreement (see [84] of chapter 1), which will lead to an account of Case-assignment in 2.2. This in turn leads us to an analysis of direct-object mutation (DOM) in 2.3.

2.1   The V-Feature

2.1.1   V-Movement and the Status of the Agreement Affixes

We have seen that there is good syntactic evidence that AgrS has a strong V-feature in Welsh. What are the correlates of this feature? Ever since Pollock (1989) (who developed an observation in Roberts 1985), it has been thought that verbal inflection may play a role in determining the strength of V-features. On the basis of well-known contrasts in main-verb placement in English and French, Pollock, following Emonds (1978), argued that French main verbs raise to I (or AgrS)[1] while English ones do not:

(1)   Adverb:
      a.   Jean **embrasse souvent** Marie.
          *Jean **souvent embrasse** Marie.
      b.   *John **kisses often** Mary.
          John **often kisses** Mary.

(2)   Negation:
      a.   Jean (ne) **mange pas** de chocolat.
          *Jean (ne) **pas mange** de chocolat.
      b.   *John **eats not** chocolate.
          John does **not eat** chocolate.

(3)   Floated quantifiers:
      a.   Les enfants **mangent tous** le chocolat.
          *Les enfants **tous mangent** le chocolat.
      b.   *The children **eat all** chocolate.
          The children **all eat** chocolate.

Pollock notes that it is likely that the value of AgrS's V-feature in a given language is connected to the "richness" of agreement morphology, since French agreement morphology is somewhat richer than that of English. Moreover, Pollock observes, following Roberts (1985), that earlier stages of English had richer agreement and V-to-AgrS movement. Similarly, Icelandic has V-to-AgrS movement and relatively rich verbal inflection, while the Mainland Scandinavian languages have neither. Also, the history of the Mainland Scandinavian languages shows a development comparable to that of English (see in particular Platzack 1987 and Vikner 1994). In attempting to account for the relationship between the loss of verbal inflections and the loss of a strong V-feature of AgrS, I have suggested elsewhere (Roberts 1999) that inflectional morphology of certain kinds can act as a trigger for a strong feature. The relationship between inflection and movement can be expressed as follows:

(4)   If there is verbal inflection of the relevant type, then AgrS has a
strong V-feature.

Here the obvious question is what constitutes "relevant inflection." A number of
proposals have been made in this connection (see in particular Roberts 1993,
Rohrbacher 1997). The most interesting of these proposals is that in Vikner (1997),
who argues that the relevant morphology is the presence of agreement in all simple
tenses. French, Middle English, and Icelandic have such agreement, while Modern
English and the Mainland Scandinavian languages lack it (see Vikner 1997 for
detailed discussion and illustration). So there is a considerable amount of cross-
linguistic evidence for a correlation between verbal agreement morphology
and a strong V-feature of AgrS. We call languages without agreement "weak-
agreement" languages, and those with it "strong-agreement" languages. I will
make a brief suggestion as to where the OV West Germanic languages fit into this
picture in 4.3.2.

Let us now look at Welsh agreement morphology in light of this correlation. As
we saw earlier (cf. chapter 1, note 1), Welsh verbs (with the exception of *bod*; see
1.2.3) have three simple tenses. King (1993: 180) gives the endings of these tenses
as follows for contemporary spoken Welsh:[2]

(5)   Non-past tense: *-af, -i, -ith/-iff, -wn, -wch, -an*
       Past tense: *-es, -est, -odd, -on, -och, -on*
       Conditional: *-wn, -et, -ai, -en, -ech, -en*

It is clear that Welsh has, by Vikner's criterion, the relevant agreement morphology
for a strong V-feature to be associated with AgrS. We can thus conclude that this
morphology is sufficient to trigger V-movement. This conclusion also means that
the V-feature of AgrS meets the learnability and typologizability criteria for
parameters. It is learnable if we assume that parameters can be morphologically
triggered (or expressed, in the terminology of Clark and Roberts 1993) and if we
assume that segmenting the endings into tense and agreement markers is an aspect
of acquisition—the correct segmentation will trigger AgrS's strong feature in line
with (4). And Vikner's work shows how the feature can give rise to an interesting
typology of verb-positions and verb morphology.

Our first conclusion is thus that Welsh AgrS patterns like that of French in
having, following (4) and Vikner's (1997) generalization, a sufficiently rich
conjugation to trigger V-raising. Welsh is a strong-agreement language, then.

The agreement system illustrated in (5) is in fact considerably richer, in an
obvious intuitive sense, than that of French. In each tense, five out of six forms are
distinct. In this respect, it resembles Spanish and Rumanian, both of which are
null-subject languages in the classical sense of Rizzi (1982, 1986a). And in fact,
Welsh is a null-subject language, as the following examples show (there appears
to be a preference to include the pronoun *ni*, "we", in (6d); there may be a functional explanation for this, as this is the one syncretic form):[3]

(6)   a.   Mi welais Megan.
                Prt saw-1sg Megan
                'I saw Megan.'

       b.   Mi welaist Megan.
                Prt saw-2sg Megan
                'You(sg) saw Megan.'

       c.   Mi welodd Megan.
                Prt saw-past Megan
                'He/she saw Megan.'

       d.   ?Mi welon Megan.
                Prt saw-1pl Megan
                'We saw Megan.'

       e.   Mi weloch Megan.
                Prt saw-2pl Megan
                'You(pl) saw Megan.'

       f.   Mi welon Megan.
                Prt saw-3pl Megan
                'They saw Megan.'

Welsh fits with the generalization made in Roberts (1993: 125–128) that verbal agreement licenses null subjects if it allows up to one syncretism, that is, if at least five out of six person forms are distinguished. Welsh is thus, as we just mentioned, like Spanish and Rumanian (note also that the vernacular variety described in Thomas [1982] and briefly discussed in notes 2 and 3 may also pattern like Italian, Greek, and numerous other languages).[4] So we can strengthen our first conclusion and observe that Welsh AgrS is sufficiently rich to both attract V and license null subjects.

However, if we compare Welsh with a classical null-subject language like Italian, we observe two very striking and important differences. First, subjects in Welsh are required to appear in the Specifier position immediately following and adjacent to AgrS, a position I have so far been identifying as SpecTP, and nowhere else; in particular subjects cannot be "freely inverted" in Welsh and cannot appear preverbally. This contrasts with the familiar Italian situation (see Rizzi 1982, chapter 4, for a detailed description and analysis). Second, non-pronominal subjects always fail to agree with the verb in Welsh (see [84] of chapter 1).

The relative restrictions on the positions of the subject are illustrated in the following examples. In each case the (a) example is Standard Italian and the (b) example is Welsh:

(7)   a.   Ha telefonato Gianni.
              has telephoned John

       b.   *Mae wedi ffônio Siôn.
              is   Asp phone John

              'John phoned.'

(8)   a.   Gianni ha telefonato.
              John   has telephoned

       b.   *Siôn mae wedi ffônio.
              John is   Asp phone

              'John phoned.'

(9)   a.   *Ha Gianni telefonato.[5]
              has John   telephoned

       b.   Mae Siôn wedi ffônio.
              Aux John Asp phone

              'John phoned.'

Difference (ii) mentioned earlier has to do with the anti-agreement property, which I illustrated at the end of chapter 1 and will discuss in detail in the next section. Clearly we need to account for these differences.

The idea that I want to pursue here is that the Welsh agreement system does not exactly correspond to that of Standard Italian but corresponds more closely (although not exactly, as we shall see) to that found in the Northern Italian dialects. In these varieties, as is well known, AgrS contains an agreement particle (see Rizzi 1986b, Brandi and Cordin 1989, Poletto 2000, Manzini and Savoia, forthcoming, and later) and the verb at the same time carries a specification of subject-agreement. The following paradigm from Padovano (given in Benincà 1995: 41–42) illustrates:

(10)   Magno   'I eat'
               Te magni   'you (sg) eat'

               Magnemo   'we eat'
               Magnè   'you (pl) eat'
               I/le magna   'they (m/f) eat'

The double realization of agreement seen in (parts of) paradigms of this kind has been referred to in the traditional Italian dialectological literature as *raddoppiamento dell'accordo* (doubling of agreement). Following an original suggestion by Rizzi (1987/2000), I interpret this phenomenon in the obvious way: a higher AgrS-head contains the clitic, while a lower head contains the agreeing verb. Both heads instantiate the properties of Standard Italian agreement, as is shown by the fact that these varieties all have the null-subject phenomenology and, just like Standard Italian, show the patterns in (7)–(9). In other words, the lower AgrS attracts V exactly as in Standard Italian, French, and so on, while the higher one contains a paradigm—often with gaps, as in (10)—of subject clitics, which I assume, owing to their morphological property of being non-affixal, repel V-movement.[6]

In fact, the very detailed recent studies of Northern Italian dialects by Poletto (2000) and Manzini and Savoia (forthcoming) provide clear evidence from the distribution of subject clitics that AgrS must be broken up into distinct projections. These projections include one for first/second person, one for third person, and one for number. For my purposes, it is sufficient to conflate the Person positions (the fact that Welsh does not provide direct evidence of as many positions as Italian dialects does not mean that these positions are absent—they may be present but inactive; compare the uniformity assumption articulated in Chomsky 2001). So from now on I refer to the higher AgrS projection as Pers and the lower one as Num; thus we have the following structure between C and TP: $[_{CP} C [_{PersP} Pers [_{NumP} Num [_{TP} T \ldots]]]]$.

So, my proposal regarding the Welsh agreement system is as follows:

(11)   The agreement markers in (5) are subject clitics in Pers that function as syntactic affixes in attracting the V-stem.

Following Kayne (1994), V left-adjoins to the affix and so the clitic always appears as a suffix. The plural endings in (5) suggest that the tense morphemes are *-w-* (non-past), *-o-* (past), and *-e-* (conditional). In turn, we can see that the plural pronouns are *-n* (1pl and 3pl) and *-ch* (2pl). The singular forms are less easy to segment and clearly involve some synchronically rather opaque morphophonemics. However, we can see that the 1sg ending in the present is *-f*, related to the pronoun *fi* and the 2sg ending in the past is *-t*, related to the pronoun *ti*.[7] Crucially, only the 3sg endings really do not look like the corresponding pronouns *e(f)/(f)o* ,"he", and *hi*, "she" (in any tense). It is also striking that the *-dd* ending shows up in the paradigms of inflected prepositions, in between what is clearly the prepositional root and the agreement ending: *i-dd-o* "to-3sgm," *i-dd-i* "to-3sgf" (cf. Rouveret 1991 for more on the possible morphosyntactic structure of these prepositions).[8] So we can observe that the unmarked person/number combination, 3sg, is literally unmarked; in its place we seem to have, at least in some tenses, a morphological placeholder *-dd*. So we see that even though more needs to be said regarding the morphophonemic details, the paradigm is considerably less opaque than a typical Romance agreement paradigm.[9]

The distinction between Welsh agreement affixes and those of Standard Italian, Northern Italian dialects, and French relies on the distinction made by

Sportiche (1998: 203–204) between syntactic and morphological (or lexical) incorporation. Syntactic incorporation is head-movement and thus always moves the stem upward and is morphologically transparent. Lexical incorporation does not depend on head-movement and thus may appear to involve downward dependencies and may be morphologically opaque. Welsh incorporation of verb and agreement affix clearly involves upward movement of the verb stem (see 1.1) and, as just observed, is morphologically transparent, at least in comparison with what we find in the Romance languages. Although Romance does not have downward movement for verb-agreement—compare Vikner's generalization as given in (4)—English notoriously appears to (see Chomsky 1957, 1991, Pollock 1989). In these terms, we can think of Vikner's generalization as deriving from the presence of agreement affixes lexically attached to V that "push V up" into Agr, since these affixes realize Agr and yet are merged in V as part of the verb and are morphologically inseparable from V (see 4.3.2, for some remarks on the nature of Germanic verbal inflection).

Now, notice that the agreement morphemes are the only ones that appear in Welsh. In other words, Welsh has no *raddoppiamento dell'accordo*. In this respect, Welsh differs from the Italian dialects and resembles Standard Italian. However, sticking to the idea that cross-linguistically Pers may contain a clitic and Num a verbal affix, we can actually observe that Welsh differs from Standard Italian, too, in that Standard Italian has only the affixal agreement (lexical incoporation in Sportiche's sense) while Welsh has only the clitic agreement (syntactic incorporation, according to Sportiche). In other words, we are taking Welsh verbs to lack an inherent, non-clitic agreement-marking. This proposal actually fills a gap in the logical space of proposals that have been made in the literature regarding agreement systems. Since the recognition that subject clitics in Northern Italian dialects are a kind of agreement head (see Renzi and Vanelli 1983, Brandi and Cordin 1989, Manzini and Savoia, forthcoming), three of four logical possibilities for the realization of agreement have been recognized:

(12)   SCL   Verb-agreement
             +   +   Northern Italian dialects
             −   +   Standard Italian, Greek, etc.
             −   −   Mainland Scandinavian

Systems like those in (12) have been extensively discussed in the literature, and the connections between the variant properties such as null subjects, verb-positions, and subject-positions are fairly well understood. However, there is clearly a fourth possibility, as follows:[10]

(13)   +   −   Welsh, Irish, . . .

This is the system instantiated by Welsh (and Irish), I propose. So we see that the Celtic languages can be made to fit very comfortably into a range of parametric space created by agreement systems that has already been proposed. Effectively, then, we are adding nothing to what is currently assumed about UG in our account of these languages. What we now have to show is that VSO and anti-agreement inevitably arise in a system like that in (13). If we can do this, we will have a very straightforward account of what makes these systems have the properties they have, one which clearly meets the learnability and typologizability requirements.

The proposal in (11) can derive V-movement to AgrS from some version of Lasnik's (1981) Stray Affix Filter, the requirement that syntactic affixes must be syntactically affixed to something (I will present a formal account of this filter in 5.1). The morphological property of Welsh—its "rich" set of verbal affixes—which arguably constitutes the trigger experience for V-movement to Pers, also constitutes the trigger for the syntactic movement (this is also true, albeit rather less obviously, for varieties of the type discussed in notes 2 and 3). Additional reference to Pers's strong V-feature adds nothing, either empirically or theoretically. For this reason, I will henceforth drop the idea that V raises to Pers in Welsh for any reason other than to satisfy the Stray Affix Filter (or whatever PF condition underlies this filter; see chapter 5). If Pers is not an affix, it can be a free morpheme (a subject clitic, as in Northern Italian dialects) or absent/unrealized (as in English). In both cases it repels movement. A further possibility, as we have seen, is that Pers is realized by features lexically affixed to V; in that case Pers triggers movement exactly as in the syntactic-affix case, only for a different morphological reason: affixes cannot detach from (or excorporate from) their stems. As Baker (1988) points out, this is a residue of the Lexical Integrity hypothesis of lexicalist theories of morphology (see Lieber 1980, Marantz 1984). Vikner's generalization holds only of languages of the last type (see note 2).

Let us now replace AgrSP in our representations of Welsh up to now with PersonP and NumberP, as follows:

(14)

```
        PersP
       /    \
   Pers     NumP
           /    \
              Num'
             /   \
          Num
```

In terms of this structure, the relevant parts of (70) of chapter 1 are replaced by (15):

(15)

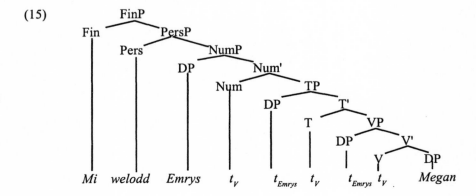

Compare this with the typical situation in Northern Italian dialects, as illustrated by the following examples from Poletto (2000):

(16) a.   A te vien.   (Loreo: Veneto)
              SCL SCL come-2sg
              'You come'

      b.   A ta vegnat.   (Lugano: Northern Lombard)
              SCL SCL come-2sg
              'You come'

      c.   A la vien.   (Padova: Veneto)
              SCL SCL comes-3sg
              'She comes'

Initial *a* here is an invariable clitic that Poletto clearly shows belongs to the C-system (possibly in Foc, as it is associated with new information, although I indicate it as dominated by C in [17] for simplicity). With this difference, which is not germane to our concerns here, these examples correspond exactly to what we have seen in Welsh, except that in (16) the second clitic (*te, ta, la* here) is not an affix and as such repels V:

(17)

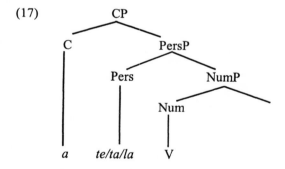

So these dialects have Pers filled by a true clitic, that is, they have the negative value for the parameter in (11). In this respect they differ minimally from Welsh, since in both languages AgrS = Pers is morphologically realized (in many persons). Poletto also mentions, citing Benincà (1995), that some varieties have clitics lower in the agreement field that function exactly as we are claiming Welsh Person clitics do, in that they attract V and so appear as suffixes on V. This is visible in the 2sg, 1pl and 2pl in various Lombard varieties, as in the forms of the Lugano dialect *vegnat*, "you (sg) come," *vegnum*, "we come," *vegnuf*, "you (pl) come" (Benincà 1995).

What I have said so far gives an analysis for Welsh which fits well with work on Northern Italian dialects and on agreement systems in general. However, we still need to account for the anti-agreement and VSO properties.

The proposals so far take us part of the way toward an account of the VSO property. In terms of the idea that Pers is occupied by a subject clitic that behaves as a syntactic affix, we can see why V must move there. But why can no DP move to SpecPersP? In other words, what underlies the differences between Welsh and Italian illustrated by (8)? To answer this, let us look again at the Northern Italian dialects. Some of them, mainly Veneto varieties, do not allow a subject clitic to cooccur with a subject DP in the Specifier of the position filled by the clitic. This can be seen with a negatively quantified subject, as these cannot topicalize:

(18)   Nisun (*el) magna.   (Veneto)
            nobody (*SCL) eats
            'Nobody eats.'

But many Northern Italian dialects allow this (the subject clitic can license a null subject, however we construe this operation as taking place, and so overt DP subjects are never obligatory). According to Poletto (2000), this is the situation in "Friulian, most Piedmontese dialects and some Ligurian varieties." Example (19) is from Friulian:

(19)   Nisun al mi capiss.   (Friulian: S. Michele a T.)
            noone SCL me understands
            'Nobody understands me'
            (Poletto 2000: 6.1)

So it seems that the presence of a subject clitic in Pers can "block" SpecPersP or not, as a parametric property. Clearly what we want to say is that Welsh is like Veneto in having this property (we must add that the Welsh "subject clitics" must always appear in order to "support", [i.e. attract] the verb stem; in the Italian dialects, this may not be obligatory, i.e. the subject clitic can be dropped in [18], since the verb is formed independently of the clitics). We can state that Welsh has the relevant Veneto-like property if we say that merger of a subject clitic values the features of Pers. In other words, these subject clitics have interpretable features that can value the uninterpretable features of Pers by merger, to phrase things in terms of the system in Chomsky (2000, 2001) (alternatively, we could simply say that the subject clitics are directly interpretable and so there is no checking or valuing of features here). So this is the status of Welsh and Veneto subject clitics.

For dialects like Friulian, Piedmontese, and such, of the type illustrated in (19), we treat the subject clitics as a manifestation of uninterpretable features of Pers, and so these have to be valued by a subject DP (note that in Chomsky's terms they also have an EPP-feature that can trigger insertion of an expletive subject clitic). It may be that the analogue of Welsh subject clitics, but with uninterpretable features, is constituted by languages like French, where a subject seems to have to raise into SpecPersP, and verbal agreement is uninterpretable. Whether we say this depends on other decisions about the analysis of French atonic subject pronouns; see Sportiche (1998) on this.

The preceding proposals account for both the null-subject property of Welsh and the fact that SpecPersP is not a possible subject-position. This is done in terms of a reasonable analysis of the agreement system that does not add anything to notions needed for the analysis of Northern Italian dialects and null-subject languages: subject clitics that occupy head-positions in a "split-Agr" system, clitics with +/−interpretable features, enclitic subject clitics, and the correlation between rich agreement and verb-movement. But what about the position that overt subjects occupy? Given the strict adjacency of the verb and (definite) subjects (see 1.1), we have to say that the subject occupies SpecNumP; see (15). Why? And how is this connected to anti-agreement? It is clear that the answer (and the crucial difference between Welsh and the Romance strong-agreement languages) lies in (12) and (13): the fact that Welsh, to put it in Italo-Romance terms, lacks *raddoppiamento dell'accordo*. This fact is what underlies both the subject's position and anti-agreement.

Everything I have said here holds only for strong-agreement languages. In weak-agreement languages like English, a DP must always appear in the highest SpecAgrP (i.e., SpecPersP). We can take this to be caused by the EPP, supposing then that the EPP applies at the Pers level where Pers lacks (significant) morphological realization. This idea can be exploited in order to cause a subject to always appear in SpecNumP in Welsh, if we stick to the idea that Welsh has weak agreement at the Num-level.

The analysis just sketched solves part of the problem, but it faces some serious difficulties. First, as we saw at the end of chapter 1, Welsh has no obligatory EPP effect: it simply is not true that SpecNumP always has to be filled (unless we make the theoretically undesirable move of assuming expletive *pro*). Second, Welsh is a null-subject language. Whether or not we assume argumental *pro* in our analysis, we see from examples like (6) that number agreement can be marked by an agreement affix. In fact, the anti-agreement phenomenon shows that number agreement is marked exactly where no subject DP appears. Clearly we have to account for this. Dealing with this point is the subject of the next section. That will then permit us to complete the analysis of VSO order.

In this section, I have sketched a parametric network for agreement systems that can account for very well known cross-linguistic variation in the realization of agreement, the position of verbs, null subjects, subject clitics, and the positions of subjects. I suggested that the Celtic VSO languages have a natural place in this network of possibilities. So we take a big step toward replacing the notions of strength/weakness of V- and D-features with the system just proposed.

2.1.2   Anti-Agreement

The anti-agreement effect is illustrated in (20) (repeated from [84] of chapter 1):

(20)   a.   Canon
             sing-3pl
             'They sang.'

b.   Canodd
     sing-3sg
     'He/she sang.'

c.   Canodd y plant.
     sang-3sg the children (pl)
     'The children sang.'

d.   *Canon y plant.
     sang-3pl the children (pl)

As (20) shows, the anti-agreement effect consists in the fact that the verb cannot agree in number with an immediately following nominal subject, (20c). Where the subject is null, as in (20a), the verb must agree. Where number agreement fails, as in (20c), the default form of the verb is third singular. So we see that number agreement, although morphologically marked, is obligatorily suspended in VSO clauses with non-pronominal subjects.

Let us consider the contrast between (20a) and (20d) first. Here 3pl -*n* is merged in Pers and attracts V. Suppose that this element also values Num's features under a head-head relation; that is, it is able to license Num as plural in virtue of its own plural feature and its structural proximity to Num. This can in fact be seen as a case of Chomsky's (2000, 2001) Agree relation. According to Chomsky (2000), Agree holds where a Probe c-commands a Goal (and there is no other potential Goal that intervenes between them) and the features of the Probe and the Goal are non-distinct. In these terms, Pers corresponds to the Probe and Num to the Goal in (20). Clearly Pers c-commands Num and no other head of any kind intervenes between them, and so the conditions for the Agree relation are met. So let us suppose that Num is an uninterpretable feature that is valued as plural (and hence rendered interpretable) by the interpretable ϕ-features on Pers (Chomsky also requires the Probe to have features that are uninterpretable; this could be the V-feature of Pers, but since saying this would represent a step backward given the result of the previous section, I will simply relax the requirement here). In that case, Num's ϕ-features do not need a value, and hence, since we know from the lack of obligatory expletives that Num does not have an EPP-feature (i.e., it does not require its Specifier to be filled), no subject can move into SpecNumP; on why this entails that no overt subject can appear at all, see the next section. In this way, the basic anti-agreement effect, illustrated by (20d), is accounted for, as well as the obligatory 3pl interpretation of (20a).

Turning now to (20b, c), I observed in the previous section that 3sg agreement does not resemble a pronoun in Welsh. So let us assume that these forms are *not* subject clitics; this person/number combination is either zero or the placeholder -*dd*. Also, let's assume, uncontroversially, that 3sg is the unmarked person/number combination. So in this case we have unmarked features without morphological realization. It is reasonable to suppose that a head with these properties cannot value anything—an unspecified head cannot give specifications to another one.

Where such a clitic appears in Pers, Num has no value and so is not interpreted. But there are in principle two ways in which Num can receive a value in this situation, either by default, in which case it will be interpreted as singular, or by getting a value from a DP that moves to its Specifier, in which case the value will depend on that of the DP. Both options are found: the former is operative in (20b), the latter in (20c). When a DP-subject raises to SpecNumP, that subject then gives Num a value, although this will have no morphological reflex. In other words, despite appearances, there is agreement, at the Num-level, here. There is no requirement for agreement in number features between the subject and Pers (in fact, the structural configuration relevant for determining agreement is lacking— see Kayne 1989, Guasti and Rizzi 2002). So this allows a plural DP to appear in SpecNumP where a default clitic appears in Pers (and attracts V). In other words, this accounts for (20c). This account carries over to anti-agreement in the type of variety mentioned in note 2 that has fewer distinctions in agreement-marking and may not allow null subjects (see note 3). We simply have to assume, quite standardly, that feature distinctions do not always correlate with morphological distinctions, that is, that syncretism exists.

Of course, the configuration of (20c) is allowed with an overt singular DP subject:

(21)   Canodd   y   plentyn.
          sang-3sg the child-sg
          'The child sang.'

In (21), everything is as in (20c), except that Num has the underspecified feature that is interpreted as singular.

It has been well known at least since Rizzi (1986b) and Brandi and Cordin (1989) that anti-agreement of a limited type is found in Northern Italian dialects. Here are some examples from Poletto (2000):

(22)   a.   A ze morto   do fiole. (Bastia di Rovolon: Central Veneto)
            SCL is dead (m.sg.) two girls
            'Two girls have died.'

       b.   A   no ze rivà   i   putini. (Loreo)
            SCL neg is arrived the children
            'The children have not arrived.'

Here there is no SCL in the agreement field (*ze* is an auxiliary, and *a* is in C). If there's an SCL of the right type, agreement is found, however:

(23)   E   son muars i   fantas. (Felletis di Palmanova: Friulian)
           SCL are dead   the boys
           'The boys are dead.'

Also, preverbal subjects trigger agreement:

(24)　　　　　I   putini   i   è   rivà.　　　(Loreo)
　　　　　　　yhe children SCL have arrived
　　　　　　　'The children have arrived.'

Compare (24) with (22b). Poletto argues that wherever a position in the agreement field is activated by an SCL, the verb shows agreement (in other words, there is agreement with locally c-commanding positions that bear φ-features; this can be analyzed in terms of Chomsky's [2000, 2001] Agree relation, as described earlier, so the situation here would be just as in Welsh). However, Northern Italian dialects differ from Welsh in that verbal agreement can assign a value to Num via verb-movement (assuming the verb always moves at least to Num); in Welsh this isn't possible and so the subject moves to SpecNumP as described earlier.[11] So we see that Welsh is like a weak-agreement language at the Num-level and like a strong-agreement language, in fact a Northern Italian dialect of the Veneto type, at the Pers level; see again (12) and (13). These observations are true up to the fact that Num does not require expletives in its Specifier, although it does allow them; see later.

Standard Italian (and, in Stylistic Inversion constructions, French) shows agreement in the equivalents of (22): for example, *sono morte due ragazze*, "are dead(f.pl.) two girls(f.pl.)," corresponding to (22a). In a non-subject-clitic, null-subject language like Standard Italian (recall also that French has null subjects in Stylistic Inversion contexts; see Pollock 1986), consistent with (12), the finite verb or auxiliary (here *sono* in Standard Italian) must move to Pers, giving rise to full agreement.

Prepositions show both agreement-marking and the anti-agreement effect (although they differ slightly from verbs in that their "default agreement" form is the bare preposition rather than the 3sg form):

(25)　　a.　　arna-f　　　　　　　'on me'
　　　　b.　　arna-t　　　　　　　'on you(sg)'
　　　　c.　　arn-o　　　　　　　'on him'
　　　　d.　　arn-i　　　　　　　'on her'
　　　　e.　　?arn-on　　　　　　'on us'
　　　　f.　　?arn-och　　　　　'on you(pl)'
　　　　g.　　?arn-on　　　　　　'on them'

(26)　　a.　　ar y plentyn　　　　'on the child'
　　　　b.　　ar y plant　　　　　'on the children'
　　　　c.　　*arnon y plant　　 'on-3pl the children'

To account for these facts, we can simply assume that the same class of clitics as found in the clausal Pers position appears in the head of an AgrP (or PersP) associated with PP (see Rouveret 1991 for discussion and further motivation of this kind of structure and Roberts and Shlonsky 1996 for the idea that these clitics represent one class that is found with verbs). So in (25) P raises and left-adjoins to the clitic. Anti-agreement with P involves no agreement at all, and so the complement of P remains in a standard complement position.[12]

We saw at the end of chapter 1 that Welsh does not always require a subject in (what we are now calling) SpecNumP. The relevant examples are repeated here:

(27)   a.   Gwelwyd plant.
               see-PASS children
               'Children were seen.'

       b.   Mae yn yr ardd blant.
               is in the garden children
               'There are children in the garden.'

The question raised by the analysis of anti-agreement just proposed is: how is Num given a value in examples like (27)? In both cases Num must be linked to a postverbal subject, as in the English and Italian examples that follow:

(28)   a.   There are several unicorns in the garden.

       b.   Ne   sono stati arrestati molti.
               of-them have been arrested many
               'Many of them have been arrested.'

Whatever the long-distance licensing mechanism that links Pers to the postverbal subject is these examples, it can serve to link Num to the postverbal subjects in the Welsh examples in (27).[13] This can clearly be expressed in terms of Chomsky's (2000, 2001) Agree relation as outlined earlier. We return to the parallel between (27) and (28) in 2.3.4.2.

Another complication in Welsh is shown by the existence of "echo pronouns." These elements show what we might call "anti-anti-agreement." In other words, the verb agrees with these elements when they appear as subject pronouns:

(29)   a.   Mi welais i Megan.
               Prt saw-1sg I Megan
               'I saw Megan.'

       b.   Mi welaist ti Megan.
               Prt saw-2sg you Megan
               'You(sg) saw Megan.'

       c.   Mi welodd ef/hi Megan.
               Prt saw-past he/she Megan
               'He/she saw Megan.'

    d.   Mi welon ni Megan.
                Prt saw-1pl we Megan
                'We saw Megan.'

    e.   Mi weloch chi Megan.
                Prt saw-2pl you Megan
                'You(pl) saw Megan.'

    f.   Mi welon nhw Megan.
                Prt saw-3pl they Megan
                'They saw Megan.'

Echo pronouns also show up with inflected prepositions:

(30)   a.   arna-f   i   'on me'
        b.   arna-t   ti   'on you(sg)'
        c.   arn-o   fo   'on him'
        d.   arn-i   hi   'on her'
        e.   arn-on   ni   'on us'
        f.   arn-och chi   'on you(pl)'
        g.   arn-on   nhw   'on them'

To account for the echo pronouns, I restate and slightly generalize Poletto's observation regarding Northern Italian dialects, that agreement in φ-features holds between a φ-position and any locally c-commanding φ-positions. I define "φ-position" as any position whose D-content is exhausted by φ-features (i.e., any non-nominal position with φ-features, e.g., an inflected verb, or any pronominal) and "local" in terms of relativized minimality (i.e., there can be no φ-distinct φ-position intervening between the one controlling agreement and the agreeing element). This guarantees that in Northern Italian dialects subject clitics in the presence of subject arguments, and verb-agreement in the presence of subject clitics, always agree with the locally c-commanding φ-features, as Poletto observed. It also derives the generalization regarding the configuration for obligatory agreement in Guasti and Rizzi (2002). For echo pronouns, we can assume that everything we said in our account of (20) earlier holds, except that the echo pronouns are constrained to show the form dictated by the φ-features of the subject clitic in Pers, following Poletto's generalization. The echo pronouns in (29) are thus subjects in good standing, forced to show a surprising morphological shape. This implies that the echo pronouns do not in fact give Num a value (in the non-3sg cases, at least). These pronouns are manifestations of a fully unspecified DP, which agrees in features as a function of Poletto's generalization.

    There appears to be cross-linguistic variation regarding how overt pronouns are treated, in that in Irish neither pronouns nor full nominals can agree with the inflected verb in VS order:

(31)   a.   Chuirfeadh Eoghain/na léachtóiri isteach ar an phost sin. (Irish)
              would-put(sg.) Owen/the teachers in for the job that
              'Owen/the teachers would apply for that job.'

       b.   *Chuirfinn   mé isteach ar an phost sin.
              would-put-1sg I in   for the job   that
              'I would apply for that job.'

Presumably, pronouns must have a Num-value in Irish and are therefore unable to appear with an agreeing verb. As McCloskey and Hale (1984) show, the generalization for Irish is that no pronoun can ever appear with an agreeing form of the verb, but one must appear with a non-agreeing ("analytic") form of the verb. Example (31a) illustrates the non-agreeing form and (31b) the agreeing form; there is considerable variation among Irish dialects as to which agreeing forms are available in which tenses (see McCloskey and Hale 1984 and Ó Siadhail 1989 for details). In terms of the analysis of Welsh just proposed, the agreeing verb forms are really verb + subject-clitic combinations, where the subject-clitic values Pers and Num, and thereby prevents any DP from occupying either Specifier (including pronouns, if we assume that Irish pronouns have a Num-value, as just suggested). The analytic forms are like Welsh (20c); here there is an expletive clitic that, being overt, values Pers as 3sg. A DP in SpecNumP fails to agree in Person-features with anything, but this causes no problem, as this DP values Num. So an example like (31a) is just like (20c).

The preceding proposal about the difference between Irish and Welsh pronouns receives one piece of interesting support. As McCloskey (1996b) shows, Irish lacks expletive DPs completely. In Welsh, however, expletive pronouns are found in some constructions, although they are not obligatory; see (33). McCloskey (1996b) argues that the absence of expletive pronouns underlies the existence of the salient unaccusative construction in Irish, that is, unaccusatives whose single argument is a PP, as in:

(32)   a.   Laghdaigh ar a neart.
              decreased on his strength
              'His strength decreased.'

       b.   Mhéadaigh ar a   neart.
              increased on his strength
              'His strength increased.'
              (McCloskey 1996b: 242–243)

McCloskey (1996b: 260–262) argues, following Burzio (1986: 73, note 9; 209–210, note 4), that this construction can only exist where there is no expletive subject looking for a PP associate. The proposals for the licensing of Agr-heads lead us to expect this. Irish is a subject-clitic language, I have suggested, and so has no expletive DPs since Pers always values Num. Welsh, however, has optional expletive DPs, as in the following:

(33)   a.   Mae **hi'n** bwrw glaw.
                is   it-Prt raining
                'It's raining.'

         b.   Mae **yna** blant   yn yr ardd.
                is   there children in the garden
                'There are children in the garden.' (cf. [27b])

In terms of the proposals made here, we can treat these expletives as echo pronouns, like those in (29) and (30). In fact, the analysis given there effectively treats the echo pronouns as expletives that agree with Pers in accordance with our modification of Poletto's agreement principle (the variation in form in true "echo-expletives" like those in [33] is not relevant here, as it involves gender—feminine vs. neuter—features, which are not encoded on Pers). The difference between Welsh and Irish reduces to a simple difference in pronoun inventories: Welsh has a class of pronouns that Irish lacks.[14] I have no explanation for why Welsh should have echo pronouns with the properties they have, although I can understand why they should be optional, why they should agree, and why their existence correlates with the existence of overt expletive pronouns. I also correlate the presence of echo pronouns, the possibility of overt expletives, and the absence of salient unaccusatives in Welsh with the opposite properties in Irish.

    Even internally to Welsh, there are subject pronouns that do not trigger agreement. Both "reduplicated" and "simple independent" pronouns can appear in the focus position, and in this case there is no agreement:[15]

(34)   a.   Myfi a   gafodd anrheg.   — reduplicated pronoun
                me Prt got-3sg present
                (Tallerman 1996: 98)

         b.   Fi a   gafodd anrheg.   — simple independent pronoun
                I Prt got   present
                'It was me who got a gift.'

To be more precise, we can say that the trace of the pronouns—*myfi* in (34a), *fi* in (34b)—in SpecNumP is not associated with agreement; it acts like an overt DP. This accords with the idea that traces and pronouns are distinct kinds of elements (however this distinction is to be made in technical terms).

2.1.3   Conclusion

In this section, we have seen that a closer look at the Welsh (anti-)agreement and pronominal system leads to a deeper understanding of the nature of the trigger for

V-movement. I have suggested that the fundamental property of Welsh is that it has a series of subject clitics that must be realized as syntactic affixes in the context of an analysis of AgrS, independently motivated by the data from Northern Italian dialects, which splits AgrS into (at least) Pers and Num. The affixal property of SCLs alone is enough to trigger V-movement, implying that the alleged "strong V-feature" has no independent existence. This property is also clearly both typologizable and learnable.

However, there is a further issue. The account of VSO and anti-agreement given here implies that the subject raises to SpecNumP to license Num, rather than to be licensed itself. It is now time to examine this idea—and the general question of how structural Case is assigned in VSO systems—more closely. This will take us into a detailed consideration of the Initial Consonant Mutation (ICM) system in 2.3.

2.2   DP-Licensing and Case

2.2.1   Introduction

We have seen that the generalization regarding subject-positions in Welsh is that an overt subject can only appear in SpecNumP (except in passive and unaccusative constructions, which we will look at later). I now need to account for this. Doing this is central to accounting for VSO order and, in fact, to accounting for anti-agreement in examples like (20c) in the previous section (in the discussion there, I assumed that subject DPs had to move into SpecNumP, without giving a reason for this).

In recent work, a number of different mechanisms have been proposed for why subjects generally have to raise out of VP into a canonical subject-position. Consider an English example like (35), assuming standardly that the subject raises from some predicate-internal position to the surface subject-position that we take to be the Specifier of a functional head F (whether this is seen as AgrS, I, T, or Pers; these choices are not crucial for the point here):

(35)   John F [t$_{John}$ left].

Here *John* has the following relations with F:

(36)   a.   *John* agrees with F.
        b.   *John* checks a D-feature with F.
        c.   *John* is attracted by F's EPP-feature.
        d.   *John* is assigned Nominative Case by F.

In the case of a simple sentence like (35) in a language like English it is very difficult to decide which of the properties in (36) is in fact responsible for triggering movement of *John* (indeed, the question was only explicitly recognized for the first time in chapter 4 of Chomsky 1995). Consider now a VS, anti-agreement sentence like (20c) in Welsh:

(20c)   Canodd   y   plant.
               sang-3sg the children
               'The children sang.'

Welsh permits us to immediately dismiss D-feature and EPP-feature checking as the movement triggers here; as we saw in the previous section, Welsh allows (and Irish, a language which is very similar to Welsh in the crucial respects, requires) the absence of expletives in SpecNumP. This means that there can be no general requirement for checking of a D-feature or an EPP-feature in this position, unless we make the dubious move of postulating expletive *pro* (cf. the discussion at the end of chapter 1). So we can eliminate (36b) and (36c) as mechanisms that trigger DP-movement in Welsh.

As we saw in the previous section, at first sight it appears that DP-subjects cannot fully agree in Welsh. So agreement with Num cannot be the mechanism that triggers raising. When a DP raises, it will value Num; otherwise Num defaults to singular.

So what causes the DP to raise? The only answer remaining open to us among the options listed in (36) is that the DP raises for Case reasons. In this section I want to develop this idea. First, I propose an account of licensing the subject. The view that I advocate is one in which DPs are licensed as bearers of Case, although there is no mechanism of Case-assignment or checking as such. Instead, the operative notion is that of configurational licensing. As we will see, it is possible to formulate this idea without making reference to Case parameters, a notable advantage of this analysis of VSO. This is described in 2.2, and the final piece of the picture regarding the position of the subject, and hence of VSO order, is presented. Section 2.3 extends the approach to the licensing of direct objects. This entails an analysis of the Direct Object Mutation (DOM), which is based on and develops the proposals in Roberts (1998). Putting together 2.2 and 2.3, we will see that the mutation system provides the morphophonological realization of Case in Welsh. This conclusion in turn leads to the question of how to analyze non-inflected direct objects (objects of non-finite verbs) and of possessors, which form the subject matter of chapter 3.

2.2.2   Licensing Subjects

Case is a good example of an "imperfection" of natural language in the sense of Chomsky's recent work (see Chomsky 1995, 2000, 2001, Chomsky, Belletti, and Rizzi 2000). It is common to regard Case-licensing as a condition on argumenthood (see Aoun 1981; Chomsky 1981, 1986), but in the context of a minimalist theory one can think the only condition we should impose on arguments is the θ-criterion (or at least the part of the θ-criterion that states that arguments need a θ-role, leaving open the possibility that they may bear more than one). Nevertheless, there is no question that in many languages DPs vary in morphological shape according (roughly) to their grammatical function. In the context of a theory that reduces grammatical functions to structural positions (cf. Chomsky 1965), this means that in such languages DPs are required to have specific morphological shapes in specific structural positions. Hence some syntactic property determines the morphological shape, and it seems reasonable to follow tradition in calling this property a Case feature. So different Case features are associated with different structural positions. Now, if we assume that languages with impoverished morphology have the same abstract syntactic features as languages with richer morphology, we are led to propose abstract Case features for all languages, whether or not individual morphological systems provide an overt realization for these features. So it is extremely natural to posit abstract Case. However, we can at least try to maintain that there are no Case parameters.

I will thus assume that UG makes available a set of Case features, including at least Nominative, Accusative, Dative, and Genitive. Following the spirit of the Visibility Condition of GB theory, which required all θ-marked elements to have Case, I will assume that DPs are associated with unvalued (i.e., unspecified) Case features, and that these features must be valued in order for the DP to be interpreted, that is in order for the DP to receive a θ-role. The configurational licensing conditions on Case are simply the statements of the contexts in which Case features can receive a value.[16]

A preliminary statement of the contexts in which the Case feature is valued as Nominative is given in (37):

(37)   Value (Case, DP) = NOM iff DP is in SpecAgrP.

Here AgrP is intended to cover Pers and Num (as well as others, as we will see in the next section and in the next chapter). Example (37), as stated, does not require Agreement heads (including Num) to have or assign a Case feature nor does it require that SpecNum, or any other Agreement Specifier, be occupied by a DP. As we have seen, this is exactly what is needed in order to account for the facts of Welsh. For this reason, it seems preferable, at least to avoid overgeneration of unassigned or unchecked Case features, to regard NOM as resulting purely from the configuration the DP occupies.

As we have seen, in Welsh (and presumably in other VSO languages) nothing needs to agree with the subject DP and the subject DP does not need to agree with anything. Hence movement to any Agreement Specifier will satisfy (37). Relativized minimality requires that the DP move to the lowest agreement Specifier, that is, the one I have been calling SpecNumP. Following Rizzi (2000), I formulate relativized minimality in terms of the notion of Minimal Configuration (MC), as follows:[17]

(38) $(A_1, \ldots A_n)$ is a chain iff, for $1 \leq i < n$
            (i) $A_i = A_{i+1}$,
            (ii) A_i c-commands A_{i+1}, and

(iii) A_{i+1} is in a minimal configuration with A_i

(39)   Y is in a Minimal Configuration (MC) with X iff there is no Z such that:
        (i) Z is non-distinct in featural and structural type from X and
        (ii) Z c-commands Y and Z does not c-command X.

Crucially, I assume that all agreement heads are of the same featural type, being positions whose content is exhausted by ϕ-features (cf. the definition of ϕ-position following [30] earlier). Given (38) and (39), then, Num functions as an intervener for a putative relation between a DP in SpecPersP and its predicate-internal trace.

More precisely, there are three cases we can imagine in which a DP moves to a Specifier in the Agreement system in order to be Case-licensed as NOM following (37). The first possibility is that DP moves to SpecNumP and no further. This does not violate relativized minimality and does Case-license the DP but of course is only possible where (a) Pers imposes no agreement requirement (i.e., has neither uninterpretable agreement features nor an EPP-feature) and (b) Num is not valued (see 1.2 on both these points). As we have just seen, this is what happens in Welsh and, in combination with the idea that Pers contains a syntactic affix that attracts V, it is responsible for VSO order and anti-agreement.

In the second case, DP moves to SpecNumP and on to SpecPersP. NOM is licensed in SpecNumP following (37), and relativized minimality is not violated. However, Pers must have some property that attracts the DP, or the second movement is not allowed. In a language where Pers does not contain a subject-clitic and instead contains features that need to be valued by a DP in its Specifier, this second movement from SpecNumP to SpecPersP will be required. This is what happens in familiar SVO languages (with the exception of Veneto-like subject-clitic varieties; see 1.1). As is standardly assumed, SVO languages vary as to the position occupied by the inflected verb; see the remarks on verb-movement to Pers in 1.1 and the speculative comment on Germanic in 4.3.2.

The third possibility is that the subject raises directly to SpecPersP, assuming Pers requires a value, skipping SpecNumP. This is ruled out by relativized minimality in the way described earlier. Hence, as I said, if the requirement is simply NOM-licensing, with no further agreement requirement at the Pers level, movement cannot go beyond SpecNumP.

Schematically, then, we have the following:[18]

(40)   a.   Pers   DP   Num $\ldots t_{DP}$ — VSO (Pers attracts V)
        b. DP Pers t_{DP} Num t_{DP} — SVO
        c. *DP Pers   Num t_{DP}

This completes the analysis of VSO and anti-agreement. The crucial steps in deriving VS as opposed to SV order are:

(41)   a.   Pers is occupied by subject clitics that function as syntactic
                affixes; otherwise V bears no agreement affixes;

b.   the Case-licensing condition in (37);

c.   relativized minimality.

As I argued in the previous section, (41a) is a specific parameter of Welsh. It was seen there that it blocks DP-movement to SpecPersP, forces V-movement to Pers, and requires plural Num to be licensed either by a subject-clitic (agreement affix) or by a DP (anti-agreement). The effect of (41b) is to trigger DP-movement into the agreement system. Finally, (41c) is the general principle of locality that applies to all instances of movement. The interaction of relativized minimality with the proposals regarding agreement and verb-movement is summarized in (40).

NOM has no morphological reflex in Welsh. It has a reflex in Irish, though; McCloskey (p.c.) points out that the analytic verb form (as in [31a] earlier) shows up with a Nominative pronoun, as in *bhris siad* (broke-analytic they-NOM = 'they broke'; Ó Siadhail 1989: 183). This fact can be readily accounted for under the analysis of anti-agreement proposed here. Also, it can be argued that the zero-realization of NOM in Welsh forms part of a highly impoverished morphological case paradigm. This idea has implications for the analysis of possessive constructions and non-finite constructions, as we shall see in chapter 3. In order to support it, I need to analyze the Direct Object Mutation (DOM) in terms of Case-licensing. This is the goal of the next section.

2.3   The Syntax of Direct Object Mutation

2.3.1   Introduction

Initial consonant mutation (ICM henceforth) is a well-known feature of the Celtic languages. Welsh is unique among these languages in showing a case of ICM that is apparently not triggered by a specific lexical item. This is the direct-object mutation (DOM henceforth). DOM applies exactly where the finite main verb moves to the pre-subject position in a transitive clause (i.e., to Pers, in terms of the analysis presented in 2.1). However, where an auxiliary appears initially and the transitive main verb is realized in a non-finite form, known as the verbal noun, occupying a position in between the subject and the object, there is no DOM. This is illustrated in (42):

(42)   a.   Mi welodd Megan **blant**.
                 Prt saw   Megan children
                 'Megan saw children.'

        b.   Mae Megan wedi gweld **plant**.
                 is   Megan Asp   see   children
                 'Megan has seen children.'

In (42a) the word for "children" undergoes mutation from *plant* to *blant*. The phonological processes involved in the mutations are summarized in table 2.1.

Table 2.1   Initial consonant mutations in Welsh

Class	Root	Soft	Nasal	Aspirate
−voice, −cont	p	b	mh	f
	t	d	nh	t
	k	g	nh	x
		—> +voice	—> +nas	—>+cont
+voice, −cont	b	v	m	
	d	ð	n	
	g	∅	ŋ	
		—> +cont	—> +nas	
+son	m	v		
	ł	l		
	rh	r—> +voice		

Here my aim is to propose an analysis of DOM and ICM that integrates these striking phenomena with what is known generally regarding phonosyntactic processes, functional heads, and parametric variation. I will argue that DOM is a phonological reflex of v and hence—plausibly—of Accusative Case (in this respect, the analysis is similar to Zwicky 1984; to the extent mutation most often occurs in the environment of lexicalized functional heads and that sometimes the only lexicalization of that head is the phonological mutation feature, the analysis is also like that proposed for Irish by Duffield 1995).[19] More generally, I assume the following condition on ACC-realization:

(43)   Val (Case, DP) = ACC iff DP is in SpecVP

I take the subject to be merged in Spec,vP (see Chomsky 1995: 331) and direct objects to be merged in SpecVP (see Larson 1988, Haider 1997). Thus ACC is not available to subjects, as they are simply generated too high in the structure. Direct objects appear in the configuration in (44):

(44) vP

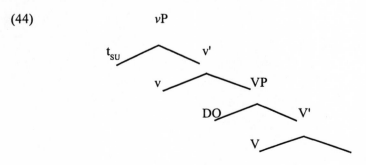

In finite contexts, V moves to *v* and through the T-system to Num and Pers, as we have seen. I will discuss the question of the position of non-finite verbs and their direct objects in chapter 3.

The morphological realization of ACC is soft mutation, whose phonological effects are summarized in the third column of table 2.1. I propose that this comes about because in the DOM context (i.e., when V moves through *v*) *v* contains a floating phonological feature (in this respect, my analysis is similar to that of Lieber 1983). This feature is assigned to an adjacent category in a structural configuration to be defined later, giving rise—under the right phonological conditions—to phonological effects in the assignee. This idea makes two important predictions: first, the phonological mutation process takes place at PF and so is sensitive to post-movement configurations only; and second, that mutation is sensitive to phonological constraints concerning linear adjacency, natural classes of sounds, and so on. As we will see, both of these predictions are fulfilled.

With this background, we can proceed to the analysis of the mutations.

2.3.2   An Initial Characterization of the Context of ICM

As table 2.1 shows, the ICMs have a certain phonological naturalness: soft mutation (or lenition) voices voiceless stops and makes voiced stops into the corresponding fricatives; as such it is a fairly standard case of consonant gradation with the single unexpected case of deletion of /g/ instead of the expected conversion to /ɣ/ (which exists in Breton as the soft mutation of /g/). Its effects on sonorants are less regular, in that /m/ is converted to /v/, while voiceless liquids are voiced. The nasal and aspirate mutations are essentially regular. I write soft mutation as *L*, aspirate mutation as *H,* and nasal as *N.*

What are the syntactic environments of ICM? It is a pervasive process in Welsh, but the basic structural generalization is clear (a number of possible counterexamples are discussed in note 20). First, ICM is characteristic of the complements of prepositions. Some Ps take soft mutation, some aspirate, and one triggers nasal mutation (in examples that illustrate ICM, the mutated word is boldfaced and its citation form is given in parentheses after the example):

(45)   a.   Soft mutation:
             i **Fangor**   (Bangor)
             to Bangor

        b.   Nasal mutation:
             ym **Mangor**   (Bangor)
             in Bangor

        c.   Aspirate mutation:
             gyda **chyfarchion** (cyfarchion)
             with compliments

Which P triggers which mutation is clearly a lexical matter—we have to indicate this in the lexical entry of a given P, so the lexical entry of *i* is *iL*, that of *yn* is *ynN*, and that of *gyda* is *gydaH*. The elements *L*, *N*, and *H* are as much a part of the lexical entries of these prepositions as the segmental structure and just as unpredictable. Non-mutation is also an option and thus part of the ICM paradigm; *ger*, "near," is a P which does not trigger ICM:

(46)   ger Bangor
            near Bangor

The syntactic context of ICM triggered by a preposition is:

(47)

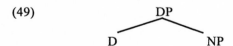

The second context of ICM is following a Determiner:

(48)   a.   pa/un/y **ferch**   (merch)
                which/one/the girl

        b.   dau **fachgen**   (bachgen)
                two boy

        c.   ei **gar/char**   (car)
                his/her car

(See Roberts and Shlonsky 1996: 186 and 3.1.3 for discussion of the idea that possessive pronouns like *ei* in [48c] are in D.) Note that the interpretation of the 3sg possessive pronoun depends on the mutation it triggers: the masculine pronoun triggers soft mutation, while the feminine triggers aspirate mutation (i.e. *eiL* is "his" and *eiH* is "her"). So (49) is a further syntactic context of ICM:

(49)

```
              DP
           ⟋     ⟍
        D          NP
```

        Third, preadjectival intensifiers can trigger mutation:

(50)   rhy/mor **wyn**   (gwyn)
            too/so white

On analogy with what is known about the functional structures associated with verbs and nouns, we might suppose that there is a functional projection DegP associated with AP (see Donati 1996). Assuming further that intensifiers occupy the head-position Deg, we then have the following structure for (50):

(51) .

Fourth, as mentioned in 1.2.2, the C-particles trigger mutation (negative particles trigger "mixed mutation," which is the aspirate mutation where possible—i.e., where the initial consonant of the mutated word is a voiceless stop—and the soft mutation elsewhere):

(52)   a.   (Fe/mi) **welais** i blant.   (gweld)
            (PRT) saw   I children
            'I saw children.'

       b.   Pwy a   **welith** Gwilym?   (gweld)
            who PRT will-see Gwilym?
            'Who will see Gwilym?'

       c.   (Ni) *welais* i ddim plant.   (gweld)
            (Neg) saw   I neg   children
            'I didn't see children.'

The particle is frequently not pronounced, but the mutation remains, indicating that the particle is subject to a late deletion rule in PF. I argued in chapter 1 that the particles are in Fin. So the ICM configuration is as follows:

(53)

The contexts discussed earlier can clearly be generalized as follows:

(54)   Mutation regularly affects the leftmost segment, if this is [−cont]
               or [+son], in XP in the configuration: Y'
                                                              /   \
                                                           Y   XP

In other words, the floating autosegment associated with Y attaches to the left edge of XP and is phonologically realized where possible (i.e., where the phonological conditions permit). This operation takes place under linear adjacency and is subject to phonological conditioning, as reference to distinctive features in (54) shows. It is clear, then, that this operation is a PF-operation, part of the operation of spell-out of mutation triggers; since we are treating mutation as part of the segmental structure of the mutation trigger, this is exactly what we expect. This is how ACC DPs are morphologically marked (and so we could say that ACC-marking is assigned to the direct object under head-government by *v*; see later).[20]

The syntactic configuration in (54) can be characterized as head-government. This conclusion parallels that of Rizzi and Savoia (1991), who show that /u/-propagation in various Southern Italian dialects is subject to a government condition. The precise nature of the government restriction varies from dialect to dialect, but one relevant parameter is F-government, government by functional head. If we take Prepositions to be functional heads, then the Welsh mutation environments fall under this characterization. Rizzi and Savoia also argue that the environments of obligatory liaison in French, analyzed in terms of c-command by Manzini (1983), can be characterized in terms of head-government. Also, Cardinaletti (1991) shows that /s/-affrication in Central Italian varieties is sensitive to a similar restriction.

So we observe that the head-government relation in (54) is relevant to phonosyntactic processes; this is a clear empirical generalization. The theoretical question is: can we reduce the head-government relation to something else, if we want to adopt a theory that eschews head-government as a primitive relation? Our proposals allow us a way of doing this. In our terms, the morpheme merged under Y contains a floating autosegment that must attach immediately to the right of Y. It follows that this element will attach to something in XP, including possibly SpecXP. This gives rise to the effect of head-government of SpecXP by Y. It may be, then, that the effect of head-government can be reduced to phonological properties of the putatively governing head (cf. Roussou 2002 for a similar idea applied to the analysis of complementizer-trace effects). A more conservative conclusion is that the configurational relation of head-government is relevant in PF, as argued by Aoun, Hornstein, Lightfoot, and Weinberg (1987) and, in the context of minimalist assumptions, by Adger (2000). I will not decide between these two positions here; further work, both on phonosyntax and on the residue of head-government, is needed. What is clear, though, is that we can describe the configurational licensing and the phonological manifestation of a given Case separately, which is desirable since the former is an aspect of UG while the latter is language-specific. Also, we leave open the possibility that the morphophonological operations that mark Case may have other functions; this is clearly true of soft mutation, in that it is highly unlikely that all instances of soft mutation are manifestations of ACC (see note 20, Borsley and Tallerman 1998, and Borsley 1999 on this).

So my basic claim about ICM is that it is a manifestation of a category F, where the element merged in F contains a floating autosegment that attaches to the left of a following category. In other words, the only odd thing about ICM is the segmental structure of the exponent of F. The effect of head-government arises from properties of PF, in particular the fact that a head is string adjacent to the specifier of its complement. This is the general characterization of ICM. What about DOM? Obviously we want it to fall under this general characterization—in this respect, accounts like those in Borsley and Tallerman (1998) and Borsley (1999) fail. As we shall see, my account achieves this goal.

In the examples we have looked at so far, the mutation trigger has further segmental structure in addition to the floating feature that gives rise to ICM, but nothing in principle prevents this autosegment from being the sole content of the relevant morpheme. This is what I will now propose for DOM, following Lieber (1983).

2.3.3 Direct Object Mutation: The Evidence and Some Proposals

The most striking example of ICM from a syntactic point of view is the DOM. As already mentioned, this mutation arises on direct objects (and other constituents; see later) when a transitive verb is fronted. DOM is illustrated in (55a), while (55b) shows that it does not arise in periphrastic tenses where the transitive verb is not fronted:

(55)   a.   Mi welodd Megan **blant**. (plant)
            Prt saw   Megan children
            'Megan saw children.'

        b.   Mae Megan wedi gweld **plant**.
            is   Megan Asp see   children
            'Megan has seen children.'

Lieber (1983) proposed that DOM is a manifestation of an empty P, which is inserted when V-movement destroys Case-adjacency (cf. *of*-insertion in early versions of GB theory such as Stowell 1981). Harlow (1989: 294f.) argues against this approach by pointing out that mutated direct objects do not behave like PPs under extraction. Clear cases of extraction of the complement of a P have two possible manifestations in Welsh, in that P can be pied-piped or apparently stranded. Where P is stranded, it must agree in person and number with the complement. These options are illustrated in (56):

(56)   a.   I **bwy** y   rhoddodd y dyn anrheg t?
            to whom PRT gave   the boy present?
            'To whom did the boy give a present?'

        b.   **Pwy** y   rhoddodd y dyn anrheg iddo?
            who PRT gave   the man present to+3sg?
            'Who did the man give a present to?'
            (Harlow 1989: 294)

There are two important things about (56). First, as (56a) shows, a Wh-word in a pied-piped constituent undergoes the mutation triggered by the P, while a Wh-word that apparently strands the P does not. Second, the particle in C is *y*. Now, when a direct object is extracted, the Wh-word cannot mutate and the particle is always *a* (see 1.2.2, 4.1, and note 3 on the *a/y* alternation):

(57)   **Pwy/*bwy** a/*y welodd Megan?
            who   Prt saw   Megan?
            'Who did Megan see?'

If the mutated direct object were in a PP, then, other things being equal, we would expect pied-piping to be possible and therefore expect the mutated form of the Wh-word to be possible. Moreover, *y* is the particle that usually occurs with extraction of or from PPs.

Harlow concludes that Lieber's analysis should be abandoned. Instead, he proposes that a constituent undergoes ICM when it is adjacent to and follows a DP. Borsley and Tallerman (1998) refine Harlow's generalization by saying that a phrase bears soft mutation if it is immediately preceded by another phrase that c-commands it; Borsley (1999) formulates this in terms of immediate precedence by a phrasal sister. The evidence for Borsley and Tallerman's conclusion comes from examples such as the following:

(58) a. Mae yn yr ardd **afr.**   (gafr)
          is   in the garden goat
          'There's a goat in the garden.'

     b. yr hen **gi**   (ci)
          the old dog

In (58a), a PP is fronted in a locative/existential construction (cf. Rouveret 1996). Here the DP *yr ardd* does not c-command the mutated DP, but the PP *yn yr ardd* does. Example (58b) illustrates the fact that prenominal adjectives trigger mutation. In both of these cases, Borsley and Tallerman claim that the triggering category is a c-commanding XP that precedes the mutation target. For Borsley (1999) *afr* is a complement in (58a), preceded by the phrasal sister $[_{PP}$ *yn yr ardd* $]$.

Borsley and Tallerman seem to reach the correct empirical generalization (although Tallerman 1999 points out a few counterexamples). It is clear, however, that the phenomenon remains unexplained on their account: it is entirely unclear why a phonological modification of a subclass of initial consonants of XP should take place exactly where XP is preceded and c-commanded by YP, where YP can be one of a range of categories. The generalization fails to relate DOM to ICM in general or indeed to any other grammatical mechanism. This kind of generalization is unprecedented in terms of Case theory, checking theory, or any other theory of licensing that I am aware of. It also fails to relate DOM to Southern Italian /u/-propagation or French liaison, both of which appear to be configurationally similar phenomena. Borsley (1999) makes reference to the notion of complement, implicitly relating it to other ICMs and to Accusative Case (although the notion of complement Borsley adopts has some rather counterintuitive consequences). If we can reduce Borsley and Tallerman's generalization to the general case illustrated in (54), we will at least have related DOM to the other instances of mutation and to /u/-propagation and liaison in a coherent way. I will now develop a proposal that does exactly this.

2.3.4 Direct Object Mutation: An Alternative Analysis

2.3.4.1 Introduction

In this section, I will present a modified version of the analysis of DOM put forward in Roberts (1998). The proposal is as follows:

(59)   DOM is the reflex of $[_v L]$.

This clearly falls under the general proposal for ICM given earlier. The relevant parts of the structure of a simple example like (54a) are as follows:

(60) $\ldots [_{vP} [_v L] [_{VP} \textbf{blant } t_V \ldots]]$

Here L has the effect of voicing the initial consonant of the object (citation form *plant*). This is because in the phonology it attaches to the first consonant to the right of v.

An important technical point needs to be clarified in connection with (60). In this kind of VSO sentence, the verb has clearly moved past v; as we have seen, V moves to Pers and the subject to SpecNumP, in such cases. If L is merged in v, how is it possible for V to move to this position and from there into higher positions?

There are basically two ways in which this question can be answered, either by appealing to Long Head Movement (LHM) of V, "skipping" v and therefore L, or by appealing to excorporation of V from the structure $[_v V [_v L]]$ formed by V-movement to v. Roberts (1994, 2000) argues that LHM must be subject to relativized minimality, essentially as formulated in (38) and (39) earlier (see also 4.2, where LHM in Breton is discussed in detail). However, if V moves through the V-related functional structure on its way to Pers, it seems implausible that it can skip an obviously V-related position such as v. Accordingly, I will not pursue this option.

This leaves "excorporation" of V from $[_v V [_v L]]$. Although no explanation has been offered for the general impossibility of excorporation (but see 5.1), it seems natural to rule this out in the case where head-movement forms a morphologically complex entity (by syntactic affixation or compounding) along the lines of some version of the Lexical Integrity Hypothesis; this was in fact proposed by Baker (1988: 73) and exploited in the discussion of different triggers for verb-movement in 2.1. But this approach offers no strong reason to think that a phonological feature cannot be stranded by head-movement. Phonological features are not obviously subject to morphological conditions of attachment to stems or to any straightforward version of Lexical Integrity (as [54] in fact implicitly states). We can formulate this idea as follows:

(61)   Phonological features do not copy (in the syntax).

See 5.1. The consequence of (61) in this context is that movement of v strands L since L is an uncopiable phonological feature. It seems possible that PF-features are in general unable to copy (or at least to be copied by the syntactic process of movement); perhaps they only spread in the sense familiar from autosegmental phonology. If we assume (61), and assume that in DOM configurations the content of v is exhausted by L, we can solve the technical problem.

My claim is that L manifests Accusative features, as I have said. In this respect, this account is rather similar to Lieber's. However, this analysis provides a straightforward account for the absence of DOM on extracted direct objects, which was Harlow's principal objection to Lieber's account, as we saw in the previous section. At the point of input to PF, (57) has a structure like the following:

(62)   **Pwy/*bwy** a welodd Megan $[_{DP}\ t_{pwy}\ ]$?

Quite simply, L is unable to attach to the Wh-trace here, as the Wh-trace does not have the relevant phonological properties (not having any phonological properties).[21] L cannot attach to the Wh-word *pwy*, as L attaches at PF while *pwy* moves in the syntax. Note that a pied-piped P triggers mutation in (56a).

We turn to the analysis of the non-finite verb (the verbal noun, VN) and the non-mutated direct object of (55b) in 3.2. For the remainder of this section, I want to consider certain implications of the analysis of DOM just sketched. The analysis has implications for three constructions in Welsh: impersonal passives, non-finite complements, and locative and existential copular clauses. I now briefly treat each one of these.[22]

2.3.4.2 Impersonal Passives

The first topic is impersonal passives (see chapter 1, note 42, for some remarks on the status of this construction). As we saw in 2.3.3, Harlow (1989) proposed that a constituent undergoes DOM when it is adjacent to and follows a DP. In a system where expletive *pro* is assumed wherever there is no overt expletive, this approach runs into problems in impersonal passive constructions, such as the following:

(63)   Gwelwyd **plant**.
        see-PASS children
        'Children were seen.'

Following the impersonal-passive form of the verb, DOM is not found. One might think that this is because *plant* in (63) is in subject position, but as we saw at the end of chapter 1, it appears that this is not so. *Plant* can be cliticized by an infixed pronoun that can in turn be optionally doubled by an echo pronoun, and the impersonal passive can appear in a periphrastic tense where the single argument follows the verbal noun and so must be in the direct-object position. These phenomena are illustrated in (64a) and (64b), respectively (cf. [80] of chapter 1):

(64)   a.   Fe   'i   welwyd   (o).
              PRT   -him see-PASS (he)

'He was seen (him).'

b.   Yr   ydys   yn gweld plant.
        PRT is-PASS Asp see   children
        'Someone is seeing children.' (=There is been seeing children)
        (Harlow 1989: 310)

Harlow observes that his generalization can be retained only if we assume that the subject is entirely absent in (63), that is, that the Extended Projection Principle doesn't hold in its standard form in Welsh. Of course, we have already observed this fact about the EPP (see 2.1). As mentioned at the end of chapter 1, expletive *pro* has no place in a truly minimalist theory (since it has neither PF nor LF properties). I therefore assume that SpecNumP is entirely absent in (63) and (64) (Num is valued by the impersonal morpheme in Pers, which in that case is extremely similar to non-argumental *si*; see chapter 1, note 42). In that case, Harlow's analysis can stand.

As we also saw at the end of chapter 1, (63) contrasts with null-subject examples that contains a referential null subject, which do trigger mutation:

(65)   Mi welais **blant**.
            Prt saw-1sg children
            'I saw children.'

The approach advocated here makes possible a very simple account of what is going on in impersonal passives, one that relates the facts just seen to other well-known facts about passives (unlike Harlow's account). The relevant parts of the structure of a simple impersonal passive like (63) are shown in (66):

(66) $[_{\text{PersP}}[_{\text{Pers}}$ gwelwyd $]\ldots[_{\text{VP}}$ plant t_{v} $]]$

Here, as in passives generally, ACC is deactivated (see Chomsky 1981, Burzio 1986); in the spirit of the analysis of passives put forward in Roberts (1987) and Baker, Johnson, and Roberts (1989), one could propose that the passive ending *-wyd* is incompatible with ACC-licensing. We can express this idea fairly mechanically in terms of the approach to DOM by ascribing the voice-feature PASS(ive) to *v* and by assuming that PASS and *L* are in complementary distribution in *v*. In this way, (65) is unproblematic; here, since the sentence is active, ACC is realized. (But cf. 3.3 for an important refinement of this proposal.)

To account for the Case-licensing of *plant* in (66), I exploit the clear similarity with Romance examples like (67):

(67)   ne   sono stati   arrestati molti.
            of-them are-3pl been-pl arrested-pl many-pl

'Many of them have been arrested.'

Modifying the Case-licensing approach along the general lines of Chomsky's recent (2000, 2001) Probe-Goal mechanism (see 1.2), we can restate the NOM-licensing condition as follows:

(37')   Val (Case, DP) = NOM iff DP is in a Minimal Configuration with Agr.

Here Minimal Configuration (MC) is to be understood as in (39) earlier. If we treat L as a ϕ-feature (but not PASS, although we retain Marantz's idea that PASS is in v), then its absence in passives will allow a DP in SpecVP to be in an MC with Num and hence be licensed as NOM in accordance with (37').

This analysis has the advantage that the lack of DOM in (63) is a further instance of Burzio's generalization: the subject is suppressed and so the object cannot be Accusative. Moreover, Burzio's generalization follows from the combination of Marantz's idea that PASS and L are in complementary distribution in v with reference to Minimal Configuration in (37'). A strange anomaly for Harlow's (1989) analysis becomes a reflex of a cross-linguistically robust generalization that is readily explicable in terms of our assumptions.

Treating *plant* as NOM in (63) means we have to reconsider the cliticization evidence in (64a). However, this evidence is not compelling; the generalization about Welsh is that diachronically Accusative forms of pronouns are restricted to preverbal clitics (exactly this generalization holds of French and Italian, at least, among the Romance languages) and preverbal clitics are restricted to diachronically Accusative and Genitive forms. Preverbal clitics surface as "infixed pronouns" in the characteristic position in between the preverbal particle and the IP-initial finite verb. In other positions, pronouns are either historically Genitive in form (we will look at the main cases of this type in chapter 3) or Nominative. The echo pronouns we analyzed in 2.1.2 are all historically Nominative, as is *o* in (64a), which is usually analyzed as the direct object in direct-object position. Historically, Nominative pronouns can occupy positions that we clearly do not want to consider Nominative synchronically—notably object of P, as seen in (30)—and so we can say that the synchronic generalization does not concern morphological case but position. A similar analysis can apply to the preverbal historically Accusative pronouns: synchronically, they are not Accusative but simply clitics. In that case, (64a) is not evidence that the single argument of the passive is ACC. On the Case-licensing of *plant* in (64b), see 3.2; note that there is no DOM here.[23]

To conclude this discussion, the lack of DOM in impersonal passives is exactly what we would expect if DOM is a reflex of ACC-licensing.

2.3.4.3 Non-finite Complements

Since I have not yet investigated verbal nouns, what I say about non-finite clauses here will not be very conclusive. Nevertheless, I can sketch an analysis that at least shows how the proposals about DOM work in this context.

In non-finite clauses we find that the non-finite verb-form of the embedded clause undergoes soft mutation under conditions exactly comparable to DOM: where the main verb is finite it mutates; where there is no verb-movement in the main clause it does not mutate. The following examples illustrate:

(68)   a.   Gall y   dyn [$_{XP}$ **ddreifio** car]
              can the man   drive   car
              'The man can drive a car.'

        b.   Mae'r dyn yn gallu [$_{XP}$ **dreifio** car].
              is-the man in able   drive   car
              'The man can drive a car.'

Also like direct objects, the VN does not mutate when the entire embedded clause is fronted:

(69)   [$_{XP}$ **Dreifio** car] (a)   all   y   dyn.
              drive   car (PRT) can the man
              'It's drive a car that the man can.'

It is tempting to conclude from this that all non-finite clauses are in fact nominals, that is, that XP = DP here. In that case, we could extend the account of DOM to these data straightforwardly. However, Borsley (1996) points out that in some kinds of complements VNs are possible, but ordinary nominals are not:

(70)   a.   Gobeithiodd Emrys [$_{XP}$ **ddisgrifio** 'r llun].   (disgrifio)
              hoped   Emrys   describe(VN) the picture
              'Emrys hoped to describe the picture.'

        b.   *Gobeithiodd Emrys [$_{XP}$ **ddisgrifiad** o'r llun] (disgrifiad)
              hoped   Emrys   description of-the picture

This seems to cast doubt on the idea that XP is DP in (68) and (69). For now, I take no view on the nature of XP in these examples (see 3.2). The important point for consistency with the analysis of DOM presented so far is that XP is the structural complement of *v*.

The relevant parts of the structure of (68a) are given in (71):

(71)   [$_{PersP}$[$_{Pers}$ gall] [$_{NumP}$ y dyn … [$_v$ *L*] [$_{XP}$ ddreifio car]]]

Following the general analysis of DOM, the first consonant to the right of *L* undergoes mutation if it can, hence the initial consonant of *dreifio* is mutated. *v* and XP are in the standard ICM configuration, given in (54). Example (69) parallels the Wh-movement examples we saw earlier (cf. [56]): the trace of the fronted XP does not contain a mutable consonant and so no mutation appears.[24]

A further point concerns finite clauses. Many finite clauses are introduced by the fronted auxiliary *bod* (cf. Hendrick 1996, Rouveret 1996, and 1.2.3 for analyses of this element). This element also undergoes DOM in the same fashion as direct objects and non-finite clauses; when the verb raises it shows DOM, and when the verb does not raise it does not:

(72) a.   Dywedodd Gwyn **fod** Emrys yn ddiog.   (bod)
             said   Gwyn be Emrys in lazy
             'Gwyn said Emrys was lazy.'
             (Borsley 1999: 283)

      b.   Mae Alys yn dweud **bod** Aled yn mynd allan.
             is Alys Asp say   be Aled Asp go   out
             'Alys says Aled is going out.'
             (Tallerman 1998: 29)

Here we can straightforwardly treat the CP as the structural complement of *v* (see 1.2.3 for evidence that this is a CP). The mutation alternation is then straightforwardly accounted for.

Finally, Wh-complements provide interesting support for a head-government approach to DOM (or, more precisely, for the idea that there is a minimality condition on the assignment of *L*). Harlow (1989) pointed out that the initial Wh-word of a Wh-complement does not mutate—and recall that such words can mutate, as illustrated by (56a):

(73) a.   Gwn i **pa/*ba** lyfr i'w ddarllen.
             know I which book to.3sgm read
             'I know which book to read.'

      b.   Gwn i **pwy/*bwy** a ddaeth yn ôl.
             know I who   Prt came back
             'I know who came back.'
             (Borsley and Tallerman 1998)

We can assume that the Wh-C, overtly realized as *a* in (73b), blocks head-government of its Specifier from outside CP by minimality. Hence *L* cannot be assigned to the Wh-words here. This favors a configurational rather than a linear approach to *L*-assignment; compare the discussion at the end of 3.2.[25]

2.3.4.4 Locative/Existential Copular Clauses

Here we find that the Theme argument undergoes what looks like DOM if it is not adjacent to the copula:

(74)   Mae yn yr ardd **gi**.   (ci)
              is   in the garden dog
              'There's a dog in the garden.'

In his very detailed study, Rouveret (1996: 134) proposes essentially the following underlying structure for locative/existential clauses:

(75) $[_{VP-1}$ CL $[_{VP-2}$ ci [bod $[_{PP}$ yn yr ardd]]]]
                                 dog be   in the garden

CL here denotes a null locative clitic to which *bod* incorporates. Leaving aside this and various other details of Rouveret's analysis, the most important point for my purposes here is that three alternative derivations are available from an underlying structure like (75). On the one hand, *ci* can move to SpecNumP, PP remaining unmoved, and be licensed in the usual way for subjects, that is with no mutation. This gives (76):

(76)   Mae('r) ci yn yr ardd.
              is (the) dog in the garden
              'The/a dog is in the garden.'

Alternatively, the expletive *yna*, "there," can be inserted in SpecNumP, and neither *ci* nor the PP move. In this situation, *yna* is licensed as Nominative and *ci* therefore cannot be licensed as NOM:

(77)   Mae yna **gi** yn yr ardd.   (ci)
              is there dog in the garden
              'There's a dog in the garden.'

If *gi* is VP-internal here, then our analysis of DOM can account for the mutation. However, examples like the following show that *gi* is higher than the aspect particle and hence presumably higher than Asp and so outside VP (and higher than *v*; see later):

(78)   Mae yna **ddyn** yn siarad efo Mair.   (dyn)
              is   there man Asp speak with Mair
              'There is a man speaking with Mair.'
              (Rouveret 1996: 130)

For these cases, I take it that *ddyn* occupies the Specifier of the position where the auxiliary (*bod*, which surfaces suppletively here as *mae*; see section 1.2.3) is generated. Rouveret (1994: 82–85; 1996: 134) proposes that *bod* is generated in a V position (see [75] and 3.2.3). Hence *ddyn* here is in SpecVP, and so ACC, and so undergoes DOM.[26]

The third possible derivation from (75) involves raising of the PP, to give (74).

Here again, *ci* undergoes DOM. It might appear that PP goes to SpecNumP here, but, as we saw at the end of chapter 1, this is probably not the case (see chapter 1, note 41). In order for *ci* to be able to be the attachment target for L in (74), the PP must be higher than v. The PP cannot move to Spec$v$P, as this is the base position of the subject. I conclude that Rouveret's abstract clitic heads a VP-external category— *contra* the representation in (75)—into whose Specifier PP moves. If this category is situated higher than v, then we can retain the general account of DOM for (74). This implies that vP is situated in between VP-1 and VP-2 in (74), in turn suggesting that VP-1 is a functional category. I suggest that this category is AspP, a category I'll say more about in 3.2.[27]

2.3.5   Conclusion

We see that it is possible to maintain an interesting and insightful analysis of DOM in terms of Case-licensing. The central hypothesis is that DOM is the PF-realization of v's Accusative Case as the floating feature L; in this I follow the basic insights of Lieber (1983) and Zwicky (1984).

The analysis proposed here has the following features:
- it is an empirically adequate analysis of ICM in Welsh, which fully integrates DOM with the other cases of ICM;
- it relates ICM to phonosyntactic processes found in other languages, notably Southern Italian /u/-propagation and French liaison;
- it fits naturally into a configurational Case-licensing theory of the sort outlined in 2.2.

I submit that, because it has these features, this analysis takes us a step further toward a genuine understanding of ICM.

2.4   Conclusion

In this chapter, I have considered the triggers for V-movement and DP-movement. The account of DP-movement tells us when we have NOM and when we have ACC in Welsh. I repeat for convenience the Case-licensing conditions I have made use of here:[28]

(79)   a.   Val (Case, DP) = NOM iff DP is in a Minimal Configuration with Agr.
        b.   Val (Case, DP) = ACC iff DP is in SpecVP.

Obviously, we can restate (79b) as (79b'):

(79b')   Val (Case, DP) = ACC iff DP is in a Minimal Configuration with v.

These proposals for Case-assignment fit in with our analyses of three salient phenomena of Welsh syntax:

(80)   a.   VSO order (see 1.1).
       b.   The anti-agreement effect (see 1.2 and 2.2).
       c.   Direct Object Mutation (see 2.3).

These features of Welsh can be accounted for in terms of the interaction of the Case-licensing conditions in (79) with independently motivated UG principles (e.g., relativized minimality; see 2.2) and the parameters of the Agr-system discussed in 2.1.

So we arrive at the result that the "V-feature" isolated at the end of the previous chapter is really a subject clitic in Pers that functions as a syntactic affix, and that the "D-feature" is the DP-movement to SpecNumP that takes place to license Num when Pers lacks the features necessary to do this. The first property, as I stressed in 2.1, is a typologizable and learnable property that interacts with a whole parametric network sketched out there. The second property is directly connected to anti-agreement and the default agreement that can be manifested by Pers (see 2.1). These results are of some interest for their implications regarding the analysis of Welsh itself, for their wider empirical implications, some of which I have briefly touched on, and for their conceptual nature: parametric variation can be maintained to be limited to very simple morphological properties, while the central principles of UG (e.g., Case-licensing, Full Interpretation, relativized minimality) remain constant.

A very simple result of 2.2 and 2.3 is that we see non-mutation as a "realization" of NOM and DOM as a realization of ACC. We have also seen that the direct objects of verbal nouns are not mutated. Is it possible that they are NOM? The general question of the nature of the verbal nouns and their objects must now be dealt with. This entails looking at Possessors and the structure of nominals generally and is the subject matter of the next chapter.

3

Genitive Case, Word Order in DP, and Objects of Non-Finite Verbs

The goal of this chapter is to analyze the other principal instances of non-mutated argument DPs aside from the subject of the finite clause. The main purpose is to complete the picture of argument-licensing developed in chapter 2 by analyzing non-mutated objects of non-finite verbs. In order to do this, though, two preliminary points—both of considerable empirical and theoretical interest—have to be established: (i) the Case/agreement properties of Possessors, which resemble the direct objects of non-finite verbs in their position in relation to the head noun, in their pronominal forms, and in lacking mutation; and (ii) the nature of the verbal noun.

Regarding word order and movement relations in Welsh DPs, and the expression of possession relations, the salient points are as follows:

(1)   a. N raises to Q, a functional position between D and N, in all DPs;
          b. N raises to D where a non-pronominal Possessor is present (in SpecNP);
          c. The GEN-licensing rule:
            Val(DP,Case) = GEN iff DP is in an MC with DP-internal Agr.

Examples (1a) and (1b) are familiar from the literature on Celtic and Semitic; see the references later. Example (1c) is clearly parallel to (79a, b') of chapter 2, and in fact necessitates the following reformulation of the NOM rule of (79a):

(2)   Val(DP,Case) = NOM iff DP is in a Minimal Configuration with CP-internal Agr.

The close similarities among these Case-assignment contexts are obvious. The content of "DP/CP-internal Agr" in (1) and (2) should be defined as follows: a given occurrence a of Agr is mP-internal if there is a category m taken from the set of categories $X = \{D, C\}$ such that m asymmetrically c-commands a and m does not asymmetrically c-command another member n of X that asymmetrically c-commands a. Where m is D, Agr is DP-internal; where m is C, Agr is CP-internal.

In 3.1, I summarize the well-known evidence in favor of (1a), essentially the (near) N-initial nature of complex DPs. Next, I discuss the equally well known evidence for N-to-D raising in possessive constructions; see (1b). In this respect, as shown by Duffield's (1996) comparison of Irish and Maltese, Welsh shares almost all the relevant features of the Semitic construct-state construction, except for the position of the Possessor DP. All of this points to the conclusion that Welsh possessive DPs feature N-to-D movement, as has been observed by numerous authors, notably Duffield (1996) and Longobardi (1996). Here I also discuss the behavior of possessive pronouns, and how they interact with what was said about the agreement system in 2.1 and with the general structure proposed for possessive DPs. Finally, I take up the question of how N-to-D movement licenses Genitive Case, justifying the GEN-licensing rule of (1c).

In 3.2, I show how the proposals made here for Possessors carry over to the objects of verbal nouns. The account of verbal nouns relies on the natural idea that these elements are participles. This makes possible a detailed comparison with Romance past participles, from which one salient property of Welsh emerges: that Voice is "inactive" in participial constructions in Welsh but not in Romance. A further aspect of the comparison concerns the absence of a Have-auxiliary in Welsh, which receives a simple account in terms of the proposals in Kayne (1993).

3.1   Evidence for N-Movement in Welsh

3.1.1   The Head-Initial Properties of DP

In this section, I briefly review the well known evidence for N-movement within DPs which do not contain a Possessor. Most of this evidence has been adduced in Rouveret (1994) and (for Irish, where the facts are parallel) Duffield (1996). Nevertheless, I think it useful to review this evidence in the light of the discussion of verb-movement and clause structure in the previous chapters and in order to lay the groundwork for the analysis of verbal nouns later in this chapter.

Nominals are parallel to clauses in Welsh in that the central lexical category precedes most of its dependents in each. Aside from in possessive constructions (which have special properties; see later), the parallel emerges clearly if we compare a DP headed by a picture noun with an impersonal passive clause, as in (3):

(3)   a.   y llun   o 'r dyn gan Megan
                the picture of the man by Megan
                'the picture of the man by Megan'
                (Rouveret 1994: 180)

b.　　　Mi/fe welwyd　y　dyn gan Megan
　　　　Prt　　saw-Pass the man by　Megan
　　　　'The man was seen by Megan/Megan saw the man.'

In each example, we have the order *functional element—lexical element—object—*
"BY-phrase." More generally, the only things that can precede the noun are the
definite article (as in [3a]), numerals, various quantifiers (including the Wh-element
pa, "which") and possessive pronouns. The latter three possibilities are shown in
(4) ([4a] shows that nouns modified by numerals do not pluralize):

(4)　　a.　　　pedwar drws
　　　　　　　four　　door
　　　　　　　'four doors'

　　　　b.　　　pob Sais
　　　　　　　every Englishman

　　　　c.　　　ei gar
　　　　　　　his car

　　　　d.　　　pa　　ferch
　　　　　　　which girl

Welsh thus requires the orders *noun—adjective* (NA), *noun—Demonstrative*
(NDem) and *noun—Genitive* (NG), conforming to rigid head-initial typology in
nominals as in clauses (and elsewhere, e.g., in PPs and in comparatives; see chapter
1, note 2):

(5)　　a.　　　yr ysgol fawr　(NA)
　　　　　　　the school big
　　　　　　　'the big school'

　　　　b.　　　y　llyfr hwn　(NDem)
　　　　　　　the book this (m)
　　　　　　　'this book'

　　　　c.　　　llyfr John　　　(NPoss)
　　　　　　　book John
　　　　　　　'John's book'

The article is optional in (5a); if the article is absent, the DP is interpreted as
indefinite. The article is obligatory in (5b) and impossible in (5c). I will consider
the implications of the impossibility of the article in (5c) in the next subsection.

　　Just as in the case of V-positions in clauses, we can find evidence that N leaves

NP in nominals. For now, I will simply suppose that adnominal APs left-adjoin to NP and to other DP-internal functional projections.[1] More precisely, suppose that AP-adjunction to N' is impossible. In that case, if we find the order *N—AP—complement of N*, where AP modifies N, then we can conclude that N has left NP. In other words, the structure of such a sequence would be (4), where XP is either a segment of NP or some DP-internal functional category:

(6)   N $[_{XP}$ AP $[_{NP}$ t_N complement of N $]]$

Orders of the kind shown in (6) are found in Welsh:

(7)   y   llun   hardd   o'r   dyn gan Megan
                       the picture beautiful of the man by   Megan
                       'the beautiful picture of the man by Megan'

We also find the order *N—Dem—complement of N*:

(8)   a.   y   llyfr   hwn am forfilod
             the book   this on whales
             'this book on whales'

       b.   y   llun   hwn o 'r   dyn gan Picasso
             the picture this of the man by   Picasso
             'this picture of the man by Picasso'
             (Rouveret 1994: 221)

Demonstratives follow APs, as (9) shows:

(9)   y   llyfr   newydd hwn gan John
                       the book new   this by John
                       'this new book by John'

It is plausible to think that Demonstratives are Specifiers (see Giusti 1997). In Welsh they must be Specifiers of a fairly "low" category. In that case, the order in (9) clearly indicates that N has left NP. It is also possible that they are adjectives, in which case the same point holds.

Having established that N leaves NP, we have to see what the landing site of N is (the analogy to the question raised in chapter 1 regarding the position of V is clear). Assuming the definite article *y* occupies D, (3a) shows that N does not raise as far as D (in non-possessives; see next subsection). We can also see that N does not right-adjoin to D from the fact that some of the elements that can precede N can intervene between the article and N, as (10a) shows. Examples (10b and c) show that other pre-N elements can cooccur:

(10)   a.   y   pedwar drws   (Det Q N)

> the four   door
> 'the four doors'

    b.   ei dri thŷ   (Poss Q N)
                  his three house
                  'his three houses'

    c.   pa   ddau lyfr   (WH Q N)
                  which two book
                  'which two books'

As in many languages (English, French, Spanish, etc.), possessive pronouns are in complementary distribution with the determiner. Given this and their initial position in the nominal phrase, it seems plausible to place them in D. Similarly, it seems plausible that *pa* occupies D here (although one can't exclude SpecDP as a plausible possibility for this element).[2] Between D and the overt position of the noun (in a non-possessive) the only items that occur are (low) numerals and a very restricted number of adjectives and quantifiers. The latter two possibilities are illustrated in (11):

(11)   a.   yr holl blant
                  the all   children
                  'all the children'

        b.   yr hen bobl
                  the old people

Certain adjectives can appear either pre- or postnominally, with different interpretations:

(12)   a.   yr unig blentyn
                  the only child
                  'the only child'

        b.   y   plentyn unig
                  the child   only
                  'the lonely child'

Note that *unig* has a quantificational interpretation when it precedes N. With the exception of *hen* (and a handful of other words, all of which can arguably be treated along the lines of prefixes like *cyn-*, "former/ex," that is, as elements adjoined to N), only quantifiers or elements capable of receiving a quantified interpretation can appear between D and N. Another category that can appear in this position is DegP as in *y [mor wyntog] dydd*, "the most windy day" (note that in this case mutation on *dydd*, which would give **ddydd*, is not triggered). This suggests that we should call the position that N moves to Q and situate these elements in SpecQP.[3] A full-fledged DP like (13) would then look like (14) (for concreteness and simplicity I'm assuming that the Demonstrative occupies SpecNP here and that the *gan*-PP occupies a complement position to N):

(13)   y   pum   llyfr   newydd   hyn   gan John
        the five   book new   these by John
        'the five new books by John'

(14)

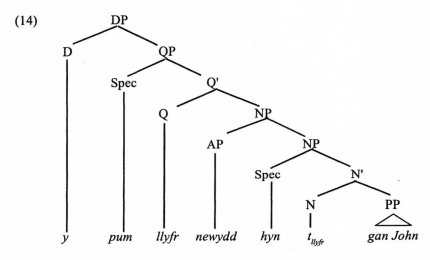

So we see that the order of elements within the Welsh DP is *Det—Q—N—A—Dem—complements*. This order can be simply accommodated into a DP that contains QP, with N-to-Q raising, as shown in (14). The alternative to postulating N-raising is to postulate rightward-movement or right-adjunction of APs and Demonstratives, along with obligatory extra-position of complements to N. Such an analysis seems more complex than the one in (14) and, if Kayne (1994) is correct, is impossible in any case.

Before going on to look at possessives, let us consider how the general characterization of ICM given in 2.3.2 can fit with the various instances of ICM that occur DP-internally (although, since we are not considering direct-object DPs, there is no question of ICM as a reflex of Case-assignment here). The cases of ICM that involve the elements considered in this section are listed in (15):

(15)

	Trigger	Target	Example
a.	*pa*	N	(4d)
b.	*y* (feminine)	N	(48a, chapter 2)
c.	possessive	N	(4c)
d.	N(feminine sg)	postnominal A	(5a) (*fawr < mawr*)
e.	prenominal A	N	(12a vs. b)
f.	numeral (<4)	N	(10b, c)

In addition, *pa* and possessive pronouns trigger ICM on a numeral that intervenes between them and the following noun, as seen in (10b) (*dri* < *tri*) and (10c) (*ddau* < *dau*).[4]

In chapter 2 I mentioned that determiners trigger ICM on N and suggested that this conforms to the general scenario for ICM, which I repeat here as (16):

(16)   Mutation regularly affects the leftmost segment, if this is [−cont] or [+son], in XP in the configuration:

$$
\begin{array}{ccc}
 & Y' & \\
 & \diagup\diagdown & \\
Y & & XP
\end{array}
$$

where Y is a mutation trigger.

Cases (15a–c) conform to (16), where Y = D and XP = Q. The fact that a numeral will mutate if it intervenes between D and N also falls under (16) in the same way. Similarly, (15d) conforms to (16), where Y = N and XP = AP, if AP is in a lower Specifier; if AP is adjoined to XP then this case falls under (16) if we assume that a segment of XP does not block ICM (this is consistent with the idea that segments of XPs do not block head-government and the idea that ICM takes place under head-government).[5]

Case (15e) does not fit into this schema, though. However, another context in which soft mutation is regularly triggered—and which does not fall under (16)—is within compounds. This can be seen particularly clearly in case of prefixation like *is-ganghellor*, "vice chancellor" (cf. *canghellor*, "chancellor"). See chapter 2, note 20.

In (15f), however, we have an instance of mutation being triggered by a numeral in SpecQP on a noun in Q. This clearly does not conform to the schema in (16). We could make this kind of case fall under (16) by introducing further structure and placing the numerals in a head that intervenes between D and N (but see note 6 for a different proposal).

As mentioned earlier, I do not want to say that these cases of ICM are manifestations of Case relations, since it's clear that the elements in question are not DPs. However, the relations that ICM marks are typical examples of morphosyntactic dependencies; this can be seen most clearly in (15b, d), where ICM marks gender. As mentioned in 2.3.2, (16) corresponds to the head-government relation of Rizzi (1990) and other work. One way to think of this is to take head-government to describe the relation where a feature (e.g., [+Feminine] in (15b, d)) is assigned by Y to X without movement of Y to X taking place (note that in [15b] this could be Agree in Chomsky's sense, but not in [15d], without further assumptions).

In conclusion, in this section we have seen that the order of elements in non-possessive DPs in Welsh can be accounted for by postulating N-to-Q movement in a DP with the structure seen in (14). The next thing to look at is the special nature of possessive DPs.

3.1.2   Possessive DPs

As I mentioned earlier in connection with (5c), in possessive DPs the order is *N–Poss*, and no article can appear. The fact that no article can appear is prima facie evidence that N moves further in these constructions than in other kinds of nominal. In terms of the structure in (14) this would mean that we have N-to-D movement in possessive DPs. In that case, the partial structure of (5c) would be (17):

(17)

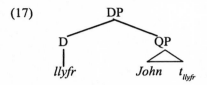

This clearly resembles what has been proposed for the Semitic construct-state construction (see in particular Ritter 1988, Mohammad 1988, Siloni 1997). In this section, I compare the Semitic construction with the Celtic one, basing the discussion on Longobardi (1996) and Duffield (1996). The same point has been made by many other authors (for references and a critical evaluation of this analysis, see Shlonsky 2000). The important difference that emerges between the two systems concerns the position of the Possessor DP in (17). The different position of N in (14) and (17) accounts for the differing word order between possessive and non-possessive DPs. In the next section, we will see that N must move to D in order to license the GEN Case of the Possessor (this kind of movement violates Greed in the sense of Chomsky 1995, chapter 3, but I do not adopt that principle here; the precise parametric property of D, however, remains rather unclear). I assume that general N-to-Q movement is simply an abstract parametric property of Q (in Roberts's 2001 terms, this is Q^*_{Move}).

Longobardi (1996) lists the following features of Semitic construct-state constructions (he argues that construct states have a marginal existence in Romance languages, too):

(18)   A.   The noun that heads the construction occurs first in the whole nominal phrase;
     B.   A phrase semantically understood as a genitive argument always follows the head noun;
     C.   The article of the head noun disappears;
     D.   The Preposition that usually introduces genitive arguments (. . .) disappears;
     E.   Strict adjacency (i.e., no intervening adjective) is required between the head noun and the argument;
     F.   The head noun occurs deaccented and often with vowels phonologically reduced;
     G   The definiteness value of the head noun depends on (is harmonic with) the ± definite status of the complement (Longobardi's [16], p. 4).

We have already seen properties (18A–C) in (5c); the structure in (17) accounts for these straightforwardly.[6] Regarding (18D), it is clear that there is no overt P in Welsh possessives. In particular, the prepositions that typically mark possession (*o,* "of," *gan,* "with," etc.) are absent.

We see then that properties (18A–D) of Semitic constructs hold straightforwardly in Welsh (the same is true of other Celtic languages). However, property (18E) does not hold in Welsh (or Irish; see Duffield 1996 and later). If the possessed noun is modified by an AP, that AP intervenes between the noun and the Possessor (this was first pointed for Welsh in Rouveret 1991):

(19)   llyfr   newydd John
            book new   John
            'John's new book'

The order *N—Poss—A* is obligatorily interpreted such that the adjective modifies the Possessor, so the following is unambiguous:

(20)   ci   y   ficer bach
            dog   the vicar little
            'the little vicar's dog' NOT 'the vicar's little dog'

The translation of the 'the vicar's little dog' would be *ci bach y ficer*. In this respect, Welsh and Irish differ from Semitic, as pointed out by Duffield (1996: 318f.) on the basis of the following contrasts:

(21)   a.   teach an tsagairt   chiúin   (Irish)
              house the priest-Gen quiet-Gen
              'the quiet priest's house' (* 'the priest's quiet house')

        b.   ħu   ir-raõel   il-kbir   (Maltese)
              brother(m.sg.) the-man(m.sg.) the-big
              'the man's big brother'/'the big man's brother'

Duffield analyzes this difference in terms of differential movement of the Possessors; in Semitic languages, Possessors appear in the immediately subjacent Specifier to D, while in the Celtic languages the Possessor remains in a lower position. Here we see an important difference between the clause structure and DP-structure in the Celtic languages, as it appears that the possessor DP remains in a "low" position in Celtic. In terms of the structure in (14), it in fact remains in SpecNP. Nevertheless, in Semitic, on the one hand, as (22) shows, the Possessor moves to SpecQP in terms of the structure in (14). In the Maltese example in (21b), *il-kbir* could be either inside the Possessor DP in SpecQP, modifying the Possessor, or in the AP-position adjoined to NP, modifying the possessee. Hence the interpretative ambiguity. In Welsh and Irish, on the other hand, if AP modifies the Possessor it will appear in the DP in SpecNP, while if it modifies the possessee it will appear in the NP-adjoined position. In the latter case it precedes the Possessor, while in the former case it follows it. Hence the lack of ambiguity in these languages. In Semitic VSO languages, the parallels between nominals and clauses may be closer than in Celtic, if VSO clauses are as described for Welsh in chapter 1 (see Fassi-Fehri 1993: 222).

(22)

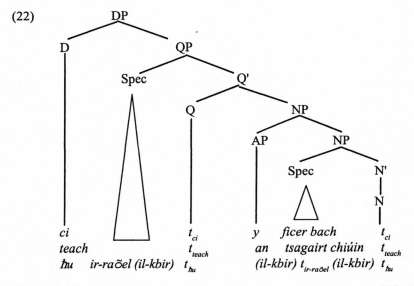

In Welsh, the head noun of a construct state cannot be modified by a Demonstrative:

(23)   *mab hwn y   brenin
            son   this the king
            'this son of the king'
            (Rouveret 1994: 220)

This may be because Demonstratives also occupy SpecNP, as suggested in (14). Then we can account for (23) in terms of the idea that Possessors are in SpecNP. If NP has a unique Specifier, there is simply not the structural space for both elements.

It seems natural to account for non-movement of Possessor DPs in possessive constructions in terms of the following Case-licensing condition:

(24)   Val (Case, DP) = GEN iff DP is in SpecNP.

It is clear that GEN lacks a morphological realization in Welsh, that is, is not associated with ICM, and as such is syncretic with NOM. In terms of what was said in 2.1, we must also assume that Q requires a noun to value it. I will reformulate (24) as we proceed.

Property (18F) does not appear to hold in Welsh. It is not clear whether this has any consequences for the analysis of the syntax of possessive DPs, however.

Finally, property (18G). What is at issue here is the interpretation of the head noun as definite or indefinite in the absence of the possibility of marking this by the presence or absence of *y*. In Hebrew, we see that the definiteness of the head noun must agree with that of the Possessor from the fact that adjectives show definiteness agreement (Longobardi 1996: 4):

(25)   a.   beyt ha-iR   ha-gadol
                house the-man the big
                'the big man's house'/'the man's big house'

        b.   beyt iR   gadol
                house man big
                'a big man's house'/ 'a man's big house'

        c.   *beyt ha-iR   gadol
                house the-man big

Example (25a) shows agreement for [+definite], and both nouns are interpreted as definite. Example (25b) shows agreement for [−definite] (the absence of *ha-* on both the Possessor noun and the adjective), and both nouns are interpreted as indefinite. Example (25c) is ungrammatical. Where the adjective is interpreted as modifying the Possessor noun, this can be accounted for by the lack of definiteness agreement between *ha-iR* and *gadol*; where the adjective is interpreted as modifying the head noun this must be due to the same factor—hence we see that the head noun must always agree in definiteness with the Possessor.

In Welsh, there is no overt definiteness marking on adjectives, and so purely interpretative evidence must be used:

(26)   mab brenin
                    'the son of a king/a son of a king'
                    (Rouveret 1994: 184)

Definiteness harmony only holds in one direction in Welsh, in that, as the translation of (26) shows, the head noun can either be definite or "inherit" indefiniteness from the Possessor. What is impossible, however, is an indefinite interpretation for the head noun where the Possessor is definite (i.e., 'a son of the king'; this must be expressed by *mab y brenin*, clearly marking the Possessor as definite). Longobardi (1996: 18) proposes that definiteness harmony in Semitic results from noun-movement through the head position whose Specifier is occupied by the Possessor (i.e., SpecQP). At this level, the Specifier and the head share a definiteness value, which is thus transferred to the head noun and retained by the head noun when it moves on to D. In terms of the structure given in (22), the relevant Specifier-head relation must hold within NP in Welsh. We assume that D is capable of being inherently definite in order to account for the fact that where such inheritance does not take place, the D targeted by N is [+definite] by default.

In this section we have seen that most of the properties of Semitic construct-state nominals are found in Welsh possessive DPs, with the important exception of (18E). As a consequence, we can adapt the widely assumed N-to-D movement analysis of Semitic constructs to their Welsh counterparts. The single difference between Welsh (and Irish, given Duffield 1996) and Semitic is that the Possessor remains in a lower position in Celtic than in Semitic. I have identified this position as SpecNP in Welsh, and proposed that this is the GEN-licensing position. These conclusions are essentially identical to those of Rouveret (1991, 1994) and Duffield (1996), with some differences in technical assumptions and node labels.

3.1.3   Possessive Pronouns

The possessive pronouns of Welsh are listed in (27):

(27)   fy nghar (i)   'my car'
               dy gar (di)   'your (sg) car'
               ei gar (o)   'his car'
               ei char (hi)   'her car'
               ein car (ni)   'our car'
               eich car (chi)   'your (pl) car'
               eu car (nhw)   'their car'

These elements are free morphemes that trigger various mutations on the following noun, as can be seen here. Note also the general possibility of a postnominal echo pronoun, a matter I will discuss in more detail later.

We saw in 3.1.1 that these elements are in complementary distribution with the definite article *y* and other likely D-elements (see [4]). This means that where the Possessor is a pronoun, we find the order *Poss—N*, exactly the opposite of what is found where the Possessor is a non-pronominal DP:

(28)   a.   llyfr   John   (N—Poss)
               book John
               'John's book'

       b.   ei lyfr   (Poss—N)
               his book
               'his book'

It seems clear from this that the possessive pronouns occupy D. In this position, they are in complementary distribution with *y*. For this reason, possessive pronouns repel N-to-D movement. They also repel DP-movement into their Specifier, of the kind found in Germanic possessive constructions (e.g., *John's/my car* in English). In these respects they resemble the subject clitics of Veneto-type Northern Italian dialects (see 2.1) and hence the Welsh Pers-clitics, with the sole (trivial) difference that they are free morphemes. It would thus be very natural to treat them as Agr-elements that raise to D (here there is a distinction between these elements and their Pers counterparts, as the latter—except when attached to *bod*; see 1.2.3— do not raise into the C-system).[7] I will now develop this idea and consider its consequences.

Possessive pronouns can be followed by a numeral, the head noun, and a postnominal AP:

(29)   ei bum   llyfr newydd
          his five   book new
          'his five new books'

Given what was said regarding (14), we want to say that *llyfr* has raised to Q here. The structure of (29) is thus (continuing to make the conservative assumption that AP is adjoined to NP):

(30)

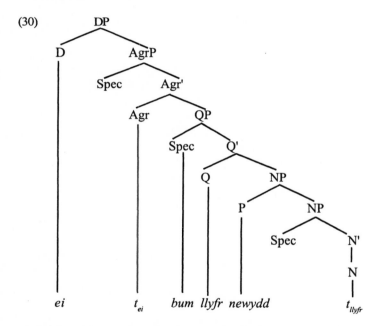

Let us turn now to the echo pronouns of (27). These elements occur in the position of a non-pronominal Possessor, that is following the head Noun and postnominal APs:

(31)   ei lyfr newydd o
          his book new   he (echo pronoun)
          'his new book'

In terms of what we have seen so far, then, these pronouns are in SpecNP. Agreement between the possessive pronoun and the echo pronoun follows Poletto's generalization of 2.1: agreement holds between a φ-position and a locally c-commanding φ-position.

However, we have to account for the impossibility of doubling a possessive pronoun and a full DP in SpecQP:

(32)   *ei lyfr John
              his book John

The natural answer to this question is in terms of Case-licensing. What I want to say is that merging a possessive pronoun in Agr prevents a full DP from being Case-licensed. This suggests the following reformulation of the GEN-licensing rule in (24):

(24')   Val(DP,Case) = GEN iff DP is in a minimal configuration with DP-internal Agr.

("DP-internal" is to be understood as defined at the beginning of this chapter.) Example (24') differs from (24) in referring to Agr rather than to SpecNP as the crucial context for Case-licensing and in using the notion of minimal configuration (defined as in [39] of chapter 2). This rule is natural and brings out a very clear parallel with the Case-licensing rules in (79) of chapter 2 (and, as pointed out in note 28 of that chapter, can be formulated in terms of Chomsky's 2000, 2001 notion of Agree). Example (24') allows us to account for the ungrammaticality of (32): when N moves to Agr a chain is formed between Agr and Q, and so Q does not act as an intervener that blocks the formation of a minimal configuration between the Possessor DP in SpecNP and Agr, and hence this DP is licensed as GEN following (24'). In this sense, the merger of a possessive pronoun in Agr "takes away" the DP's Case by preventing the formation of the chain that relates Agr and Q, since N-movement is pre-empted. Then Q intervenes in the formation of the minimal configuration between Agr and the DP in SpecNP.

3.1.4   Conclusion

This concludes the discussion of the salient points regarding the internal structure of DP. I have attempted to substantiate the points in (1), repeated here:

(1)   a. N raises to Q, a functional position between D and N, in all DPs;
          b. N raises to D where a non-pronominal Possessor is present (in SpecNP);
          c. The GEN-licensing rule:
             Val(DP,Case) = GEN iff DP is in an MC with DP-internal Agr.

None of these points are substantially original, although the details of formulation differ somewhat from the proposals elsewhere in the literature. The purpose of this discussion has been to lay the groundwork for the analysis of verbal nouns and the Case-licensing of the objects of verbal nouns. The next section deals with this and pursues some of the implications of the analysis I will propose.

3.2 Verbal Nouns and Their Complements

What I am interested in here is the form of the direct object in a periphrastic tense, for example:

(33)   a.   Mae   Megan   wedi   gweld   Iolo.
          is   Megan   Asp   see-VN   Iolo .
          'Megan has seen Iolo.'

      b.   Mae   Megan   wedi   ei   weld (o).
          is   Megan   Asp   3sg see   3sg (echo pronoun)
          'Megan has seen him.'

There are several things to note about this construction, as follows:

(34)   a.   The auxiliary is *bod*, "be"; there is no Have-auxiliary in Welsh (but cf. note 10).
      b.   An aspectual particle introduces the VN.
      c.   The object pronominalizes as a pre-VN possessive pronoun, with the usual option of a post-VN echo pronoun.
      d.   The pronoun triggers ICM on the VN (cf. *weld* without initial /g/ in [33b] and table 2.1).
      e.   The nominal direct object of the VN does not undergo ICM (see [55b] of chapter 2).

In this section, I will show how all these properties can be deduced from a simple structure for what I will call "participial clauses." Moreover, we will see that simple morphological parameters distinguish (33) from the rather different-looking Romance periphrastic tenses as in (35):

(35)   a.   Gianni ha visto Maria.
          Gianni has seen Maria

      b.   Gianni l'ha   vista.
          Gianni her-has seen-f.sg.
          'Gianni has seen her.'

To the extent that the analysis to be proposed works, it provides strong support for our approach to clause structure and parametric variation, in its application both to Welsh and to Romance.

3.2.1   Verbal Nouns

The term "verbal noun" is a translation of the traditional term *berfenw*, which designates the basic non-finite verb form in Welsh (J. Morris-Jones 1913: 386f.

points out the historical relations between these forms and non-finite forms elsewhere in Indo-European, including Latin/Romance infinitives in -*ere*). The traditional name is a very appropriate one, as VNs show some verbal properties and some nominal ones.

VNs are verb-like in that they contribute to the formation of the periphrastic tenses. I repeat the relevant periphrastic forms from chapter 1, note 1:

(36) *present*   mae e'n prynu   'he buys/is buying'
      imperfect   roedd e'n prynu   'he was buying'
      perfect   mae e wedi prynu   'he has bought'
      pluperfect   roedd e wedi prynu   'he had bought'
      preterite   naeth e brynu   'he bought' (. . .)
      future   bydd e'n prynu
                             neith e brynu   'he will buy'
      future perfect   bydd e wedi prynu   'he will have
                                       bought'   bought'
      conditional   basai fe'n prynu   'he would buy'
      conditional perfect basai fe wedi prynu   'he would have bought'

Here *prynu* is the VN that means "buy"; the mutated form *brynu* shows up in a number of cases (all of them quite regular: it appears where the finite auxiliary raises and there is no aspectual particle; see 2.3). Recall also that I pointed out in note 1 of chapter 1 that the generalization regarding Welsh tense forms is that any tense can be expressed periphrastically, but no tense has only a synthetic form, although some have both periphrastic and synthetic forms.

Borsley (1996) argues that VNs are non-finite verbs. First, the external distribution of VNPs (the constituent that contains the VN, its complement, and the pre-VN *ei*-pronoun) is different from that of DPs in various contexts (control contexts, raising contexts, and ECM contexts). I illustrate this here with what I take to be the control complement to a deontic modal:

(37)   a.   Dylai Gwyn ddisgrifio'r llun.
              ought Gwyn describe-VN the picture
              'Gwyn ought to describe the picture.'

       b.   * Dylai Gwyn ddisgrifiad   o'r llun.
              ought Gwyn   description-N of the picture

Second, the internal properties of VNs are quite distinct from those of DPs. VNs in fact fail most of the standard diagnostics for nominals. They cannot cooccur with the article, and they are modified by adverbs and not adjectives. Adverbs and adjectives are distinguished in Welsh by the presence of the predicative particle *yn* on adverbs, which is absent on (adnominal) adjectives:

(38)   a.   Mae Rhiannon yn canu *(yn) hyfryd.
             is   Rhiannon asp sing-VN Pred pleasant
             'Rhiannon is singing pleasant*(ly).'

       b.   Clywais i'r swn (*yn) hyfryd.
             heard I the sound Pred pleasant
             'I heard the pleasant(*ly) sound.'

More interestingly, there are differences regarding extraction and binding properties, in that VNs are more transparent to both movement and coreference than true DPs. In the case of extraction, this means that a resumptive pronoun is not possible when extracting the object of a VN embedded under *bod* but is optional when extracting a Possessor (see also Willis 2000: 545, 569):

(39)   a.   y   ferch   roeddet ti'n   ei   hoffi   (*hi)[8]
             the woman were   you-Pred 3sgf like-VN she
             'the woman you used to like (*her)'

       b.   y dyn y gwelais i ei fab (ef)
             the man Prt saw   I his son (he)
             'the man whose son I saw'

Following Roberts and Shlonsky (1996), and as we will see in more detail relative to (45) in the next subsection, I take the *ei*-pronoun in (39a) to be a kind of past-participle agreement. No echo pronoun is possible in object position because this position is occupied by the Wh-trace (cf. the remark on the complementary distribution of the echo pronoun in *cael*-passives in note 10). Example (39b) illustrates the general fact about Wh-extraction in Welsh that a resumptive echo pronoun is available where the extraction is long-distance (in the sense that it crosses two bounding nodes; see note 2 of chapter 4 and the references given there).

    Regarding binding, the pronominal argument of a VN must be disjoint in reference from the subject, but this is not required of a Possessor:

(40)   a.   Mae ef yn ei   daro (ef).
             is he ASP 3sgm hit
             'He is hitting him.'   — no coreference

       b.   Mae ef yn ei dy (ef).
             is   he in his house
             'He is in his house.'   — coreference possible

All these facts point very clearly to the conclusion that VNPs, despite certain appearances, are not DPs (see note 10 on *cael*-passives in this connection).

    However, VNs clearly have certain important "noun-like" properties. These include those of (34c, d, e) above: the object pronominalizes as a pre-VN possessive pronoun, with the usual option of a post-VN echo pronoun, except under extraction, as in (39a); the pronoun triggers ICM on the VN; and the nominal direct object of the VN does not undergo ICM. The full paradigm for object pronouns of a VN is given in (41) and should be compared with (27) earlier:

(41)   fy ngweld (i)   'see me'
             dy weld (di)   'see you (sg)'
             ei weld (o)   'see him'
             ei gweld (hi)   'see her'
             ein gweld (ni)   'see us'
             eich gweld (chi)   'see you (pl)'
             eu gweld (nhw)   'see them'

The lack of DOM after VNs is illustrated by (42):

(42)   Mae Megan wedi gweld   plant/*blant.
             is   Megan Asp see-VN children
             'Megan has seen children.'

A further important property is that VNs themselves can undergo DOM, as we saw in 2.3.4.3. The following pair, repeated from there, illustrates this:

(43)   a.   Gall y dyn **ddreifio** car.
             can the man drive   car
             'The man can drive a car.'

        b.   Mae'r dyn yn gallu **dreifio** car.
             is-the man in able drive car
             'The man can drive a car.'

In (43a) the VN *dreifio* mutates where the finite verb moves to Pers. In (43b) *dreifio* follows another VN, *gallu,* and so does not mutate. As we saw in chapter 2, this corresponds to the basic generalization regarding DOM—DOM affects the objects of moved (and therefore finite) verbs.

    The basic observation is that VNs themselves and their complements are licensed like head nouns and Possessors in possessive constructions, as described in the previous section. We might thus want to assign essentially the structure of (31) to the VN-part of examples like (33), which would give (44). The DP that contains the VN would be embedded under the aspectual particle, which I assume to be selected by *bod* (which I take to be V; see 2.4 and Rouveret 1994: 82f.). Above *bod,* the structure is as described in 2.1. This is very close to what Rouveret (1994) proposes. However, the difficulty lies in the fact that Borsley has given good evidence that VNPs are not normal DPs. We need to find a way of reconciling these two approaches.

(44)

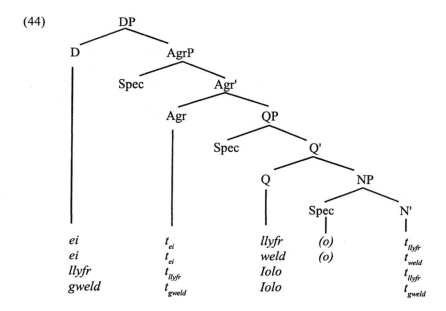

3.2.2   VNs as Participles

My proposal is to exploit the idea that VNs are participles, appearing in the following structure, selected by Asp:

(45)

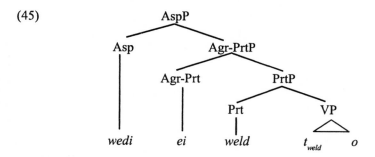

In (45) there's no DP, and so Borsley's points can be captured. (This is straightforward regarding [37], [38] and lack of articles; regarding the binding facts in [40], I assume standardly that non-finite participial clauses are not binding domains while DPs are. The extraction facts are much more complicated—see chapter 4, note 2, and Willis 2000—but it suffices to note that extraction from participial phrases is generally easier than extraction from DPs; in this connection, compare the English contrast between *Who do you remember [John [$_{PrtP}$ visiting t$_{who}$]]* and *?*Who do you remember [$_{DP}$ John's visiting t$_{who}$]].*) So in these respects I am following Borsley and treating the VN as a non-finite verb. Its "nominal" properties follow primarily from the nature of Agr-Prt. Let us look at the properties discussed in the previous section and see how (45) accounts for them. I will say more about the nature of the Prt-category in the next section.

First, *ei* is associated with Agr-Prt (cf. Willis 2000: 541, who treats these elements as occupying AgrO). There is no reason to postulate raising to D, as there is no D and no possibility of an article for *ei* to be in complementary distribution with (recall that this was the reason for assuming that *ei* raises to D in nominals; see 3.1.3). Agr-Prt is clearly different from subject agreement (the Pers and Num categories discussed in chapter 2). This is a property Welsh shares with Romance languages: in those languages participial agreement is restricted to gender and number like DP-internal agreement. So it may be that Agr-Prt is inherently more "nominal" than subject agreement. Another possibility is that the subject-agreement elements are clitics on finite V and hence cannot appear where there is no finite V (cf. the discussion of *bod* and *i* in 1.2.3; the agreement forms that appear there follow this generalization). I will return to this point in the discussion of *bod*-clauses later (see 3.2.4).

The *ei*-elements are free morphemes and as such repel V-movement. In this way, they also prevent Case-licensing on an overt object in SpecVP, following (24') if the Case is GEN and (2) if the Case is NOM. This accounts for the ungrammaticality of examples like (46):

(46)   *Mae Megan wedi ei   weld   Iolo
               is   Megan Asp 3sg see-VN Iolo

All of this directly parallels what I said about DPs earlier in this chapter.

Second, the VN undergoes ICM triggered by the *ei*-pronouns as Prt is "head-governed" by Agr-Prt. This can be readily seen by inspecting (45).

Third, the object of a VN fails to show DOM because the context of ACC-licensing is not met. The ACC-licensing condition we arrived at in chapter 2 was as follows:

(47)   Val (Case, DP) = ACC iff DP is in a minimal configuration with v.

Example (47) clearly captures the link between V-movement (through v; see 2.3) and DOM. We can also see why DOM, that is, ACC-licensing, is not available inside Agr-PrtP: there is simply no occurrence of v (or none close enough; the verb that selects Asp may be associated with v but this V will not be linked by chain-formation/movement to any position inside Agr-PrtP). However, the object of the VN is licensed by either (2) or (24'), depending on whether we regard Agr-Prt as IP-internal or DP-internal. Given Borsley's arguments and the structure in (45), we should regard it as IP-internal and therefore licensed as NOM. I will discuss the question of how the objects of participles are licensed as ACC in Romance and why they are not licensed as ACC in Welsh later.

Fourth, the VN shows DOM when it raises to Agr-Prt, as it does where no pronoun is present. Presumably this happens in order to value Agr-Prt (see later for some remarks regarding the apparently defective nature of Agr-Prt). When the

VN does not raise to Agr-Prt, that is, when there is an *ei*-pronoun in this position that repels VN-movement, it raises to Prt. We do not need to think of DOM of the VN (synchronically at least) as a realization of ACC, although it is triggered by v outside the participial phrase, since the leftmost consonant inside VP, the category in the relevant configuration with the trigger v, as in (16), is mutable. This gives a structure like (48) for the relevant parts of (43a). The *ei*-pronouns are generated in Agr-Prt. In general, then, XP in the discussion of non-finite clauses and DOM in 2.3.4.3 may be PrtP.

(48)

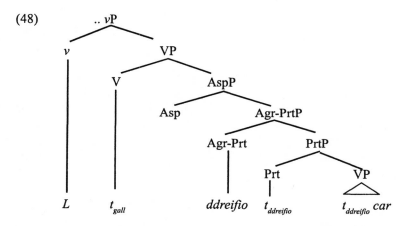

This structure matches that in Romance participial constructions as analyzed by Friedemann and Siloni (1997) rather closely (taking their AgrO to correspond to Prt in [48]; they do, however, propose a different structure for the complements to Have-type auxiliaries; see the next section for some discussion of such complements). In examples like (35), the participle raises to AgrPrtP (it may raise further, depending on the language, cf. Belletti 1990, Cinque 1999, but I leave that point aside here):[9]

(49)

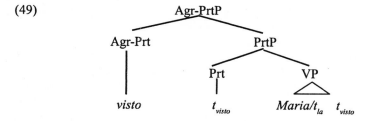

In fact, Belletti (2000) proposes a more complex structure, as follows:

(50)

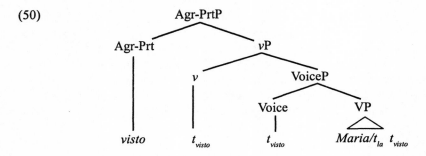

One advantage of this structure is that it provides a base position for the subject in participial clauses in Spec,*v*P. In Romance, participles raise all the way to AgrPrt in certain constructions (see the remarks on auxiliary-selection in the next section for more details). However, if we adopt this structure for the Welsh counterparts to these clauses, we must rather arbitrarily assume that *v* here lacks the ability to license ACC (i.e., to trigger mutation on the verbal noun). Suppose instead that we equate Prt with Voice and assume that the subject is merged in SpecVoiceP (this has the immediate advantage that implicit arguments of passives can be seen as empty categories licensed by Voice). So now we have the following structure in place of (49):

(51)

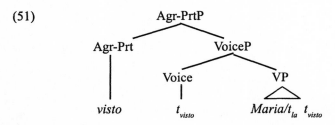

We are now in a position to understand one major difference between Welsh and Romance. Romance differs from Welsh in not allowing participial objects to be NOM (in the usual case, cf. the discussion in 2.3.4.2) or GEN (ever). How do we prevent the Case-licensing conditions licensing such a complement as NOM or GEN following (2) and/or (24'), given a structure like (51) (and given that in exactly this structure Welsh allows exactly this kind of Case-licensing)? The answer has to do with differing properties of the Voice position. Let us now ascribe to Voice in the context of Romance participial clauses the properties I have been assigning to *v* (see Kratzer 1994), in particular the ability to license ACC (this entails the relevant simple modification of [47], substituting Voice for *v*). So Romance Voice can license ACC or contain PASS. In fact, these two properties can be seen as a single feature, which either licenses an implicit argument in its Specifier (PASS) or Case-licenses an argument in a minimal configuration (ACC). Both properties are suspended with unaccusative and raising verbs, so we can observe that in these cases Voice is inert (but, for unclear reasons, not in locative/existential constructions; see 2.3.4.4 and note 26 of chapter 2). This observation is of course connected to Burzio's (1986) generalization. Let us call this PASS/ACC feature Voice's D-feature (this feature does not trigger movement since it is not associated with a strong EPP-feature). The idea1 that Voice in Romance has a PASS/ACC feature of this kind, but Welsh does not (or, alternatively, this feature is weak in Welsh) can be linked to the fact that Romance languages have passive participles, while the Welsh VN does not really have a voice property. Moreover, Welsh simply lacks a participial passive construction; the impersonal passive discussed in 2.3.4.2, is a synthetic form like the Romance non-argumental *si* (see note 42, chapter 1). The impersonal construction allows implicit arguments and is associated with lack of DOM on the direct object, as we saw in 2.3.4.2, so we have to say that in finite clauses Voice has a strong D-feature; only in non-finite clauses when it is selected by Agr-Prt, is this feature weak.[10] Voice is closer to the canonical object position in SpecVP than Agr-Prt and thus prevents the object from receiving NOM or GEN. Since this element is not a Case-licenser in Welsh, Agr-Prt functions as described in the previous section. Where Voice does not license Case in Romance, that is, in passive and unaccusative constructions, Agr-Prt may do so. In these cases the relevant argument is associated with past-participle agreement (it may move to subject position but does not have to; this is presumably connected to the independent question of T's EPP-feature in Italian; cf. Borer 1986, Alexiadou and Anagnostopoulou 1998 on this matter):

(52)   a.   É arrivata   Maria.   (unaccusative)
            is arrived(f.sg.) Mary(f.sg.)
            'Mary has arrived.'

       b.   É stata   vista   Maria.   (passive)
            is been(f.sg.) seen(f.sg.) Mary(f.sg.)
            'Mary has been seen.'

The fact that such objects are clearly NOM and not GEN suggests that Agr-Prt licenses NOM and not GEN in Welsh, too.

In Romance, where the direct object is a clitic, it raises through SpecAgrPrtP triggering agreement in number and gender as seen in (35b). The basic difference between the two systems lies in the morphological nature of Agr-Prt: this position can be filled by a pronoun, and hence repel movement in Welsh, on the one hand, while this is impossible in Romance. In Romance, on the other hand, a clitic can trigger agreement at this level by passing through the Specifier, something that is impossible in Welsh. In both systems, Agr-Prt is defective compared to subject agreement; it may have features that need a value, in which case it gets them by merger of a pronoun in Welsh and by Spec-head agreement with a clitic in Romance, but it may also lack ϕ-features altogether and simply trigger V-movement in both languages (cf. also the comments on participle movement in Romance in note 9).

So we arrive at the following general picture for Welsh and Romance (where "Pro" denotes whatever property of the relevant head is responsible for its attracting just pronouns):

		Agr-Prt	Voice
(53)	Romance:	sPro, (sV)[11]	sD, sV
	Welsh:	sPro, sV	wD, sV

Leaving aside a possibly independent difference between the two systems regarding the status of clitic pronouns just mentioned (i.e. that they are merged in a head position in Welsh but moved from a complement DP-position in Romance), the basic distinction between Romance and Welsh resides purely in the strength of Voice's D-feature. The strong V-feature abbreviated as "sV" here simply denotes the possibility of V-movement; in Welsh, this is pre-empted if an *ei*-pronoun is inserted in Agr-Prt. The notation is intended as a shorthand for what we assume are deeper properties (cf. the discussion of V-movement in IP in 2.1). As already mentioned, a strong D-feature does not necessarily trigger movement unless an EPP-feature is also present. The variation in the value of Voice's D-feature is linked to a morphological property: the presence of participial-marking. In this sense, the parameter is learnable, and the preceding discussion illustrates that it is typologizable. Voice's D-feature is analogous to lexically incorporated agreement in Romance verbs as described in 2.1.

This section completes the picture regarding Case-licensing, verb-movement, agreement, and ICM in Welsh. We now have a full account of all these properties, and one that allows us to see the similarities and differences with other languages fairly clearly. In the next section, I will pursue the comparison with Romance in another direction and provide an account in terms of the structure of participial clauses just given for the absence of a Have-auxiliary in Welsh.

3.2.3   AspP and Auxiliary Selection

The sketch of the Romance participial phrase in (51) did not include Asp. While it is clear that this position can be occupied by particles like *wedi* and *yn* in Welsh (see [36]), the Romance languages do not at first sight have any counterparts to these elements. Here I want to relate this to the fact, mentioned several times up to now, that Welsh lacks any alternation in its aspectual auxiliary system; that is, it has no Have-auxiliary. This can be done by adopting the account of Romance auxiliary selection in Kayne (1993). Kayne accounts for the familiar alternation between Have- and Be-auxiliaries in languages like Standard Italian by postulating: (i) that Have-auxiliaries are the result of incorporation of an abstract prepositional element (which Kayne designates D/P but I will call simply P) into a Be-auxiliary, (ii) that Universal Grammar thus has only the "archi-auxiliary" BE, and (iii) that the category headed by P is absent in unaccusatives (see Ledgeway 2000: 190ff. for a thorough exposition of Kayne's analysis).[12] Kayne shows how this proposal can capture the variation in auxiliary-selection that has been observed in Central Italo-Romance varieties (see Kayne 1993 for details; see also Vincent 1982, Tuttle 1986, Cocchi 1995, Ledgeway 2000).

We can integrate this idea with the structure proposed for participial clauses in the previous section by assuming that P is merged in Asp. So a fuller structure for (35a) than that given in (51) would be as follows:

(54)

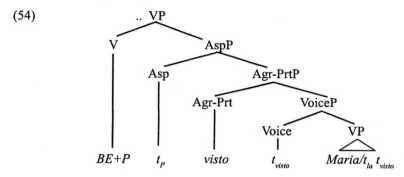

Now we are able to straightforwardly account for the existence of a Have-auxiliary in Romance but not in Welsh. In Welsh, the elements that correspond to Asp here are *wedi* and *yn* and they simply do not incorporate, as (55) shows:[13]

(55)

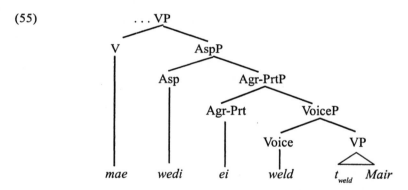

This analysis complements Mahajan's (1994) proposals regarding the absence of Have-auxiliaries in OV languages. Mahajan in fact proposes that P is merged as part of a constituent with the subject (in SpecVoiceP in terms of the structure in [55]) and, assuming P-incorporation depends on string adjacency (of a subject in SpecVoiceP and V in the structure in [55]), incorporation will always be impossible in head-final languages where V and SpecVoiceP will be separated by all the other material in VoiceP. We can in fact modify Mahajan's system in the light of Kayne (1994), in such a way as to weaken the correlation between OV order and the lack of a Have-auxiliary (an empirically justified move, given the presence of a Have-auxiliary in the OV West Germanic languages) and retain the idea that P is a head that takes the category that contains the subject as its complement, rather than an element that forms a constituent with the subject.[14] Suppose that the universal auxiliary, BE, is a head that triggers a standard kind of variation in movement: no movement, movement to its Specifier, movement to the head, or both types of movement. Welsh (and Celtic languages generally) instantiates the first option, as

I have just proposed. Hindi and other OV languages with no Have-auxiliary discussed by Mahajan instantiate the second. Romance instantiates the third, following Kayne (1993). And West Germanic OV languages with a Have-auxiliary instantiate the fourth option (this accords with the proposal by Haegeman 2001 and Biberauer 2003 that verb-final order in these languages is derived by movement of the complement of the position of the finite verb to the specifier of that position). Of course, in Roberts's (2001) terms, all these languages also instantiate the Merge option; the -Merge, -Move option would be instantiated by a language that lacks aspectual auxiliaries. In other words, the four varieties of BE under consideration here are all "strong."

Let us now consider auxiliary-selection in Romance in slightly more detail. This phenomenon can also in fact be handled in terms of feature strength, at least for Standard Italian. The basic generalization, subject to considerable variation across the Romance languages and dialects, is that the Have-auxiliary appears with transitive perfects and the Be-auxiliary with passives and with perfects of unaccusatives:

(56)   a.   Gianni ha telefonato.
              Gianni   has phoned   (unergative intransitive: HAVE)

       b.   Gianni ha visto Maria.
              Gianni has seen Maria   (transitive: HAVE)

(57)   a.   Gianni è arrivato.
              Gianni is arrived
              'Gianni has arrived.' (unaccusative: BE)

       b.   Maria è stata vista (da Gianni).
              Maria is been seen (by Gianni)
              'Maria has been seen.'   (passive: BE)

Following the basic idea in Kayne, although implementing it rather differently in technical terms, I propose that where the Be-auxiliary *essere* appears Asp does not contain the abstract P. To put it another way, Asp is strong when it contains P (Asp^*_{Merge} in the terminology of Roberts 2001) and weak when it does not. This appears to be linked to the obligatory presence of agreement morphology in Agr-Prt and to the absence of ACC in Voice. In other words, assuming as in the previous section that Voice's ability to license ACC is the reflex of a strong (D-)feature and that participle-agreement is a reflex of strong (D-)features on Agr-Prt, we have the following situation:

(58)   **Asp**   **Agr-Prt**   **Voice**
       Have: strong   weak   strong
       Be: weak   strong   weak

Here we just observe this pattern. In 5.2, I will suggest that the Be-pattern is an EPP-effect.

Direct confirmation for the analysis of the contrast between Welsh and Romance regarding the nature of P comes from the form of the Breton Have-auxiliary *kaoud*. As Schafer (1994: 106) describes, the forms of *kaoud* "consist of a proclitic on a base corresponding to (and in many cases identical to) the third-singular form of *bezañ* 'be' in the same tense." The proclitic agrees in person, number, and gender with the Possessor or subject of *kaoud*. Schafer goes on to present an analysis of these forms in which the proclitic is treated as an agreeing preposition (like Welsh, Breton has these in general) that incorporates into *bezañ*. Clearly we can integrate this analysis into the proposals regarding the structure of Welsh and Romance participial phrases, by simply inserting the proclitic under Asp in (55) andrequiring it to incorporate into V. So an example like (59) has the structure in (60) at the relevant stage of the derivation—ignoring both the fact that both the PP and *kaoud* seem to move into the C-system (see 4.2) and the fact that Breton has genuine participles, hence it's not clear where *kerzhet* might be inside Agr-PrtP:

(59)   D'ar ker o deus kerzhet.
           to-the town 3pl 'have' walked
           'They have walked to the town.'

(60)

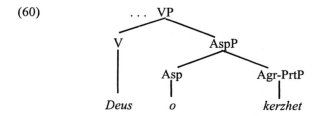

The analysis of participial constructions in Welsh and the absence of a Have-auxiliary has further possible consequences. In Welsh, the combination of Be and a preposition appears where in many other languages, notably in Romance, Have appears. In addition to perfects, this situation is found in possessive constructions, in various psych-constructions, and in some modal constructions:

(61)   a.   Mae gan John gar.
              is   with John car
              'John has a car.'

        b.   Mae gen i   ofn . . .
              is   with me fear . . .
              'I am afraid' (cf. 'J'ai peur,' 'Ho paura,' etc.).

        c.   Mae'n well ganddo fynd   adref.
              is Prt better with-3sg go-VN home

'He prefers to go home.'

These constructions are structurally like the locative/existentials we looked at briefly in 2.3.4 (see Rouveret 1996 for a comprehensive treatment). Of course, Kaynian preposition-incorporation is not an option in that case, hence there is no possibility of a Have-word appearing.

The Welsh psych-constructions with a Be-auxiliary and an overt preposition fit interestingly into a cross-linguistic paradigm observed by Freeze (1992) and Freeze and Georgopoulos (2000). They observe the locative paradigm in (62):

(62) a.   The Jaguar is in the garage.   — predicate locative
      b.   There is a Jaguar in the garage.   — existential
      c.   Mary has a Jaguar.   — possessive

(63) Russian:
      a.   Kniga   byla na stole.   — predicate locative
            book-NOM was on table
            'The book was on the table.'

      b.   Na stole byla kniga.   — existential
            on table was book-NOM
            'There was a book on the table.'

      c.   U menya   byla sestra.   — possessive
            at me-GEN was sister
            'I had a sister.'

The contrast between English (62c) and Russian (63c) can be accounted for if, as I have been assuming here, *have* is the derivational result of the incorporation of a Preposition into the archi-auxiliary BE; English has such incorporation, while Russian does not (see also Kayne 1993).

The locative paradigm has an interesting parallel in psych-constructions, as we can observe if we compare (62) and (63) with Belletti and Rizzi's (1988) paradigm for the latter:

(64) a.   John fears inflation.   — Type I
      b.   Inflation worries John.   — Type II
      c.   I soldi   piacciono a Gianni.   — Type III
            the money pleases   to John
            'Money pleases John/John likes money.'

Attempting to align the two paradigms in terms of thematic relations, we observe the following:

(65)   LOC   PSYCH
         a. Theme Pred Locative (63a/64a) Theme Pred Experiencer (64b)
         b. Dative-Locative Pred Theme (64c) Theme Pred Dative-Experiencer (64c)[15]
         c. Proform Pred Theme Locative (63b)   ??
         d.   ??   Experiencer Pred Theme (64a)

We can make the two paradigms more similar if we make two empirical observations. First, the LOC counterpart of (64a) (i.e., the left-hand column of [65d]) might be cases where the "locative content" generally encoded in a preposition (including P in languages like English) may be lexicalized in the verb as, to varying degrees, the "psychological content" (i.e., specification of the actual psychological state, rather than the theme or the experiencer of the state) of psych-predicates is in all the examples in (64). So we can suggest (66) for the left-hand column of (65d):

(66)   The garage contains a Jaguar.   (Locative Predicate Theme)

Most important for my purposes here, the Welsh psych-construction in (61) fills the gap in the righthand column of (65c), with the result that we can align the two paradigms very nearly exactly. This invites the inference that Experiencers are animate Locations, an idea supported by expressions like *put the fear of God in someone, put the wind up someone,* where an Experiencer role is assigned in a canonical locative syntactic frame.

Very roughly, all of these structures may derive from a structure of the following type (cf. Rouveret's 1996 structure given in (75) of chapter 2; [67] differs from that structure in that BE/*bod* is outside of the core thematic domain in [67], and Rouveret's CL-position is identified with Asp in (67), as I suggested in the discussion of [75] in chapter 2):

(67) $[_{IP} \ldots [_{VP}$ BE $[_{AspP}$ Asp $[_{XP}$ Location/Experiencer X Theme]]]]

I take no stand as to the finer structure or categorical nature of XP here. The most important point is that X is the head responsible for assigning the two θ-roles Location/Experiencer and Theme. In terms of (67) we can see why Welsh (or Celtic more generally) differs from other languages in allowing psych-constructions like those in (61). Since prepositions can appear in Asp (in [61] this is *gan*), no P-incorporation into BE is possible, as in perfects. Hence no Have-auxiliary appears in locative, existential or psych-constructions in Welsh. Similarly, the heads in IP above VP are not associated with EPP-features, as we saw in 2.1 and 2.2. For this reason, the various XP-raising operations that must be at work in the English, Italian, and Russian examples in (62)–(64) are not found in Welsh. More speculatively, we can think that the "psychological content" of a psych-predicate does not have to be realized on the finite verb in Welsh because of the presence of the morpho-logically isolating P in Asp. This element does not itself incorporate, as we have seen, and does not allow anything to incorporate to or through it. Hence X (or perhaps the result of incorporation of the head of Theme into X) cannot be mani-fested as the main predicate of the clause. Thus, although many questions remain open, we see that the analysis for the lack of a perfect Have-auxiliary has interesting and wide-ranging implications in other areas and that the assumptions made here can do some work in accounting for the properties of the Welsh constructions in (61). I leave the further elaboration of these isues, in particular the structure in (67), for future research.

In this section we have seen that the proposals regarding VNs have consequences in three areas, all of which open avenues of further research: why Welsh lacks a Have-auxiliary, why it has no passive participles, and the nature of the constructions in (61). The generalization in each case concerns the parametrically variable morphological properties of the Kaynian abstract P, which in Celtic is not in fact abstract.

3.2.4   Agreement Markers and *Bod*-Clauses

Here I want to take up a suggestion made earlier regarding the distinction between Agr-Prt and subject agreement. This will also lead to a closer comparison of DPs, clauses and "participial clauses," and extend the account of VNs to the *bod*-clauses discussed in 1.2.3.

What we have seen is that (i) subject agreement consists of PersP and NumP, where Pers is occupied by affixal subject clitics that trigger V-movement (2.1); (ii) DP contains Agr and Q, the former containing possessive clitics that are non-affixal, the latter attracting N; and (iii) "participial clauses" contain Agr-PrtP, which contains the same clitics as the DP-internal Agr, and Voice, which always attracts V.

We can clearly see that each system contains a true agreement position, into which agreement morphemes are merged, and a head that simply attracts the lexical head.[16] But why are the agreement morphemes different? The natural answer, alluded to earlier, is that the subject clitics are clitics on the finite V and the *ei*-clitics are the default agreement elements. It is well known that finite verbs trigger particular cliticization patterns (this is pervasive in Romance), and so I am not saying anything special in this. So now we see why the subject-agreement pattern is different from the others. Of course, the same (or a subset of) these clitics also cliticize to P (see 2.1 for a discussion of inflected prepositions).

The preceding idea makes a clear prediction: if we can find clauses where Pers and Num are present, but where V can't be finite, then we expect to find the *ei*-clitics. This is what happens in the *bod*-clauses and the past-tense *i*-clauses discussed in section 1.2.3.

As we saw in chapter 1, *bod*-clauses appear as the complements to certain types of declaratives, as in (68):

(68)   a.   Dywedodd Gwyn **fod** Emrys yn ddiog.   (bod)
             said   Gwyn be Emrys in lazy
             'Gwyn said Emrys was lazy.'
             (Borsley 1999)

b.   Mae Alys yn dweud **bod** Aled yn   mynd allan.
       is   Alys Asp say   be Aled Asp go   out.
       'Alys says Aled is going out.'
       (Tallerman 1998: 29)

Since the non-finite form of *bod* is a VN, it can, like other VNs, be associated with an *ei*-pronoun, be mutated, and be followed by an echo pronoun:

(69)   Mae o 'n   deud **fy mod** i 'n   dwp.
              is   he Asp say   my BOD I Asp idiot
              'He says I am an idiot.'

In chapter 1, I suggested that the *ei*-pronoun here is in AgrS. Following the proposals in 2.1, I now modify this to Pers. As we saw in chapter 1, this means that we have a root-embedded asymmetry that involves *bod*: it fails to raise to Fin in these examples. What is more important here is the fact that *ei* is in Pers, *bod* presumably in Num, and the echo pronoun therefore in a lower position (perhaps SpecTP, although this is unclear—this problem was already anticipated in note 37 of chapter 1, although at that point it seemed more acute, as I was assuming a unitary AgrS). The structure of the embedded clause in (69) is thus:

(70)

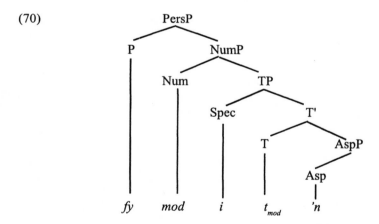

This idea supports the contention that the *ei*-clitics are the default clitics. It also supports the idea that Num in "IP," Q in DP, and Voice in participial clauses are the same element and always trigger V/N/VN raising (for reasons that are unclear in the case of participial clauses but clear in the other two cases). Furthermore, it supports the analysis of *bod*-clauses given in 1.2.3, the proposals about the root-embedded asymmetry made there, and thus in fact the idea that finite verbs do not raise into the C-system.

3.2.5   Conclusion

The preceding analysis of the VN treats it as a kind of participle. This allows me to accommodate Borsley's (1996) points but at the same time make sense of its apparently "nominal" properties regarding pronominalization and DOM. I also pursued a fairly close comparison with Romance and showed that the same structure can be maintained with mostly very simple parametric variation. The principal variation concerns (a) the fact that Agr-Prt, when it realizes overt φ-features, repels the participle in Welsh but attracts the participle in Romance (with the possible complication regarding Romance mentioned in notes 9 and 13), (b) the fact that Voice has a weak D-feature, and (c) the fact that Asp contains a Kaynian abstract preposition in Romance but overt, non-incorporating preposition-like particles in Welsh. These aspects of parametric variation, like many others that we've seen in the previous chapters, are signaled by morphological properties of the heads in question. In this way, the desideratum of learnability is met, and the cross-linguistic validity of the analyses shows that the typologizability desideratum is met.

3.3   Conclusion

This concludes the analysis of DPs and the licensing of objects of non-finite verbs. What I have said about the structure of DP is no doubt too sketchy and simplified, but the goal here was to account for GEN-licensing, N-to-D movement, and the similarities to VNs. The core of the chapter is the analysis of VNs in the previous two sections, and this completes the account of Case, agreement, and word order in Welsh. Two important theoretical conclusions emerge from this discussion: (i) that I have not needed to appeal to the EPP at all (although I recognized in 2.1 that I need it for the subject requirement in weak-agreement languages like English) and (ii) the idea that "strength" may not be a primitive parametric property of single heads but derivable from morphological properties of heads.

In the next chapter, I return to the discussion of the C-system begun in 1.2. Here we will see that both of the preceding points are relevant. We will see that Welsh and other Celtic languages are subject to a version of the EPP that holds at the C-level. Establishing this entails a fairly detailed analysis of the C-systems of Welsh and other Celtic languages, which is the empirical focus of the next chapter.

4

The C-System and the Extended Projection Principle

In this chapter, I return to a question already addressed in the discussion of the landing site of V-movement in VSO sentences in 1.2: the nature and structure of the C-system in Welsh and in at least some of the other Celtic languages (the discussion will focus mainly on Breton and rather sketchily mention Old Irish but leave aside Scots Gaelic and Modern Irish; for some remarks on the latter, see McCloskey 2001). The purpose of the discussion here is more general than in chapter 1, however. Now that I have established that we don't need to refer to the EPP as a separate principle at the "IP"-level, we need to consider whether it holds at the CP-level and, if so, in what form. Doing this entails a discussion of Germanic verb second, since it has been proposed that the obligatory XP-movement into the C-system that makes up part of this phenomenon is a consequence of the EPP (cf. Chomsky 2000, 2001, Haegeman 1996, Laenzlinger 1998, Roberts 1993, Roberts and Roussou 2002).

In 4.1, we look at the Welsh particle system and compare it with the V2 system of Germanic languages. At the relevant level of abstraction, the two systems are alike, as we shall see. Section 4.2 deals with the Breton particle system. This system differs from Welsh in one crucial respect, which appears to be connected to the existence of long V-movement in Breton. Following Borsley, Rivero, and Stephens (1996), and Roberts (2000), I will show that this construction is a genuine violation of the standard Head Movement Constraint and also show how the version of relativized minimality adopted in (39) of chapter 2 can account for this and for the constraints on long V-movement that have been observed. In both of these systems we observe variants of a default "filled-Fin" requirement that is reminiscent in significant respects of the Germanic V2 property. In 4.3 I attempt to account for this observation in terms of the EPP.

4.1   Welsh Particles

The "sentential particles" of Welsh are illustrated in (1):[1]

(1) a. Root affirmative *fe, mi, y*:
     Fe/mi welais i Siôn.
     Prt   saw   I John
     'I saw John.'

  b. Subordinating *y*:
     Dw i 'n meddwl y dylech chi ddeud wrtho fo.
     am I Asp think   Prt ought you say   to-3sg he
     'I think you ought to tell him.'

  c. Interrogative *a*:
     Tybed   a   geith   hi ddiwrnod rhydd wythnos nesa.
     I-wonder Prt will-get she day   free week   next
     'I wonder if she'll get a free day next week.'

  d. Root negative:
     Ni   ddarllenodd Emrys y llyfr.
     Neg read   Emrys the book
     'Emrys didn't read the book.'

  e. Subordinate negative:
     Dan ni 'n gobeithio nad ydach chi yn   siomedig.
     are we Asp hope   neg are   you Pred disappointed
     'We hope that you're not disappointed.'

  f. Direct relative:
     y dynion a ddarllenodd y llyfr
     the men   Prt read-3sg   the book
     "the men who read the book"

  g. Indirect relative:
     y dynion y dywedodd Wyn y byddant yn   darllen y llyfr
     the men   Prt said   Wyn that will-be-3pl Asp read the book
     'the men who Wyn said will read the book'

Let us look at these one by one. The root affirmative particles, like most of the other particles, are natural candidates for membership in the C-system. This is apparent from the fact that these elements must be adjacent to the finite verb (only an "infixed pronoun" can intervene, for example, *mi'ch gwelais i*, "I saw you(pl)"; see the brief discussion of these elements in 1.2.1). In particular, as we saw in 1.2, adverbs cannot intervene between these particles and the finite verb:

(2) a. Bore 'ma, fe/mi glywes i'r newyddion ar y radio.
    morning this, Prt heard I the news   on the radio
    'This morning, I heard the news on the radio.'

  b. *Fe/mi bore 'ma glywes i 'r newyddion ar y radio.
    Prt morning this heard I the news on the radio

Root affirmative *y* only appears with the tenses of *bod* associated with movement of *bod* to Fin, as argued in 1.2.3. As I suggested there (see note 35), it may be that *y* is morphologically part of *bod* in these cases.

Subordinating *y* seems to correspond to English *that* and similar elements in other languages. Following Tallerman (1996), we observed in chapter 1 that it, too, must be adjacent to V:

(3)   *Dywedodd ef y, gyda llaw, bydd yn gadael.
    said   he that by the way will-be Asp leave
    'He said that, by the way, he will be leaving.'
    (Tallerman 1996: 104)

I concluded that, like Irish *go* but unlike English *that* and German *daß*, *y* does not raise to Force (see 1.2). There are some further complications regarding the availability of *y* in certain tenses, as we saw in 1.2.3.

Interrogative *a* is to be distinguished from the *a* that alternates with *y* in clauses where an XP undergoes Wh-movement. The former may be in Force, while the latter are in Fin. The motivation for this is that interrogative *a* can occur with the present and imperfect forms of *bod*:

(4)   A ydych chi 'n mynd?
    Prt are you Asp go?
    'Are you going?'

I do not intend to propose an analysis of the Welsh negation system here (cf. the brief remarks in 1.1, and Borsley and R. Morris Jones 2000), and so I do not have much to say regarding the negative particles. As is clear from the fact that it can precede the sequence of a fronted XP and a focus particle (see 1.2 and later), *nid* must be able to appear in Force. Whether it is merged there or is moved there from Fin in simple negative clauses like (5) is unclear:[2]

(5)   Ni redodd Siôn i ffwrdd.
                Neg ran   John away
                'John didn't run away.'
                (Rouveret 1994: 127)

The "subordinating" negative particle *nad* introduces negative *bod*-clauses, as seen in (1e) (on these clauses, see 1.2.3 and 3.4). This particle also appears in negated focused clauses:

(6)   a.   Mi wn   i nad y dyn a ddaeth.
                Prt know I neg the man prt came
                'I know it was not the man who came.'
                (Tallerman 1996: 119)

        b.   Nid y dyn na ddaeth.
                Neg the man neg came
                'It's not the man who didn't come.'
                (Watkins 1991: 332, cited in Tallerman 1996: 119)

So *na(d)* seems to be able to occupy both Fin and (selected) Force.

The "direct" and "indirect" relative particles illustrated in (1f, g) have very interesting properties. They appear in relatives, as in (1f, g), in Wh-questions, in focused clauses, and in abnormal sentences, which, following Tallerman (1996), I analyze as topicalization (see note 15, chapter 2):

(7)   a.   Pa   ddynion a werthodd y ci?   — Wh-question
                which men   prt sold   the dog
                'Which men sold the dog?'

        b.   Y   dynion a werthodd y ci.   — focused clause
                the men   Prt sold-3sg the dog
                'It's the men who have sold the dog.'

        c.   Y dynion a werthasant y ci.   — abnormal sentence
                the men prt sold-3pl   the dog
                'The men, they sold the dog.'

As I mentioned in chapter 1, the "direct" particle appears when an object, subject, or VP is fronted: otherwise the "indirect" particle appears.[3]

A focused clause like (7b) can be embedded under another complementizer, as we have already seen:

(8)   Dywedais i mai ['r dynion a   werthith y ci].
                said   I MAI the men   Prt will-sell the dog
                'I said that it's the men who will sell the dog.'

I propose that the sentence-initial particles of Welsh fit into Rizzi's (1997) split-C system in the following way, as we saw in (66) of chapter 1:

(9)   **Force**   **Fin**

          mai/ai/nad/nid   *a/y/fe/mi/bod*(Pres/imperf)

With these points in mind, let us now compare the Welsh particle system with the V2 system of the Germanic languages.

The obvious similarity lies in the fact that full V2 is characteristic of root affirmative clauses:

(10)   a.   Yesterday John danced.
      b.   Gestern hat Johann getanzt.
      c.   *Gestern Johann hat getanzt.

Continuing to take the movement here to be V-movement to Fin, it is natural to see this V-movement as directly analogous to the merger of the root affirmative particles in Welsh. Following Roberts's (2001) notation for functional categories that require PF-realization, we can understand this similarity as a manifestation of the fact that Welsh actually has the same parametric property as German, namely Fin*. Welsh differs from German in having particles that can be inserted into root Fin, pre-empting movement of the finite verb. Like V-movement to Fin in German, the particles appear only in finite clauses. This can of course be simply stated: Fin requires a PF-realization when [+finite]. Non-finite Fin is subject to different PF-realization conditions (which, unsurprisingly, are not quite the same in the two languages; see Tallerman [1998] on infinitival *i*, as opposed to finite *i* discussed in 1.2.3, in Welsh).

Both German V-movement and Welsh *fe/mi*-merger are root phenomena, as I have mentioned. Let us suppose that root declarative Force has no feature content, such clauses being interpreted as declarative by default (cf. the discussion of root-embedded asymmetries in 1.2.2). In fact, following what was proposed in 1.2, we can go a step further and assume that selection for a [+finite] Fin automatically implies a declarative clause, and thus that there is no declarative feature. This is directly supported by Stowell's (1981: 422) observation that selection for a Wh-feature pre-empts selection for finiteness (see the paradigm in [47] of chapter 1), and we will see further support for it in 4.3. Hence the generalization about languages like German and Welsh is that unselected Fin requires PF-realization. In German, unselected Fin has no lexical realization and so V-movement is triggered. In Welsh, unselected Fin can be realized by *fe/mi*.

It is clear from (1) that the Welsh interrogative, negative, and relative particles manifest substantially the same features as those that are manifested by residual V2 (see 1.2.2, for a discussion of this phenomenon). These features are naturally treated as associated with Force (interrogative, negation) or Focus (Wh, negation). Although most of the Welsh particles are in Fin, as we have seen, negative *ni(d)/ na(d)* can be, and interrogative *a* is, in Force. The particles that clearly occur in

Fin are root *fe/mi*, embedded *y*, and the Wh-particles *a* and *y*. None of these is inherently associated with a marked clause type; *fe/mi* and *y* are declarative, and *a/y* can mark a focused or relativized constituent, hence a Wh-dependency in an otherwise declarative clause. The *a/y* particles can also, however, appear in indirect questions; I account for this by saying that these particles may be— but do not have to be—selected by a Q-morpheme in Force. Evidence that the *a/y* particles can be associated with different features in Force comes from the embedded focused clauses discussed in 1.2.2, of the type in (8). Alongside (8), we find such clauses embedded under a negative and an interrogative Force:

(11)   Ai [ceffyl a   fuasai hi'n   gwerthu]?
          AI   horse Prt would she-Asp sell?
          'Is it a horse that she'd sell?'

(12)   Nid [y   dyn a   ddaeth].
          NEG the man Prt came
          'It wasn't the man who came.'

Presumably, in all these cases Fin containing *a/y* is selected by Focus.

In this section, we have looked at the particle system of Welsh and shown how, at the relevant level of abstraction, it can be seen as a manifestation of the same parameter value as that which gives rise to full V2 in the Germanic languages. In these terms, I gave an account of the root nature of both the affirmative *fe/mi* particles and of V2. This account relies on the idea that declarative clauses are the unmarked clause type, in the sense that there is no distinct declarative feature, [+finite] Fin being interpreted as declarative. From this, an important observation regarding full V2 emerges. If the Welsh particles manifest a default value of Fin* and so does the V-movement component of V2, then it follows that the XP-movement component of V2, since it takes place where there is V-movement but not where there is merger of a particle, must be systematically related to the V-movement operation. To put it more succinctly, the Welsh data lead to the following observation about V2 (this observation was anticipated in Roberts and Roussou 2002):

(13)   Observation I:
        The second-position effect only arises where Fin is realized by Move.

We now turn to a consideration of the Breton data, which will lead to a confirmation of this observation and a refinement of what I have said about declarative Fin.

4.2   Breton

Breton has a very similar particle system to that of Welsh, with one very significant difference that emerges immediately upon inspection of the list in (14) and a comparison with (1):

(14) subordinating: *e*
            interrogative: *hag-en*
            negative: *ne*
            "direct" relative: *a*
            "indirect" relative: *e*

The difference from Welsh is that Breton has no root affirmative particles (see Borsley and Roberts 1996: 26). The significance of this observation will emerge later.

As observed by Borsley, Rivero, and Stephens (1996), Breton, although a VSO language (as we saw in chapter 1), does not allow simple verb-first clauses with an initial main verb:

(15)   *Lenn Anna al levr.
          reads Anna the book

Instead, the equivalent of the Welsh focus construction must be used, as illustrated in (17):

(16)   Al levr a lenn Anna.
          the book Prt reads Anna
          'Anna reads the book.'

Example (16) is directly equivalent to a Welsh example like (7b) (in fact, [16] probably corresponds to the Middle/Biblical Welsh abnormal sentence; following Willis 1998, we take this to be the same construction as the Modern Welsh focus construction of [7b]; see chapter 2, note 15). In neutral clauses, Breton makes use of "long V-movement" (LVM),[4] illustrated in (17):

(17) a.   Lenn a ra Anna al levr.
             Read-inf Prt does Anna the book
             'Anna reads the book.'

       b.   Lennet en deus Anna al levr.
             Read-pprt has Anna the book
             'Anna has read the book.'

In (17a) the infinitive has been fronted and the finite auxiliary is a form of *ober*, "do." In (17b) the past participle has been fronted and the finite auxiliary—the compound element *en deus* here—is a form of "have."[5]

At first sight, examples like (17b) resemble the German remnant-topicalization construction (see den Besten and Webelhuth 1989, Müller 1998), as in (18):

(18)   Gelesen hat Anna das Buch nicht.
          read-pprt has Anna the book not
          'Anna has not read the book.'

However, the two constructions can be shown to be quite distinct (much of the argumentation and many of the examples in what follows are from Borsley, Rivero, and Stephens 1996; henceforth BRS). The standard analysis of the German construction in (18) involves the postulation of scrambling of the object *das Buch* and topicalization of the ("remnant") VP that contains the trace of scrambling. The postulated structure of (18) is thus (18'):

(18')   [$_{VP}$ Gelesen t$_{das\ Buch}$] hat Anna das Buch nicht t$_{VP}$

There are several reasons that this analysis does not carry over to Breton examples like those in (12).

First, Breton has a VP-fronting operation that has quite different properties from the LVM construction in (17). Comparing these two constructions, we see that VP-fronting can occur across clause boundaries, while LVM is clause-bounded:

(19)   a.   [$_{VP}$ O lenn al levr] a ouian emañ Yann. — VP-fronting[6]
                Prog read the book Prt know-1sg is   Yann
                'I know Yann is reading the book.'

         b.   *Desket am eus klevet he deus Anna he c'hentelioù. — LVM
                learnt 1sg have heard 3sgf has Anna her lessons
                'I have heard that Anna has learnt her lessons.'

In (19a), the VP (or larger category; see note 6) has been fronted from the complement clause into the C-system of the main clause and the example is fully grammatical. In (19b), however, the participle of the lower clause is unable to be fronted to the initial position in the main clause.

A second important difference between VP-fronting and LVM is that VP-fronting is possible in negative clauses, while LVM is impossible in this context:

(20)   a.   [$_{VP}$ O lenn al levr]   n' emañ ket Yann. — VP-fronting
                Prog read the book neg is   neg Yann
                'Yann isn't reading the book.'

         b.   *Lennet n'en   deus ket Tom al levr.   — LVM
                read   neg.3sgm has neg Tom the book
                'Tom hasn't read the book.'

Third, the two constructions differ as to which auxiliaries they may occur with. In particular, LVM is impossible with progressive *bezañ*:

(21)   *O lenn emañ Yann al levr.
                Prog read is   Yann the book

This leads to a further point: it is impossible to front the verb and strand the object where the auxiliary is progressive *bezañ*:

(22) a.   [$_{VP}$ O voueta ar moc'h] e   oa Helen.
            Prog feed   the pigs   Prt was Helen
            'Helen was feeding the pigs.'

      b.   *O voueta e   oa   Helen ar moc'h.
            Prog feed   Prt was Helen the pigs
            (Schafer 1994: 2)

This straightforwardly shows that German-style remnant VP-fronting is unavailable in Breton.[7] From the data in (19)–(22) we can conclude that the LVM construction is not a case of remnant VP-fronting.

A third difference between German VP-fronting and Breton LVM has been brought to light by Borsley and Kathol (2000). In German, certain types of infinitival complements (so-called "coherent infinitives") can be fronted separately from their selecting verb or together with that verb, but the selecting verb cannot front separately from the infinitival complement :

(23) a.   . . . daß Peter das Buch wird finden können.
            . . . that Peter the book will find   can
            . . . 'that Peter will be able to find the book.'

      b.   [Finden] wird Peter das Buch können.
            find   will Peter the book can
            'Peter will be able to find the book.'

      c.   *Können wird Peter das Buch finden.
            can   will Peter the book find

      d.   [Finden können] wird Peter das Buch.
            find   can   will Peter the book
            'Peter will be able to find the book.'

These data can be straightforwardly accounted for by assuming that the fronting operation is VP-fronting in every case and that *können* does not form a VP that excludes *finden* (see Wurmbrand 1999 for a recent analysis of coherent infinitives, which argues that such complements are in fact VPs that are associated with no T- or C-level).

Now, Breton allows structures that contain a non-finite auxiliary and a non-finite main verb, a kind of *temps surcomposé* shown in (24) (with a PP in initial position and an agreement proclitic occupying the particle position; see note 5):

(24)   Er   gegin am eus bet kavet al levr.
            in-the kitchen 1sg have had found the book
            'I have found the book in the kitchen.'

What we find here as regards verb- and VP-fronting is precisely the opposite of the German facts seen in (24), in that either non-finite form may undergo movement, but not both together:

(25)   a.   Kavet am eus bet al levr.
                     found 1sg have had the book
                     'I have found the book.'

          b.   Bet am eus kavet al levr.
                     had 1sg have found the book
                     'I have found the book.'

          c.   *Bet kavet am eus al levr.
                     had found 1sg have the book

The contrast with German can be simply accounted for if we analyze the Breton construction as V-, and not VP-, movement.

In addition to what we have seen in contrasting the construction with (remnant) VP-fronting, LVM has a number of interesting properties that are compatible with the fact that it involves movement into the C-system. First, LVM is a root phenomenon (this was first pointed out by Stephens 1982 and also by Schafer 1994 and BRS):

(26)   *Lavaret he deus Anna [lennet en deus Tom al levr].
              said   3sgf has Anna   read 3sgm has Tom the book
              'Anna said Tom had read the book.'

Note also, as mentioned earlier, that LVM is subject to what Schafer calls "strict locality", that is, it cannot take place out of an embedded clause into a main clause, unlike VP-fronting; see also (19). Here I illustrate with an infinitival embedded clause:

(27)   a.   Gellout   a   reont goro ar saout.
                     be-able(infin) prt do-3sg milk the cows
                     'They can milk the cows.'

          b.   *Goro a c'hellont ober a   saout.
                     milk   prt can-3sg do   the cows
                     (Schafer 1994: 145)

Second, LVM cannot take place in negative clauses. Since negation is partly indicated by a negative particle in C (*ne*; see [14] and [20]), we can see this as a case of sensitivity to properties of C. Third, LVM is impossible where some XP is fronted:

(28) *Al levr lennet en deus Tom.
the book read-3sg has Tom

This can clearly be seen as a further case of sensitivity to a property of C.

Two other properties of LVM are relevant here. First, nothing can intervene between the fronted non-finite verb and the particle/auxiliary, not even a pronoun (Schafer 1994: 141—142):

(29) a. Plijout   a   ra din   eo tomm an heol.
         please-infin prt do to-me be warm the sun
         'I am happy the sun is warm.'

      b. *Plijout   din   a   ra eo tomm an heol.
         please-infin to-me prt do be warm the sun

(30) a. Gwardet   deus   he breur gant aked.
         looked-after has-3sgf her brother with care
         'She looked after her brother with care.'

      b. *Gwardet   gant aked deus   he breur.
         looked-after with care has-3sgf her brother

Second, Schafer (1994: 146f.) shows in detail that the construction is discourse-neutral; it is associated neither with topic nor with focus interpretations.

From all of the preceding arguments we can conclude that Breton LVM is a genuine case of Long Head Movement of a non-finite verb. It appears to move the verb into the C-system, to a position immediately preceding the *a* particle or a form of the "have"-auxiliary. More precisely, I propose that this is a case of movement of the non-finite verb to Fin. The verb left-adjoins to the particle or auxiliary in this position, creating the structure in (31) for an example like (17a):[8]

(31)

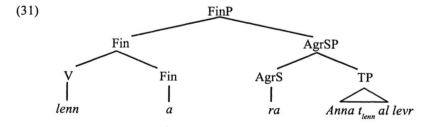

Here movement of the non-finite verb clearly crosses AgrS (i.e., its constituent heads; see note 8) and presumably at least also T. This is in fact allowed by the version of relativized minimality given in (38) and (39) of chapter 2, which I repeat here:

(32) $(A_1, \ldots A_n)$ is a chain iff, for $1 \leq i < n$
                         (i) $A_i = A_{i+1}$,
                         (ii) A_i c-commands A_{i+1}, and
                         (iii) A_{i+1} is in a minimal configuration with A_i.

(33)   Y is in a Minimal, Configuration (MC) with X iff there is no Z
                         such that:
                         (i) Z is non-distinct in structural and featural type from X and
                         (ii) Z c-commands Y and Z does not c-command X.

If we take Fin to be of a distinct featural type from (the heads that make up) AgrS
and T, then it will be possible for the moved V in (31) to form an MC with its trace
according to the definition in (33) (the moved V is Y, its trace is X, and the intervening
heads fail to count as Z owing to the fact that they are of a different type). Hence
the moved V can form a well-formed chain with its trace according to the definition
in (32). What is the basis for saying that Fin is of a distinct featural type from AgrS
and T? Suppose that heads (and indeed categories of all types) can in general be
divided into operators and non-operators, and that this is one property that is
relevant for the creation of intervention effects and hence for the definition of MC
in (33) (see Rizzi 1990, 2000). More generally, as a first approximation we can propose
the following partition of heads:[9]

(34)   a.   Operator heads: Force, Topic, Focus, Fin, Neg . . .
        b.   Non-operator heads: Agr, T, Asp . . .

It certainly seems very natural to propose that Agr-heads are not operators. For T
this is perhaps less obvious, although Roberts and Roussou (2002) propose that T
contains a variable that is bound by an operator in Fin as a way of accounting for
the well-known observation that there is an inherent link between the temporal
properties of the C-system and those of the I-system (in this they follow a long line
of analysis going back through, inter alia, Holmberg and Platzack 1995, Pollock
1989, den Besten 1983, and Pesetsky 1982 to Stowell 1981). Assuming Roberts
and Roussou's approach, then, T is not an operator and the preliminary classification
in (35) can be maintained. In turn, this means that we can postulate long-movement
of the non-finite verb in structures like (32) with no violation of relativized
minimality.

    The proposed account of Breton LVM gets the locality facts just right. In
addition to allowing long movement where it is needed, for example, in core cases
like (31), it also accounts for the "strict locality" of LVM discussed by Schafer and
BRS and illustrated in (19) and (27). There I observed that LVM can never cross a
C-position and so is strictly clause-bounded. Now we see that this follows from
relativized minimality: an intervening Fin (or any element of the C-system; see note
9) blocks the formation of a minimal configuration between the moved head and its
trace in examples like (27b) and (19b). Also, we can account for the possibility of
long-movement of either of a sequence of non-finite verbs, as illustrated in (25a,

b). The formulation of relativized minimality just given combined with (34) means that if the entire structure is contained within a single IP, neither non-finite verb will block long-movement of the other.

More generally, the approach to the locality of head-movement embodied in (32)–(34) implies that head-movement will always be local except in one context, which we can schematize as follows:

(35) $[_{Fin}$ V[−fin] Fin . . . $[_I$ Aux[+fin]] . . . t_V . . .

In other words, where Fin has some property that triggers head-movement and a finite auxiliary checks the relevant tense and agreement features in the I-system, a non-finite V can move into Fin without violating relativized minimality. Within the I-system (possibly modulo "low" negative markers; see note 9), within the C-system, and, trivially, between the highest position in the I-system and the lowest position in the C-system head-movement is always strictly local; that is, the traditional Head Movement Constraint of Travis (1984) and Baker (1988) holds. The contention here is that this is an artefact of the nature of the heads involved and relativized minimality; the locality system allows for a very limited and precisely defined range of cases of Long Head Movement. Other cases that appear to fall under the general schema in (35) have been discussed in the literature; see BRS for a range of Slavic and Romance languages, Cavar and Wilder (1992) on Croatian, Rivero (1991, 1994), and the references given there.[10]

Given the preceding analysis of Breton, I now need to relate the LVM construction to what was said in the previous section regarding Welsh and German. It seems clear, given the almost minimal difference between the Breton particle system and that of Welsh (basically just the absence of neutral *fe/mi*-type particles in Breton) and given the discourse-neutrality, declarative root nature of the LVM construction, that this construction is a way to fill a non-selected Fin* (see also Schafer 1994 for a similar proposal). In this respect it is in a sense the functional equivalent of the *fe/mi* particles and therefore of full V2. So Breton has the same parameter value as Welsh and German. The Breton construction differs from the Welsh one in that the presence of *fe/mi* in Welsh means that merger of these elements pre-empts movement in Welsh, while merger of *a* causes it in Breton (consistent with the fact that Breton *a* is always associated with movement). The availability of particles also distinguishes Breton from German; the Breton particles are such that they allow Breton to satisfy Fin* with one movement, whereas German requires two, so we can see that the LVM possibility pre-empts full V2.

Diachronic evidence from the history of Welsh confirms the minimal nature of the difference between Breton and Welsh. According to Willis (1996, 1997, 1998), Welsh had the LVM construction until the Early Modern Welsh period (1400–1600):

(36)   Gwyssyaw a oruc Arthur milwyr yr ynys honn.
              summon   prt did Arthur soldiers the island this
              'Arthur summoned the soldiers of this island.'
              (CO 922–923: Willis 1997: 17)

Interestingly, at this period the *fe/mi* particles did not exist. These elements developed out of fronted pronouns soon after the Early Modern period (the earliest written examples are from the mid–eighteenth century, as documented in detail by Willis 1998: 225f.). The following are examples of the historical antecedents of *fe* and *mi* cooccurring with particles (note that *ef* is an expletive in [37a]; in Middle Welsh as in Modern German, overt expletives only appeared in the fronted position):[11]

(37)   a.   Ef a doeth makwyueit a gueisson ieueinc y   diarchenu . . .
            it prt came squires and lads   young to-him disrobe
            'There came squires and young lads to disrobe him' . . .
            (PKM 4.8–9: Willis 1998: 154)

       b.   . . . mi a rodaf   Pryderi a   Riannon it . . .
            . . . I   prt will-give Pryderi and Rhiannon to-you . . .
            . . . 'I shall give Pryderi and Rhiannon to you' . . .
            (PKM 64.18–20: Willis 1997: 13–14)

It seems then that the loss of LVM in Welsh is connected to the development of the *fe/mi* particles as true Fin-elements from topicalized pronouns.[12]

So, if LVM has the structure in (31) and is the functional equivalent of *fe/mi* and full V2, we can make the following further observation about V2, in addition to the one already given in (13):

(38)   Observation II:
       The second-position requirement can be satisfied by Long Head
       Movement.

Putting together this observation and Observation I in (13) earlier, we can observe the following range of properties of non-selected declarative Fin*:

(39)   a.   Merger of a head: Welsh
       b.   Adjunction to a head: Breton
       c.   Creation of a Spec-head relation: full V2
       d.   No morphophonological realization: English, and so forth.

Example (39c) subsumes the Observation I in (13), in that V-movement to Fin does not seem to be tolerated on its own: in just this case an XP must be fronted.[13]

In 2.1, we saw that there were three principal morphological ways of valuing Agr, as follows:

(40)   a.   merger of a subject clitic
       b.   DP-movement to Spec
       c.   Head-government by an overt head of the relevant type

Reformulating (40a) in terms of the more general notion of merger of a head and recalling that subject clitics can be inherently enclitic (this was a very important aspect of the account of VSO order in chapter 2), we can see that it corresponds to (39a, b). Example (40b) corresponds straightforwardly to (39c). We can assume that the requirement for a DP in (41b) is a reflex of specific properties of agreement systems, that is, that DPs bear φ-features. The configurational property that unites (39c) and (40b) is clearly the Specifier-head relation. Example (40c) applies to Fin in non-declarative clauses and selected declaratives but not in non-selected declaratives, where, as I proposed in the previous section, the higher heads in the C-system are inactive. Whether (39d) applies in the Agr-system is unclear: perhaps this is the East Asian situation (cf. note 4, Chapter 2).

So we see that there is a real parallel between the ways in which the Agr-system is licensed and the ways in which Fin is licensed. To the extent that the EPP in its IP-internal application can be reduced to licensing the Agr-system, then it is plausible to think that its CP-level application can be likewise reduced to licensing Fin. These parallels will be explored further in the next chapter, which also takes into account the parallels with AspP that were noted in chapter 3.

A further point arises from the parallel between (39) and (40). Alexiadou and Anagnostopoulou (1998) have proposed, developing ideas in Borer (1986), that in a fully null-subject language like Standard Italian the rich verbal agreement is able to satisfy the EPP: to put it in the terms of 2.1, rich agreement of this type triggers V-movement and values the features of Pers and Num without the need for any DP or subject clitic (this implies that rich agreement features are interpretable, which seems natural). Is there an analogy in the C-system? As we briefly indicated in 1.2.1, it is in fact possible that Old Irish provides the relevant case (for much more detailed description of Old Irish than is possible here, see Carnie, Pyatt, and Harley 1995, Doherty 1999, 2000). A salient characteristic of Old Irish is that there are two sets of verbal inflectional paradigms, traditionally called the independent and dependent inflections. The two paradigms of the present tense of a simple, regular verb are illustrated in (41) (see Thurneysen 1946/1980: 360, Doherty 1999: 3):

(41)		Independent	Dependent
	1sg	biru	-biur
	2sg	biri	-bir
	3sg	berid, berith	-beir
	1pl	berm(a)i	-beram
	2pl	beirthe	-berid
	3pl	ber(a)it	-berat

Dependent forms appear when the verb follows a "dependent particle," that is, negative *ní*, interrogative *in*, and other elements that are rather clearly C-elements, as well as in other contexts where the verb is non-initial (see Doherty 1999 for an interesting interpretation of traditional observations regarding these contexts). Independent forms appear exactly when the verb is in initial position. Hence we find pairs such as the following:

(42)   Independent versus dependent verbal forms (Doherty 1999: 3):
      beirid 'carries' (independent) ní.beir/*ní.beirid 'does not carry'(dependent)
      gairid 'calls' (independent)   ní.gair/*ní.gairid 'does not call' (dependent)

The only material that is able to intervene between the dependent particle and the dependent verb form (leaving aside the archaic and non-productive "tmesis" construction; see Doherty 1999) is enclitic pronouns and preverbs. Enclitic pronouns always directly follow a dependent particle, when one is present:

(43)   a.   Ní-m.accai
           Neg-me.PreV-see(3sg)
           'He does not see me.'

      b.   Ní-m.ben
           Neg-me.strike(3sg)
           'He does not strike me.'

The verb form in (43a) contains a preverb. Where there is no dependent particle, this element precedes the enclitic pronoun (with considerable morphophonemic modification):

(44)   ato-m.chí
        PreV-me.see(3sg)
        'He sees me.'

Independent forms precede enclitic pronouns:

(45)   Bertaigth-i
        shake(3sg,ABS)-him
        'He shakes him.'

There are good grounds for thinking that dependent verbs are in C; they appear immediately following the Wh-word in one type of Wh-question, and in an archaic V2-like construction:

(46)   a.   cia beir   búar o   thig   Temrach?
           who bears-dependent cattle from house Tara-GEN
           'Who brings cattle from the house of Tara?'
           (LL 1566; Bergin 1938: 205; Doherty 1999: 10)

      b.   Bangluinn   gni   glenn   gaeth.
           bloodless-deed   does-dependent valleys-GEN   wind
           'The wind of the valleys does a bloodless deed.'
           (Corp. Gen. 6; Carney 1979: 433; Doherty 1999: 8)

Since it is extremely natural to place the dependent particles in Force, if the dependent verbs are in C they must be in Fin. Supposing, for the sake of concreteness, that the enclitic pronouns occupy Top, this gives structures like the following:[14]

(47) a. $[_{ForceP} [_{Force}$ Ní $] [_{TopP} [_{Top}$ -m $] [_{FinP} [_{Fin}$ accai $] \ldots]]] = (43a)$
      b. $[_{ForceP} [_{Force}$ ato $] [_{TopP} [_{Top}$ -m $] [_{FinP} [_{Fin}$ chí $] \ldots]]] \quad = (44)$

Naturally, then, we can analyze verb-initial examples as in (49):

(48) $[_{ForceP} [_{Force}$ bertaigth $] [_{TopP} [_{Top}$ -i $] \ldots]] \qquad = (45)$

In terms of this analysis, it seems that Old Irish required both Force and Fin to be filled. More importantly it seems that where V raises to Force it has special morphology. This happens essentially in root, declarative clauses and so is a case where Fin is licensed by rich agreement, analogous to the licensing of Num discussed in 2.1.

The main goal of this section was to analyze the particle system of Breton. We have seen that this system is very similar to that of Welsh, with the sole difference that long V-movement applies to license root declarative Fin, "neutral" particles analogous to Welsh *fe/mi* not being available. Putting this together with the discussion of full V2 in the previous section, we see that there are several ways to license root declarative Fin and that these are parallel to the ways of licensing Agr that we observed in 2.1. The brief discussion of the alternation between independent and dependent agreement in Old Irish completed this picture. It is now time to consider these results and attempt to arrive at a definitive picture both of the nature of the V2 phenomenon and of the EPP.

4.3   Second Position and the EPP

4.3.1   The Status of the Declarative Feature

Let us begin our investigation of the relation between second-position phenomena and the EPP by looking again at the question of the status of the declarative feature. I suggested in 4.1, building on the account of root-embedded asymmetries put forward in 1.2.2, that there is no such feature, declarative clauses being interpreted as such in the absence of any feature specification on Force. In this case, Fin remains simply unselected in root declarative clauses (where no higher position is activated). In this section, I want to give a general argument that there is no declarative feature in UG.

The argument is based on the following two candidate implicational universals for finite clauses:

(49)   a. If a language has V2 in declarative clauses, then it has V2 in non-declarative clauses.
    b. If a language has declarative particles, then it has non-declarative particles.

As far as I am aware, these two generalizations hold across languages. (49a) states that languages may be fully V2, like German and most of the other Germanic languages, or may be V2 in interrogative and other marked clause types but not in declaratives (like English, French, etc.), but rules out the existence of a residual V2 language with V2 in declarative clauses but not in, for example, interrogative clauses. Roughly speaking, such a language would have the pattern in (50) (using English words to represent words in the language):

(50)   a.   Yesterday danced John.
    b.   *Yesterday John danced.
    c.   Which song John sang?

I know of no example of such a language.[15]

Example (49b) states that, while there may be languages with interrogative (etc.) particles and declarative particles (Welsh is an example of such a language, in fact, but certainly not the only one) and languages with interrogative particles and no declarative particles, there are no languages with declarative particles and no interrogative particles. Again, this claim is empirically correct as far as I am aware.

The two generalizations in (49) are really a single generalization, with (49a) referring to Move and (49b) to Merge. We can thus restate (49) as follows:

(49')   If Fin requires PF-realization in declarative clauses, then it requires it in non-declarative clauses.

It is possible to account for (49') by assuming that selected features of a head may be subfeatures of that head. In general, then, suppose that functional heads, as features F, G, H . . . , can come with various further feature specifications f, g, h . . . (I write the selected subfeatures in lowercase italics and the labels of autonomous functional categories with initial uppercase). We can then treat the autonomous functional feature F as simply the unmarked value of the functional head in question, while the marked value will have a further subfeature, giving F + f. Now suppose that unspecified Force means "declarative," while Force + f, where f is a clause-type feature, means non-declarative. The same is true of Fin (where the subfeature is the feature selected by Force). On this view, [+/−declarative] does not exist and a clause is interpreted as declarative in the absence of clause-type features. What exist are other clause-type features: Q, Exclamative, Imperative, and so on. These are all subfeatures of Force that may be selected on Fin. In other words, instead of saying that we have Force with the two values [±declarative], we have Force = Declarative by default and Force = Imperative, Interrogative (etc.), as marked subfeatures.

Now, I mentioned in 4.1 that one way to construe parametrization is very simply in terms of the idea that any functional category F may or may not be associated with a diacritic requiring it to have a PF-realization. This realization may be obtained by Merge or Move, with Merge standardly pre-empting Move if appropriate lexical material is available. So we can think that the (functional) lexicon of every language contains a parametrization operator, which randomly assigns the diacritic to functional features. Now, if we assume that the parametrization operator applies equally well to both autonomous functional features and to selected subfeatures in the sense in which these were described in the previous paragraph, then we can see that $F + f$ will have two chances of PF-realization, while F will only have one. Thus, marked feature values are more likely to be overtly realized than unmarked ones and we derive implicational statements of the form in (49') from the fact that where F* must be realized then so must all subfeatures of F* (this follows directly if we think of the subfeatures in terms of feature geometry). From this it follows that, to the extent that (49') is correct, there is no declarative feature.

A further important point in this connection is that root non-finite Fin is never declarative:

(51)   a.   Oh! to be in England, now that April's here!   (optative)

        b.   Ne pas cracher par terre.   (imperative)
               Neg not to-spit on ground
               'Do not spit on the ground.'

        c.   Tornare   a casa? Mai!   (exclamative/interrogative)
               To-return to home? Never!
               'Go back home? Never!'

Given the marked clause type of these examples, we must conclude that Force selects Fin (despite the fact that neither has an apparent overt realization in these examples). So wherever Fin is not selected it is finite. Embedded non-finite Fin does not have to be non-declarative, but here it seems most natural to say that embedded infinitivals very often have no specific clause type of their own, implying that Force is inert in such cases.

We can thus conclude that since there is no declarative feature, the operations in (39), including full V2, cannot be triggered by this feature. Instead, as already suggested in 4.1, they seem to simply be different ways of realizing unmarked, finite, root Fin. This makes sense for (39a, b, d) in terms of Roberts's (2001) system of lexicalization parameters: (39a and b) are just slightly different ways of lexically realizing Fin* by merger, and (39d) is the opposite parametric value. But what of (39c)? In place of this, we expect simple verb-movement. As I mentioned earlier, it seems that simple verb-movement is not tolerated on its own. In fact, there is a clear cross-linguistic generalization here (which emerges from the study of the Celtic languages, since they are VSO and have fairly rich C-systems):

(52)   Independent V1 in C is not allowed in root declaratives.[16]

(Note that Old Irish is not a counterexample to [51] as it has rich, clause-type sensitive agreement, as we saw in 4.2.) Example (52) combines with the Fin* parameter in its Move manifestation to give V2. (52) also has the flavour of the EPP. I will attempt to flesh this intuition out in the next section.

4.3.2   The EPP and Second-Position Effects

In this section we focus on the link between the EPP and V2. The core V2 phenomenon of the Germanic languages has four main components:[17]

(53)   a.   V-movement to Fin
         b.   XP-movement to SpecFinP
         c.   The restriction to just one XP
         d.   (The root-embedded asymmetry)

Example (53d) was discussed in 1.2, and I have nothing further to add here. (53a) follows from the fact that (finite) Fin has the parametric property of requiring a PF-realization in V2 languages and that these languages lack particles like Welsh *fe/mi,* which can be merged into Fin. Hence Fin attracts a head that it selects. This head is T, assuming that Fin selects directly for T (there is abundant cross-linguistic evidence for this, and the Agr-heads arguably do not intervene for the Fin-T Probe-Goal relation, which depends on an Agreement relation in temporal features). V clearly moves to T in Icelandic (Platzack 1987, Vikner 1994) and in at least some varieties of Faroese (Jonas 1996). Following Sabel (1999), I assume that it does so also in German, and, following Haegeman (2001) and Biberauer (2003), I take it that in the Continental West Germanic languages the complement of T moves into a specifier position higher than T, creating the effect of verb-final order. Finally, following Roberts (1993), I take it that V moves to T in Mainland Scandinavian (in all these cases, with the likely exception of Icelandic and Faroese, we have weak agreement in the sense of 2.1; all we're interested in here is V-to-T—it may be that Vikner's generalization for Germanic can be kept in terms of V-movement to Num, but I will not speculate on that matter here). Thus T, containing V, raises to Fin where we have Fin*.[18]

Crucially, the EPP applies where we have both V-movement to Fin (caused by Fin* and the lack of relevant particles) and no feature in Fin (other than [+finite]). Although V-movement to Fin satisfies the lexical-realization requirement, this clearly is not enough to license Fin under these conditions, as (52) states. V2 arises in languages with rather poor agreement systems, no root declarative C-particles, and Fin*.[19] It seems to be the case, then, that Fin that lacks features and exponents (i.e., particles) to this extent must have an EPP-feature and hence triggers movement of an XP. Since this case of Fin* has no specific features to value (in the terminology of Chomsky 2000, 2001), it does not enter into an Agree relation with any XP.

The preceding characterization of the relation between V2 and the EPP has analogues in the Agr system. I mentioned in 2.1 that weak-agreement languages have EPP at the Agr-level. Like Agr, Fin has an EPP-feature when it has no other substantive feature. We can note that the "pure" EPP-effects that involve Agr, where expletives are required (as in *For there to be a riot would be a disgrace*; cf. chapter 2, note 16), are characteristic of languages with poor agreement marking. In languages where agreement features are more fully realized by morphology, the requirement to fill some position in the Agr-field does not hold in the same way, as we saw in 2.1.1. However, the way in which Fin realizes EPP-features is unlike Agr in one important respect: unlike Agr, Fin does not require a DP to occupy its Spec. This can be attributed to the fact that Agr is a D-element but Fin is not.

So I propose that (52) is an observation about feature content: Fin* with so little content (no selected features, just [+finite]) is not allowed. Such an element seems to be too impoverished to survive. This tells us something about the restrictions on the feature content of categories. Of course, the parametric diacritic * is crucial here, as we can certainly leave root declarative Fin empty, and indeed the entire C-system. This suggests that since the EPP-feature and the * are both PF-sensitive features, one PF-feature entails the other (where substantive features are absent). I return to this point in 5.2.

Concerning (53c), the question is: why is V exactly second under the conditions of full V2 as just described? I have proposed that the finite verb occupies Fin and the fronted XP SpecFinP in V2 constructions. This leaves a range of higher positions, which in V2 clauses are unavailable. Given the discussion of long head-movement in 4.2, it should be clear why no head-movement to higher positions is available: all the heads in the C-system are Operator heads, like Fin, and so Fin blocks movement to all those positions. The only thing that could move into a higher head-position is Fin itself, but this can only happen if one of the higher heads is activated, that is, not in an unmarked declarative clause. Concerning the ban on XP-movement to higher Specifier positions, I would like to reason, following a suggestion by Luigi Rizzi (p.c.), along the following lines: XP-movement to SpecFin in full V2 clauses is movement caused only by Fin's EPP-feature, as we have just seen. The moved XP is thus of no particular type in terms of the typology of potential interveners and so is able to block any type of movement. Thus, since Fin has the null featural specification, XP-movement to value it "blocks off" all higher head and specifier positions in the clause. The fact that the verb is second where we have Fin*, poor agreement, and no particles, even in an elaborately structured left periphery, thus follows straightforwardly from the statement of relativized minimality given in (32) and (33) earlier. This also underlies the "last resort" effect of full V2: once XP-fronting for V2 takes place, no more movement operations are available in that CP.

We can extend the same account to Breton-style LVM, but with one major difficulty. Here we want the movement of the non-finite verb to block off all movement to higher positions, creating the second-position effect and the last-resort effect. This can apparently only be achieved with the statement of relativized minimality in (32) and (33) if the fronted verb is treated like an XP for relativized minimality (Rizzi 2000). In that case, the long-moved head will thus act like the topicalized XP in V2, that is, in the manner just described. Obviously, there are serious technical difficulties with this; I'll come back to it in 5.2.

However, this account of the second-position effect does not prevent merger into higher positions. In matrix clauses, this won't happen since by assumption all higher heads are inactive. But this is the required result for embedded V2 of both the symmetric and non-symmetric varieties. Also, this analysis correctly predicts that embedded V2 clauses are islands (cf. Müller and Sternefeld 1993):

(54)   a.*Radios glaube ich [$_{CP}$ gestern   hat [Fritz t$_{gestern}$ t$_{Radios}$ repariert]].
        radios   believe I   yesterday has   Fritz   repaired

        b. *Was glaubst du [$_{CP}$ gestern   hat [Fritz t$_{gestern}$ t$_{was}$ repariert]].
        what believe you yesterday has   Fritz   repaired

The analysis does not predict the strength of the island directly (note that the examples in [54] involve long object-movement), but we can clearly see how relativized minimality, construed as done earlier, accounts for the intervention effect of V2 topics here.[20]

We might also need the option of merger into C-positions above Fin for the "abnormal sentences" of Welsh, if these are to be reduced to a V2-like system that features obligatory topicalization; see Willis (1996, 1998) for arguments that in cases of apparent multiple fronting in this construction all XPs but one are merged in the C-system and the one that is not merged there but moved there "counts" for determining the form of the particle as *a* or *y* (cf. also note 15 of chapter 2 and the remarks on Rhaeto-Romansch in note 15 of this chapter). It is also consistent with this analysis that material can be moved to positions higher than *fe/mi*:

(55)   Yfory   fe fydd Ifan yn mynd adref.
            tomorrow Prt will-be Ifan Asp go   home
            'Tomorrow Ifan will be going home.'
            (Willis 1998: 202, [30b])

Modal adverbs cannot appear in the pre-*fe* position, presumably because Fin has modal feature-content here and so is incompatible with merger of *fe*:

(56)   *Hwyrach fe fydd   Ifan yn mynd adref yfory.
            probably Prt willp-be Ifan Asp go   home tomorrow
            (Willis 1998: 203, (31b))

Finally, I need to say something about cases of embedded V2 again, such as German examples like (45) of chapter 1, repeated here:

(57)   Ich glaube, gestern   hat   Maria dieses Buch gelesen.

I believe yesterday have Maria this book read
'I believe Maria read this book yesterday.'

To account for V2 here we have to say that Fin* acts as if it were in a root context. It seems that Force in this type of case imposes no requirement on Fin and at the same time structurally protects Fin from outside selection. I have no proposal for what happens in symmetric V2 languages beyond what was mentioned in note 24 of chapter 1.[21]

4.4　Conclusion

In this chapter I have developed an account of parametric variation in the C-system or, more precisely, involving non-selected, root, finite Fin, which covers several of the Celtic languages (Welsh, Breton, and, somewhat sketchily, Old Irish) as well as the V2 Germanic languages. The account also extends in a straightforward way to selected Fin and to residual V2 (which in fact is treated as a case of selected root Fin).

I was also able to account for the main features of V2, as listed in (53). The most important of these is (53b), the fact that moving V + T into Fin as a consequence of the Fin* parameter combined with the absence of Celtic-style particles causes XP-fronting exactly in root declaratives. I accounted for this by saying that a category that is so impoverished in feature content requires an EPP-feature, triggering XP-movement of any XP. This can be thought of as analogous to expletive-insertion in the agreement system of a language with impoverished agreement morphology; this is always third-person agreement (which may represent the absence of features in an underspecified system of agreement features; see 2.1.2). In that case, it comes as no surprise that the fronted XP can be an expletive in V2 languages, as well-known examples such as the following show:

(58)　　a.　　Es wurde getanzt.　　(German)
　　　　b.　　Þaþ verið dansað　　(Icelandic)
　　　　　　　'It/there was danced'

Given that it is crucial for the analysis of V2 presented in the previous section that the initial XP be treated as moved in all cases, the expletive must have raised from SpecIP (i.e. presumably SpecPersP) here. In this I follow Cardinaletti (1990).

The analysis of V2 led to the conjecture that a head has an EPP-feature when it is in some sense defective in substantive features. I noted that this may carry over to Agr systems. Although this idea still needs to be made more precise, it certainly points in the direction of further investigation of the feature structures that may be associated with heads. I also need to explicate the relation between the EPP-feature, the lexical-realization requirement indicated as F*, and head-movement. This is important, since the V2 effect does not arise in the absence of head-movement. This suggests that the EPP feature must be sensitive to head-movement,[22] a matter that requires further investigation in the light of Chomsky's (2001) proposal that head-movement is not part of narrow syntax.

In the next chapter, as part of an attempt to make the preceding remarks and analyses more technically precise and in line with minimalist goals, I will investigate this point in more detail and try to show that it is both feasible and desirable to incorporate a "head-movement" operation into Chomsky's system. This "head-movement" operation is somewhat different, at least technically, from the standard notions of head-movement deriving from Travis (1984) and Baker (1988), however. Once this is done, I can reformulate the parametric options relevant for Welsh in a coherent way.

5

Head-Movement and EPP-Features

Here I try to incorporate Roberts's (2001) F* notation into Chomsky's (2000, 2001) system. The purpose of doing this is to see whether we can take a further step toward understanding (52) of chapter 4. Section 5.1 presents a technical sketch of a way to incorporate head-movement into the approach in Chomsky (2000, 2001). Section 5.2 looks at the two EPP cases, the C-level case (V2) and the Agr-level case (expletive requirement in weak-agreement languages), in these terms.

5.1   Head-Movement

Chomsky (2001) outlines a conception of movement based on the combination of three separate, independently needed mechanisms: Agree, Pied-Pipe, and Merge.

As we briefly saw in 2.1.2, Agree is the Matching relation that holds between a Probe P and a Goal G in its domain:

(1)   a. Probe: a category (label) with uninterpreted features;
         b. Goal: a category (label) with uninterpreted features in the local domain
            of the probe;
         c. Matching: non-distinctness of features.

Locality is defined in terms of the Minimal Link Condition (MLC) and the Phase

Impenetrability Condition (PIC). The MLC is very close to relativized minimality and for our purposes here can be assumed to be the same thing.[1] The PIC states that the domain of the head of a strong phase H is not accessible to operations at the level of next phase H' (see the discussion in Chomsky 2001). Strong phases are XPs headed by categories that may have an EPP-feature: C and v^* (an occurrence of v with full argument structure, i.e. the v associated with non-passive, non-unaccusative VP; this corresponds to what was called Voice with a strong D-feature in 3.2). Among other things, the PIC forces long-distance Wh-movement to operate successive-cyclically, much in the manner of Chomsky (1986).

Pied-Pipe is the operation that causes the category of the Goal to be displaced along with the features that enter into Agree, and Merge is the structure-building operation that creates a binary-branching, labeled structure out of two syntactic elements. As we have seen, the EPP-feature of a category requires something to be merged into its Specifier.

Concretely, suppose the derivation has reached the following stage (here I use a simplified structure, following Chomsky in ignoring the Agr-field and ignoring for the sake of exposition functional structure in between T and vP):

(2)

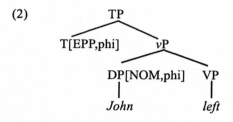

T has two uninterpretable features, EPP- and ϕ-features. The ϕ-features are unvalued and hence uninterpreted. The ϕ-features of *John* are valued (third person, masculine, singular), while NOM, a structural Case feature, is uninterpretable. The uninterpretable features of T and DP (really D or N, but I gloss over this point here) render them active. Thus T can be the Probe and *John* the Goal of the Agree relation (T, *John*). This relation does two things: it values and deletes the ϕ-features of T, and it values and deletes the structural Case of *John*. Finally, an active Goal determines a category that can be pied-piped under (second) Merge into SpecTP and thereby eliminate the uninterpretable EPP-feature of T. In this way, the sentence *John left,* with *John* bearing interpretable ϕ-features and all uninterpretable features deleted, can converge at the interfaces.

The utility of distinguishing EPP-features from Agree can be seen in pairs like the following:

(3)   a.   There arrived a train.
        b.   A train arrived.

In (3a), the lexical array that is the input to syntactic computation contains the expletive *there*, which only has a Person feature. T and the DP *a train* are in the Agree relation, just as described for T and *John* in (2). However, here T's EPP-feature is satisfied by merger of *there*, and so *a train* cannot and does not get moved. Nevertheless, its ϕ-features value and delete those of T, and T values and deletes the structural Case feature of the DP. Example (3b) is like (3a) except that there is no expletive in the lexical array, and so *a train* undergoes second merge to SpecTP to delete T's EPP-feature.

How does head-movement work in such a system, and can head-movement satisfy an EPP-feature? Chomsky casts doubt on the existence of head-movement in "narrow syntax" (the computation from the lexicon to LF, excluding PF), but in fact this can be achieved at the cost of introducing just one further feature and one further operation. The nature of these features is such that we could reasonably conclude that head-movement is a morphological operation or, more precisely, an operation with a significant morphological component.

Consider a standard case of head-movement, say English subject-auxiliary inversion under residual V2, as in:

(4)   Will John leave tomorrow?

For ease of exposition, I revert to a simple C-system and a simple I/T-system, and so we take it that in (4) T, containing the modal *will*, has raised to C. How can we formalize this operation in terms of Agree/Pied-Pipe/Move? This is fairly straight-forward: interrogative C, call it C[+Q], has an uninterpretable EPP-feature and an interpretable Q-feature, and C[+Q] selects T with an uninterpretable Q-feature. The uninterpretable features make C and T active, and hence C can be a Probe and T a Goal. Since the relevant locality relation is respected (there are no intervening heads),[2] C and T are able to agree, thus valuing and deleting the uninterpretable Q-feature of T. Since T is an active Goal, it can be pied-piped to C, and since C has an uninterpretable EPP-feature, this must happen. All of this straightforwardly derives the following substructure at the C-level:

(5)   C[+Q]

            T   C[+Q]

This structure is the result of second merge of T. Two very important questions arise at this point, though: (i) How do we ensure that only the modal, and not the entire contents of T' or TP, is pied-piped with T in (5)? (ii) If only T is pied-piped, leaving behind its Specifier and complement, where are these elements in relation to T? If they are directly c-commanded by T, and therefore dominated by C in (5), then what would prevent successive-cyclic movement of T (i.e., excorporation) under the right conditions (i.e., if there was something in a higher position capable of attracting T)? If they are not contained in C but are the sister of C in (5) (as is standardly assumed in the literature on head-movement), how is T able to c-com-mand its trace? These are among the reasons that are given by Chomsky (2001) for doubting that head-movement takes place in narrow syntax; I return to some of the others later.

I would like to propose that the answers to both of those questions can be found if we allow that the narrow syntax may contain formal features that are also PF-features. Chomsky (2001) observes that there are three types of features in lexical entries: (A) phonological features, (B) semantic features, and (C) formal features. Features (B) and (C) intersect, so that there are interpretable formal features (e.g. Q in C in [4]), where "interpretable" means "having LF-relevant content." We might therefore expect (A) and (C) to intersect, giving rise to PF-sensitive formal features (PFS-features), features that, in addition to entering the syntactic computations, are sensitive to phonological and morphological properties.[3] I would like to propose one such feature: Affix. This feature is "interpreted" at PF by causing the head that bears it to enter into a particular morphological structure: that of [Stem + [Affix]]—as such it arguably underlies Lasnik's (1981) Stray Affix Filter, which was invoked in 2.1, as underlying Welsh V-movement. So let us suppose that C[+Q] also has the PFS-feature [Affix] rather than the EPP-feature (in the next section we deal with the relation between the EPP-feature and Affix). Since in PF (taking this term to cover the morphological component, however construed) affixes cannot attach to anything bigger than a word, the [Affix]-feature prevents Pied-Pipe from selecting anything larger than T. This answers question (i) (I will slightly reconstrue this in the next section).

Concerning question (ii), suppose that the [Affix]-feature of C[+Q] derives the following structure:

(6)

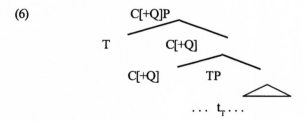

This kind of structure is problematic since, on the one hand, it could allow T to move on, giving rise to some kind of excorporation, and, on the other hand, it does not allow T to form a constituent with the head of C[+Q]. Although these points may not give rise to observable ill effects in the example under discussion, if we think of V to I to C movement (or any standard case of iterated head-movement) we clearly want exactly the opposite in each case: we do not want to allow excorporation, and we want iterated head-movement of the familiar kind to result.[4] However, note that the c-command relation between the moved head and its trace is perfectly regular in (4) (the conjunction of Sister and Contain, two relations that derive directly from Merge).

A solution to this problem, inspired by proposals in Halle and Marantz (1993), is to suppose that [Affix] converts a structure like (6) into one like (7):

(7)

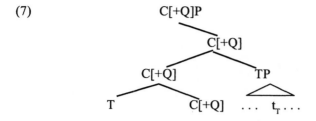

In this structure, excorporation is impossible, and T+C[+Q] behaves as a morphological word (it happens that C[+Q] is silent in English, but of course it is phonologically realized in many languages). Let us call the operation that converts (6) into (7) Incorporation (although it is similar to Halle and Marantz's 1993 operation of Fusion). It is natural to think of Incorporation as taking place at the end of each phase, as this is where a part of the derivation is "handed over" to PF; in that case Incorporation would be part of PF and we would not have to countenance such an operation in the narrow syntax. In fact, the only thing we would have added to the narrow syntax is the PFS-feature [Affix], which does not seem like a radical departure from minimalist guidelines. However, simply in order to ensure that head-movement can iterate through the T-system and possibly on into C in the standard way we need to assume that Incorporation can take place phase-internally (sticking to the idea that just *v*P and CP are phases).

There is, however, another possibility. We can exploit two aspects of the system in Chomsky (2001) to get a different result: (i) the idea that movement leaves copies, and (ii) the idea that uninterpretable features are only deleted at the end of each phase. Suppose we have a structure like the following, where F, G, and H are functional heads in the I-system, each endowed with a strong [Affix]-feature. Suppose also that V, like T in (2), has uninterpretable features, that correspond to interpretable features in F, G and H (these might, for example, be features of Aspect, Tense, and Mood):

(8)

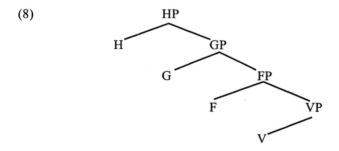

Now V moves through the structure, owing to its own uninterpretable features and the Affix-features of F, G, and H, giving:

(9)

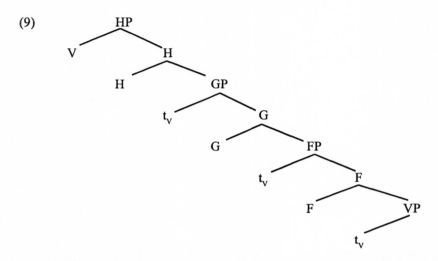

At the end of the phase, all uninterpretable features will be eliminated in the handover to PF. Suppose that Incorporation applies at exactly this point. Then the uninterpretable features that trigger each V-movement will be visible and each copy of V can be matched to the appropriate interpretable feature on each head. More precisely, Incorporation matches V_F, an uninterpretable feature on V, with F_F, an interpretable feature of the functional head, forming a morphological constituent with F_F as the Affix and V as the Stem each time.[5] If Incorporation applies cyclically in this way, we can derive Baker's (1985) Mirror Principle (see also Brody 1999). Assuming iterated Incorporation, we derive the structure in (10) from that in (9) (I indicate the structure as left-adjunction: we can integrate the LCA in this approach by assuming that Incorporation does not reorder elements):

(10) $[_H [_G [_F V F] G] H]$

It is thus possible to integrate head-movement into the system of Chomsky (2001). What we see is that head-movement is distributed between narrow syntax and PF; the basic movement computation can be seen (phase-internally) to be like other cases of movement, but it is associated with a PF-sensitive feature that constrains Pied-Piping and, at the handover to PF, triggers Incorporation. The consequence of this result for the discussion at the end of the last chapter is that Roberts's (2001) F*-notation emerges as equivalent to an Affix-feature in Chomsky's system as modified here. I return to this point in the next section.[6]

In addition to the points mentioned earlier, Chomsky (2001) gives other arguments that head-movement should not be considered part of narrow syntax. First, head-movement never affects interpretation. In fact, this is not true of certain English modals, where inversion (i.e., T-to-C movement) can affect the available interpretations. In (11a) *may* is ambiguous between a permission and an epistemic interpretation, while in (11b) the epistemic interpretation is strongly preferred (for contemporary speakers), as shown by the availability or not of the adverb *well*, which seems to be a diagnostic for epistemic readings. The embedded clauses in (11c, d) show that the interpretative difference is connected to head-movement rather than the interrogative nature of the clause:

(11)   a. John may (well) leave.   permission/possibility
        b. May John (?*well) leave.   permission only
        c. ??May it well rain tomorrow?   permission only
        d. ??John wonders if it may well rain tomorrow. permission only

Similarly, head-movement can license NPIs. This is particularly clear in the following contrast (thanks to Jason Merchant for discussion of these examples):

(12)   a.   ??Why did anyone leave?
        b.   Why didn't anyone leave?

Although Wh-elements are usually said to license NPIs, the subject NPI in (12a) is somewhat marginal. It clearly contrasts with (12b), which is fully natural. The only difference between the two examples is that negation appears in C in (12b), and so this is the element that licenses the subject NPI. On standard analyses, negation reaches C via head-movement (I-to-C movement). Assuming that NPI licensing is an LF matter (which it must be in a minimalist model, as mentioned in 1.2), this is a case where head-movement affects LF. It then follows that head-movement cannot be confined to the mapping to PF.[7]

    A second very important objection that Chomsky raises is that given T with a strong D-feature and a strong V-feature (as in French, in standard analyses), we have no way of preventing VP-fronting and D-movement taking place instead of the desired DP-fronting and V-movement, something we do not seem to find. Technically, this objection can be met in terms of the mechanics just described if we associate [Affix] with a particular feature, that is, V but not D in the case given. However, this makes [Affix] a feature of a feature and at the same time does not tell us why the observed situation holds. A more interesting approach has to do with locality: it appears in fact that head-movement pre-empts XP-movement, in the sense that the head-movement option is always the more local one compared to XP-movement and apparently always applies first. In the example given, assuming that there is functional structure between T and the merged position of the subject and that the intervening Specifier positions are not A-positions (they would be adverb positions in Cinque's 1999 system), but assuming that V moves successively through the functional structure (as again Cinque shows), then V is closer to T at the point in the cycle when T is merged with its active uninterpretable features. At this point in the derivation, the structure looks like (13). So the head undergoes the more local movement. The same is true with Wh-movement. In fact, we can observe that where the Wh-XP is closer to the Probe than the relevant head the resulting structure is ill-formed, as in (14).[8]

(13)

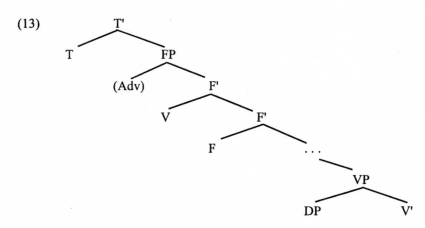

(14)   a.   *Who did leave?
        b.   *Que sent bon?
              'What smells good?'
              (Friedemann 1990)

In these cases, head-movement is in fact banned. The generalization is clear: head-movement must always be more local than XP-movement. In cases where both XP-movement and head-movement are triggered (as in the DP- and V-movement case discussed earlier), head-movement must place the head in a position adjacent to the target and hence must apply before XP-movement because of the cycle (i.e., the requirement that movement always extend the structure). We can explain the locality observation in these terms if features of the same type are involved in head- and in XP-attraction (see the discussion of long head-movement and relativized minimality in 4.2). In that case, the first movement to take place will have to be the more local one in relation to the target. Because of the (PF-imposed) adjacency requirement on Incorporation, the first movement must be head-movement. And so we may actually have here an argument that head-movement is syntactic. In (14) the Wh-XP is closer to the target than T and so raises to C, satisfying the PF-realization requirement of Q in C on its own. Head-movement is thus impossible on two counts: it would be both countercyclic and uneconomical. For this account to go through, the affixal property of Q must be a subcase of its PF-realization requirement, in principle satisfiable by mechanisms other than head-movement. I return to this point later.

    Third, Chomsky mentions that V2, due precisely to its sensitivity to the asyntactic notion of "second position," may be a PF property. However, we saw in 4.3, how second-position effects can be derived from relativized minimality. Again, this in fact gives us a reason to draw the opposite conclusion from Chomsky's.

    Fourth, Chomsky observes that head-movement in the classical sense does not have the formal properties of other operations. However, previously I noted a way to integrate it with other operations.

Finally, head-movement seems, on standard approaches, to observe slightly different locality conditions from other operations. Again, the version of relativized minimality adopted here (see [32] and [33] of chapter 4) in fact fully accounts for the local nature of head-movement, including, crucially, cases like Breton LVM, which violate the classical Head Movement Constraint and yet are subject to locality exactly as dictated by relativized minimality.

One of Chomsky's objections remains: that head-movement is countercyclic; that is, in cases where both a head and XP target the same category, the XP is always moved from a lower position than the head. In fact, if the observation made earlier that head-movement always pre-empts XP-movement is correct, then this is always true. One speculation as to why this is the case relates to the fact that head-movement is sensitive to PF-properties. Presumably, Incorporation as described earlier is subject to strict adjacency (another PF-property) and so head-movement has to apply before XP-movement in order to create a structure in which Incorporation can apply. But if the XP is closer to the target, then it can move and satisfy all properties of the target and so the head cannot move (and, if it did, it would violate the extension condition). So the countercyclic nature of head-movement is actually the consequence of the interaction of locality, the adjacency condition on Incorporation and the extension condition.

On the basis of this discussion, I conclude that it is possible and in fact desirable to maintain that head-movement is part of "narrow syntax" in Chomsky's sense, albeit with a certain sensitivity to PF (or at least morphology). In the system described here, the [Affix]-feature is equivalent to Roberts's (2001) F* notation. Given the role played by that notation in analyzing EPP-effects in chapter 4, we can now ask what the relation between this feature and the EPP-feature is.

5.2   A Formal Characterization of EPP-Effects

The question I need to address here, then, is how [Affix] and a strong EPP-feature might be connected. One observation immediately arises: it seems natural to regard the EPP-feature as a PFS-feature, too. This in fact arises in the discussion in Chomsky (2001), which is worth quoting at length:

> Some heads H have a property P that determines that H heads an occurrence; P is the EPP property of H, commonly taken to be a selectional feature satisfied by merging K. K may be an expletive or a category determined by probe-goal agreement and pied-piping; the latter is the case of multiple Merge. With no apparent substantive change, we may dispense with multiple Merge and reconstrue Move as the operation Agree/Pied-Pipe/Mark, where Agree holds of (probe H, goal G) as before, and Mark identifies H as the head of an occurrence H^P of the Pied-Piped category K determined by G. . . Under the simplest assumptions, a principle of phonology spells K out at its highest . . . occurrence in the course of the cyclic derivation.

(An occurrence of a category is a copy of that category, distinguished from other copies by its mother.) EPP-features are thus fairly directly connected to Spell Out, and hence to PF. So let's say that, like [Affix], EPP is a PFS-feature. We could in fact see the difference between the EPP-feature and [Affix] purely in terms of what is required to be spelt out on H: EPP requires that this be an XP and [Affix] that it be a Stem. More precisely, perhaps [Affix] is a version of the EPP-feature that imposes the extra condition on Pied-Pipe that only Stems (heads) can be pied-piped; this means that they are in fact interface-interpretable features: these features are interpreted at the PF interface, unlike more familiar (LF-)interpretable features.

In these terms, I can rephrase the analysis of full and residual V2 given at the end of the last chapter. As we briefly saw in the last section, residual V2 involves a clause-type feature on Fin (which may in fact be selected by Force; cf. the discussion in 1.2.2). Associated with this feature is an Affix-feature. The Affix-feature functions just like Roberts's (2001) Fin*. The reason the Affix attracts T is because Fin can only enter into Agree with T, as T is the only accessible category with temporal features (there may be other heads with temporal features, e.g., perhaps V, or Asp, but they are lower than T and hence unreachable from Fin by relativized minimality). Crucial to this idea is that no nominal has temporal features (thus the temporal features of a noun like *tomorrow* are purely semantic and thus inaccessible to the computational system). Also, the Agr-field does not contain relevant features, unless V + T has moved there, as in a strong-agreement language like French (see 2.1). So Fin Agrees with T and attracts it as an affix.

In residual V2 constructions where a Wh-XP is fronted, everything is as just described, with the addition of an uninterpretable Wh-feature on Foc (cf. the discussion in 1.2.2), which Agrees with a Wh-XP and attracts it in virtue of having an EPP feature. Languages with Wh-in-situ presumably lack the EPP-feature on Wh-Foc.[9]

Turning to full V2, the account of V-movement is substantially as earlier, but the question, as always, is: why is there both an EPP-feature and an Affix-feature on Fin in just this case? As I observed in 4.3, this must be connected to the fact that Force is inert in full V2 clauses. In fact, we can note an interesting parallel with anti-agreement, as follows:

(15)   a.   V2:

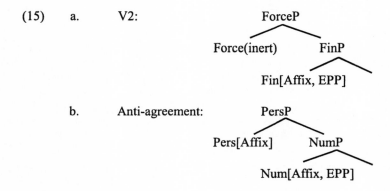

    b.   Anti-agreement:

What the two structures here have in common is that the upper head has unmarked features that have no morphological realization (recall that we treated the 3sg ending -*dd* in Welsh as a placeholder rather than as a 3sg clitic; see 2.1). As I said in section 2.1, an unspecified category cannot value a feature, and so cannot be a Probe. As the discussions in 1.2.2 and 4.3 indicate, the same holds for Force in full V2.[10] This links to the intuition expressed in the previous chapter that EPP-effects must thus arise in categories with defective feature content. It seems that where a category has a PFS-feature but is not selected as a Goal, an EPP feature automatically arises. In other words, the EPP-effect activates non-Goals in positions that are canonically Goal-positions. This is why EPP-effects show up in root position (Fin, Foc) and Agr, another unselected position (recall that we follow Roberts and Roussou 2002 in assuming that Fin selects T but not Agr). This idea also carries over to the Have-Be alternation discussed in 3.3; in this case, where Asp has no properties (triggers neither Merge nor Move), Agr must trigger movement (recall that complements move through SpecAgr-Prt where Be appears in Romance; see Kayne 1989). Again we see an unselected category that otherwise has no properties that trigger movement, so this appears to be a further EPP-effect.

We can account for the range of possibilities for licensing Fin and Agr that we observed in chapter 4 in terms of the presence or absence of the two PFS-features I have identified. In 4.2, I identified the mechanisms available for feature-valuing as selection, merger, and Spec-head agreement (see the discussion following [41] there). Let us now leave aside selection, as we are interested in cases like (14), where the standard selection (Agree) relation does not hold for any substantive features. Let us also leave aside merger, since there is little to say here: merger takes place if the relevant lexical material is available. That leaves the following schema:

(16)	Affix	EPP	C	I
a.	+	+	V2	anti-agreement
b.	−	+	*a/y*-particles	weak-agreement SVO
c.	−	−	non-V2	possible null-subject language[11]
d.	+	−	V-initial (no clause-type)[12]	V-initial (no agreement)

It is clear from what we have seen that (16d) does not exist. I discussed the significance of this with respect to V2 in 4.3.

Why can no head have the feature combination [+Affix, −EPP] alone? The answer, I believe, lies in the idea adumbrated earlier that Affix is a variant of EPP; if we say that Affix is the variant of EPP that is forced to appear when EPP appears, then we account for (16) (this does not prevent Affix from appearing on a head with other features, as in residual V2). So: why is EPP forced to manifest itself as Affix in this case? It is possible to answer this question in terms of relativized minimality.

The idea is simply that two EPP-features cannot cooccur on a single head. If they did, each one would effectively block movement for checking of the other, as long as each moves purely for checking of EPP (see the discussion at the end of chapter 4, and Starke 2000, where a much more far-reaching variant of this proposal is developed). A way to avoid this is for one of the two features to realize itself as an Affix-feature, thus becoming a different structural type and not acting as an intervener in terms of our formulation of relativized minimality. This cannot happen twice, since two Affix-features will interact in just the same way as two EPP-features. Hence it is never possible for a head to bear more than two EPP-/Affix-features. So we allow in principle for multiple Specifiers (and indeed they are present in representations that feature head-movement prior to phase-final Incorporation, as we saw in the last section), but we see that, with the exception of a narrow range of cases, they are ruled out—not by X'-theory, which we assume does not exist, but by locality.

5.3   Conclusion

The conclusion of this discussion is that we adopt a variant of Chomsky's (2000, 2001) EPP-features, construed as PFS-features, features that are "interpretable" at the PF interface (this conclusion converges with Roberts's 2001 idea that heads may have a diacritic that indicates they require PF-realization). "EPP-effects" arise when such features are associated with otherwise unselected heads. This seems to be a requirement. Note that (root) Fin and Pers (i.e., the highest Agr-position in IP) are probably the only unselected positions (other than Force, which is the true root category, but in that sense it is not a possible Goal): T is selected; lower Agr-positions are selected by higher ones, Foc is selected (residual V2) and all lexical heads, all Ds, and all Mood, Tense, and Aspect heads in the Cinque hierarchy are selected. Agr-Prt, which may also bear an EPP-feature in this sense if the remarks at the end of the previous section are correct, may also be unselected where Asp lacks a P. So we observe that the EPP-effects that arise in Fin and Agr indicate an important constraint on the possible feature makeup of heads, although it is not clear exactly how to formulate this constraint in the absence of any general theory of the possible feature content of heads. In this sense, it is unsurprising that the EPP is rather mysterious given our current state of knowledge.

Returning to the variation noted in chapter 4 regarding the realization of Agr and Fin, I can now construct the following table:

(17) (unselected)	Fin	Pers	Asp	Agr-Prt
a. Merger	Welsh *fe/mi*	Padovano subject clitics	*yn, wedi*	*ei* (etc.)
b. Merger + EPP	Breton *a*	VSO agreement	Breton *kaoud*??	
c. EPP	*a/y*	"weak" SVO (Germanic)	P (Kayne 1993)	French Participles
d. EPP, Affix	V2	"strong" SVO?? (Romance)		Italian Participles
e. No properties	English	East Asian (?)	BE	English

Table (17) is fairly self-explanatory, except for (17b). Breton *a* has an EPP-feature; hence it triggers XP-movement and LVM. LVM is incompatible with XP-movement, as we saw (cf. [28] of 4.2). This seems then to be a case of head-movement without subsequent Incorporation, presumably because *a* is not lexically specified as an affix (being lexically specified as an affix is disjoint from having the formal feature Affix, since the latter is actually EPP with the associated consequence for Pied-Pipe). The VSO agreement affixes have the same property, and so no XP-movement to their Specifier is possible, either. In both of these cases the verb moves to attach to the affix as it is the nearest available head; in Breton the auxiliary cannot satisfy EPP (perhaps because it is not a constituent, having not undergone Incorporation at the Pers level), and in Welsh V in Num moves to adjoin to Pers.

Table (17) also contains two gaps. It may be that the Merger + EPP option for Agr-Prt is instantiated by object agreement. This would present the exact parallel to the VSO subject-agreement pattern. The EPP, Affix option remains mysteriously unattested for Asp. I will leave both of these points for future research.

Table (17) is the result of the discussions in 2.1, 3.2, chapter 4, and here. It is clear that in this way a very simple system can account for a very wide range of cross-linguistic data. In this way, these proposals meet the criterion of typologizability mentioned in the introduction. Since the variant properties are simple and are directly connected to inflectional morphology (realization as a free morpheme, or a clitic, an affix, a Specifier, or no realization at all) and since we know that inflectional morphology is something language acquirers are sensitive to (see Fromkin et al. 2000, chapter 6), these proposals also meet the criterion of learnability. In this way, they meet the criterion of explanatory adequacy of Chomsky (1964). Whether they meet the goal of minimalist explanation, showing how apparent imperfections reduce to optimal design (see the discussion in Chomsky, Belletti, and Rizzi 2000), is another matter: in attempting to follow the technical apparatus of Chomsky (2001), which was explicitly designed with this goal in mind, I have tried to keep to the minimalist goal. The only operation that was added to the technical operations proposed in Chomsky (2001) was Incorporation, which I take to be a morphological operation that applies at the interface to PF.[13]

Notes

Introduction

1. There is almost certainly not a single VSO parameter. Other VSO languages around the world vary considerably in relevant respects, as many of the essays in Carnie and Guilfoyle (2000) attest. How far the conclusions reached here can apply to VSO languages in general is a question for further work. The work presented here is, as the subtitle states, a case study. I believe, however, that a great deal of what follows is valid for most of the Celtic languages at most of their attested historical stages (see Doherty 2000 and Willis 1998 for analyses of various aspects of the historical syntax of Irish and Welsh, respectively).

Chapter 1

1. In fact, the generalization is that any tense can be expressed periphrastically, but while no tense has only a synthetic form, some have both periphrastic and synthetic forms. King (1993: 137) gives the following list of the tenses of the verb *prynu,* "buy," in modern spoken Welsh:

present	mae e'n prynu	'he buys/is buying'
imperfect	roedd e'n prynu	'he was buying'
perfect	mae e wedi prynu	'he has bought'
pluperfect	roedd e wedi prynu	'he had bought'

preterite	brynodd e	
	naeth e brynu	'he bought' (. . .)
future	brynith e	
	bydd e'n prynu	
	neith e brynu	'he will buy'
future perfect	bydd e wedi prynu	'he will have bought'
conditional	basai fe'n prynu (prynai fe)	'he would buy'
conditional perfect	basai fe wedi prynu	'he would have bought'

Here *(f)e* is the 3sg masculine pronoun (the occurrence of initial *f-* is phonologically conditioned; this pronoun shows up as *[ʃ]o* in many Northern varieties and in some of the examples here). The forms *mae, oedd, bydd,* and *basai* are the present, imperfect, future, and conditional forms of the auxiliary *bod,* "be." The forms *naeth* and *neith* are the preterit and future respectively of *gwneud,* "do." Note that there is no "Have"-auxiliary— we return to this point in 3.3. I will leave aside the question of the nature of the aspectual particles *(y)n* and *wedi* here, simply assuming that they instantiate an aspectual functional head (see again 3.2). I analyze the alternation in the initial consonant (soft mutation of / p/ to /b/) in 2.2.

Various tenses that are more characteristic of the literary language are not included here: the pluperfect and the subjunctive. The future and conditional are historically present and imperfect, respectively, and are often described as such in traditional grammars.

2. Welsh is a typologically very regular language. It is VO/Pr/NA/NG; i.e., it conforms to a general "head-initial" pattern. Welsh conforms to every one of Greenberg's (1966) universals concerning VSO languages: namely, Universals 1, 2, 3, 6, 8, 9, 10, 12, 16, 17, 19, 21, 22. Following the criterion of typologizability, one would like whatever parameter accounts for VSO to account for the other properties, too. See chapter 3.

3. See also Alexiadou and Anagnostopoulou (1998), Chomsky (2000, 2001), Platzack (1998), and the essays in Svenonius (2002) for relevant considerations regarding the nature and functioning of the EPP.

4. Chomsky (1995: 329f.) excludes VP-adjoined adverbs. However, under the specific assumptions about clause structure made there, the subject is merged outside the core VP in the specifier of a higher phrase, *v*P. Adverb-adjunction to *v*P is not excluded in this system (and there is no strong motivation for such exclusion); in fact, this is arguably the position of *often* in (i):

(i)   John often reads books.

Hence the argument in the text goes through—if the subject were not raised from its merged position and V is raised to T, then we expect at least some adverbs to intervene between V and the subject, viz., adverbs adjoined to *v*P. V must leave *v*P in order to derive VSO order, if the subject is merged at Spec*v*P. In 2.2, I will adopt the idea that the subject is merged in Spec*v*P (this is further refined in 3.2).

5. There is evidence that Welsh negation follows the diachronic pattern noticed by Jespersen (1917: 195–196). Jespersen observed that English negation developed from a preverbal clitic negation in Old English (*ic ne secge*), to a French-style "double" negation in Middle English (*I ne seye not*), to a postverbal-only negation in Early Modern English (*I say not*) (the development is then complicated by the introduction of obligatory *do*-insertion, which is not relevant here). Different registers of Modern Welsh show all three patterns of negation, although it is a reasonable conjecture that the registers correlate with

diachronic stages (see Willis 1997). Literary Welsh has a preverbal negation *ni* before a verb that begins with a consonant, *nid* before a verb that begins with a vowel:

(i)   Ni   redodd Siôn i   ffwrdd.
                  Neg ran   John to far
                  'John didn't run away.'
                  (Rouveret 1994: 127)

A "double-negation" pattern is also possible, with *(d)dim*, "at all/anything" (the initial *d-* of the auxiliary is the survival of *nid* in the spoken language—I'll say more about forms like *dydy* in 1.2.3):

(ii)   Dydy Ffred ddim fan   hyn.
                  Neg-is Fred neg   place this
                  'Fred isn't here.'

J. Morris-Jones (1913: 314) remarks that "this adverbial *ddim* is nearly as frequent in the spoken language as *pas* after a negation in French." In sentences without an auxiliary, the only visible form of negation in modern spoken Welsh is *(d)dim*:

(iii)   Chafodd Ffred ddim gwobr.
                  got   Fred neg prize
                  'Fred didn't get a prize.'

Although a number of issues are unclear, the basic development appears to parallel that of English. French, too, shows the same development, viz., from *ne* V in Old/Middle French, to *ne* V *pas* in Modern Literary French, to V *pas* in the contemporary spoken language.

Borsley and R. Morris-Jones (2000: 20ff.) distinguish quantifier *dim* from adverbial *dim*. Quantifier *dim* shares the distribution of non-negative quantifiers like *peth* or *rhai* (both "some"), in appearing as a pronominal modifier or preceding partitive *o*, "of":

(iv)   a.   Does [dim dyn/dim o'r   dynion] yn yr ystafell.
                  is   neg man/neg of-the men   in the room
                  'No man/none of the men are in the room.'

          b.   Welish i [ddim dyn/ddim o'r dynion].
                  saw   I neg   man/none of the men.
                  'I saw no man/none of the men.'

          c.   Mae [rhai dynion/rhai o'r dynion] yn yr ystafell.
                  is   some men/some of the men   in the room
                  'Some men/some of the men are in the room.'

          d.   Welish i [rai   dynion/rai o'r   dynion].
                  saw   I some men/some of the men
                  'I saw some men/some of the men.'

It seems clear then that quantifier *dim* is a DP-internal element, as the bracketing in the preceding examples indicates.

Adverbial *dim* is in complementary distribution with other sentential negators such as *byth*, "never," and can appear as part of a sequence of adverbs:

(v)   a.   *Dw i byth ddim yn yfed cwrw.
                  am I ever neg in drink beer
                  (Borsley and R. Morris-Jones 2000: 29 [63])

         b.   Dydy'r   ceffyl ddim bob tro yn y cae.
                  is   the horse neg each turn in the field
                  'The horse isn't always in the field.'
                  (Borsley and R. Morris-Jones 2000: 27 [57])

This is the element that is comparable to French (sentential) *pas* and which we might thus think of as occupying SpecNegP. See later and note 6 on a peculiar restriction on the distribution of adverbial *dim*.

6. Borsley and R. Morris-Jones (2000) point out that adverbial *dim* cannot cooccur with a nominal object:

(i)   *Wela' i ddim Gwen eto.
                  will-see I neg Gwen again
                  'I will not see Gwen again.'

Although a surprising restriction and one for which we have no immediate account, it does not affect the point being made in the text: for this point to hold it is sufficient for adverbial *dim* to occupy a position that is structurally higher than the position into which the subject is merged. If the subject is merged in SpecVP and *dim* can precede VP-adverbs, as in (vb) of the previous note, then this is clear. Cf. also chapter 2, note 22.

7. Subjects can also appear in front of *ne*:

(i)   a.   Ne goll ket Yann e hent ar   c'hoad.
                  Neg lose neg Yann his way in-the wood
                  'Yann does not lose his way in the wood.'

         b.   Yann ne goll ket e hent ar   c'hoad.
                  Yann neg lose neg his way in-the wood
                  'Yann does not lose his way in the wood.'
                  (Stephens 1982: 128)

This is an instance of a general rule of XP-fronting to a position in front of the preverbal particle (*ne* in a negative clause). Other XPs can be fronted to this position:

(ii)   a.   [Al levr nevez] ne lenn ket ar vugale.
                  the book new   neg read neg the children
                  'The children didn't read the new book.'
                  (Object-preposing: Stephens 1982: 256)

         b.   [Debrin krampouezh ed-du]   ne ra   ket Yann.
                  eat   pancakes   buckwheat neg does neg Yann
                  'Yann does not eat buckwheat pancakes.'
                  (VP-preposing: Stephens 1982: 105)

It seems clear that the order in (ib) involves an A'-movement rule and so is not relevant for determining the "neutral order" of constituents. In this matter, I agree with Borsley and Stephens (1989) and not with Stump (1984). See 4.2.

8. Stump (1984) gives the following example of a pronominal subject between the verb and *ket*:

(i)   Ne gouskont-int   ket.
            Neg sleep   -they neg
            'They do not sleep.'

This example and the corresponding one where the pronoun follows *ket* are of unclear grammaticality (see in particular Borsley and Stephens 1989: 414, Schafer 1994: 38, n. 19, Stump 1989: 435–437). It may be that in at least some dialects of Breton pronominal subjects can or must raise further than nominal subjects; this point is not central to the text discussion, however, and so I leave it aside.

9. Things are apparently more complex in Breton, at least according to Schafer (1994). Schafer observes that there is an object-shift rule. This operation places the object pronoun in front of the subject and, in a negative clause, after *ket*:

(i)   a.   Ne wel ket anezhañ   Maia.
              Neg see neg it (*a*-pronoun) Maia
              'Maia doesn't see it.'
              (Schafer 1994: 38)

        b.   Breman e   wel anezhañ Maia.
              now   Prt see it   Maia
              'Now Maia sees it.'
              (Schafer 1994: 37)

Schafer (1994: 40) suggests that Neg is situated above AgrOP and that object shift places the object pronoun in SpecAgrOP. She also argues against a rightward-subject-movement analysis of (ia, b). Whatever the correct analysis of object shift, this construction appears to confirm that the subject occupies a "low" position in this language.

10. Rouveret (1994: 140) suggests that in more literary varieties of Welsh where the principal negator is *ni(d)* and *(d)dim* is not required, there may be a similar variation in the position of the subject. Without the diagnostic afforded by the medial negation, this variation is hidden, he suggests. This conclusion is not readily compatible with minimalist assumptions, which entail that the convergence of a derivation without subject-raising over the position of medial negation renders ungrammatical a derivation with such movement. In the absence of direct evidence in favor of two distinct positions for definite subjects in varieties of Welsh other than the Pembrokeshire dialect, I will assume that there is a single (VP-external) one.

11. Example (13a) is an instance of the "perfective passive." For reasons that I don't need to go into, this passive construction is always perfective in interpretation. Irish, like Welsh, has a synthetic impersonal passive. However, in both languages, there is some reason to think that there is no movement of the logical object in these cases; see Stenson (1981) on the Irish construction and Comrie (1977) on the Welsh one. See also 2.3.4.2. See McCloskey (1996b) for arguments that the object is raised to subject-position in (13b).

Example (13c) involves raising of a null subject, as the 2sg agreement on the matrix predicate shows. The 2sg argument is clearly the logical subject of the lower predicate.

12. For more on the *cael*-passive, see note 11 of chapter 3.

13. Here we have definite subjects. Indefinites are possible in (18b) because the verb is unaccusative, as we have just seen.

14. For a general alternative to Huang's account, see Heycock (1995).

15. Interestingly, the same judgments carry over to Breton, according to Schafer (1994: 90). If this is so, then we have a further indication that, despite the fact that they must follow *ket*, subjects are raised out of VP in this language. If the subject is generated in Spec,*v*P, as I will assume in 2.2, then this result implies that what is fronted here is at least *v*P and that the subject moves out of that category.

16. The subject can always be optionally realized as an Accusative DP in non-finite clauses in Irish. See Chung and McCloskey (1987: 211), Bobaljik and Carnie (1996: 238), and the references given there.

17. For further discussion of this issue and a summary of a number of analyses of SOV order in non-finite clauses in Irish, see Carnie (1995: 81–118). For my purposes here, it is enough to show how these orders argue for the idea that the subject leaves VP in Irish.

18. In English the movement is restricted to auxiliaries, owing to the interaction of the absence of main-verb movement to T and the Head Movement Constraint; see Pollock 1989. In French, the subject must be a clitic pronoun when V moves to C; see Kayne 1972, 1983, Rizzi and Roberts 1989, Roberts 1993, and Sportiche 1998.

19. Many non-standard varieties of English allow residual verb second in indirect questions. The phenomenon has been carefully studied in Hiberno-English by McCloskey (1992). In this variety, examples like the following are fully acceptable:

(i)   a.   Ask your father does he want his dinner.
        b.   'Would a woman of this area dress herself like that?'
               'I don't know would she.'
               (McCloskey 1992: 15)

McCloskey notes that embedded residual verb second is only possible with verbs whose complements have a truly interrogative interpretation (verbs that introduce "true questions" in the terminology of Suñer 1993). Verbs that take Wh-complements with a "semi-question" interpretation do not allow embedded residual verb second, e.g.:

(ii)   a.   *It was amazing who did they invite.
        b.   *The police couldn't establish who had they beaten up.
               (McCloskey 1992: 16)

It seems clear that Q- and Wh-features should be distinguished on the basis of data like this. See McCloskey (1992) for further discussion and analysis.

20. There are languages where it seems that the root-embedded asymmetry of verb second does not hold. The two best-known cases are Icelandic and Yiddish: because they lack the usual asymmetry, these languages are often referred to as symmetric V2 languages. Verb second appears to be generalized to all types of embedded clauses in Icelandic. This order is optional in relative clauses and adverbial clauses and impossible in topicalized object clauses (cf. Sigurðsson 1989: 44f.). The other Germanic language that has been claimed to allow generalized embedded topicalization is Yiddish (cf. Diesing 1988, 1990, Santorini 1990, 1994). The following examples should be contrasted with those in (30):

(i)   a.   Ég spurdi **hvort   þegar   hefdi María** lesid þessa bók.   (Icelandic)
                    I   asked   whether already had   Mary   read this   book
                    'I asked whether Mary had already read this book.'
                    (Rögnvaldsson and Thráinsson 1990)

         b.   Ikh veys nit far vos **in tsimer iz** di ku   geshtanen.   (Yiddish)
                    I   know neg for what in room   is the cow stood
                    'I don't know why the cow has stood in the room.'
                    (Vikner 1994)

Various analyses of these phenomena have been proposed (for a summary see Vikner 1994). See later for a suggestion as to what might be the situation in these languages, which does not extend to the differences noted by Sigurðsson.

21. Assuming that the initial element is always in C, this is one way of accounting for what is traditionally known as Bergin's Law, as Carnie, Pyatt, and Harley (2000) point out. Bergin's Law states that non-initial verbs are dependent (Bergin 1938: 197, cited in Doherty 2000: 6); on the analysis sketched in the text, non-initial verbs will not be in C and thus will have the dependent form. See Doherty (2000: 28–31) for some counterexamples to this, which, as he argues, probably represent a change in progress in the Old Irish period. The suggestion that absolute forms are the morphological realization of C-features is supported by the fact that there is a third set of verb-paradigms that is found in relative clauses. These forms can be viewed as morphological reflexes of a different feature associated with relative C. I will briefly return to the question of these different verbal paradigms in Old Irish in 4.2.

22. Rizzi proposes that complementizers may vary in their position in the articulated structure of Comp. In particular, he argues that *that* is in Force while *for* is in Fin, on the basis of contrasts like the following:

(i)   Yesterday I said that, tomorrow, John will leave.
(ii)   *Yesterday we preferred for, tomorrow, John to leave.

The adjacency requirement that holds between *for* and the lower subject that it Case-licenses can be accounted for if there is no available adjunction site for adverbs between Fin and IP. (This can be achieved by assuming that there are no adjunction sites at all, as Rizzi proposes.) Note the analogy with the way in which Pollock's system derives the observed adjacency requirement that holds between verbs and their direct objects in English.

This system predicts that the reverse order of *for* and the adverb will be grammatical:

(iii)   *Yesterday we preferred tomorrow for John to leave.

As (iii) shows, this is not so. Rizzi (1997: 330) suggests that *for* may be "syncretic" for Fin and Force. He also points out that the Italian prepositional complementizer *di* allows the analogous example:

(iv)   Penso, a Gianni, di dovergli   parlare.
                 I-think, to Gianni, to have-to-to-him speak
                 'I think, to John, to have to speak to.'

(v)   *Penso di, a Gianni, dovergli   parlare.
                 I-think to, to Gianni, have-to-to-him speak

The proposal in the text is that Irish *go* is a finite version of *di*, at least as far as its position is concerned.

    23. McCloskey (1996a) shows that an adverb can intervene between the fronted negative constituent and (the relevant form of) *ní*, which, in the terms adopted here, shows that the fronted negative constituent must at least be higher up than SpecFin.

    24. It may seem uneconomical to posit two differences between Irish and English. However, Welsh supports the analysis being presented in the text, as there is reason to think that Welsh is like Irish regarding property (a) (see later for examples of C-elements that do not raise from Fin to Force) but unlike Irish in that negation is not located in C. The evidence for the latter assertion comes from the following paradigm, given by Borsley and R. Morris-Jones (2000: 19–20):

(i)   Dw i ddim wedi gweld unrhyw un.
                 am I neg after see   anyone
                 'I haven't seen anybody.'
                 (Borsley and R. Morris-Jones 2000: 19–20 [15])

(ii)   *Does unrhyw un yn yr   ystafell.
                 is   anyone   in the room
                 (Borsley and R. Morris-Jones 2000: 19–20 [17])

The pattern is similar to the familiar one with *any* in English (which is not to imply that Welsh is in general like English as regards NPIs and n-words; see Borsley and R. Morris-Jones 2000 for further discussion).

    25. Many authors have proposed that there is covert I-to-C raising universally (e.g., Stowell 1981, Pesetsky 1982, and den Besten 1983, among others). Roberts and Roussou (2002) propose that there is universally a chain between T and Fin. We must assume that this chain does not go further into the C-system than Fin.

    26. Roberts also assumes that the presence/absence of a PF-realization requirement is the only form of parametric variation. Hence there is no possibility of, for example, Fin and Force being ordered differently in different languages (in fact, to my knowledge, all versions of minimalism since Chomsky 1993 have assumed that functional heads are invariant in order).

    27. This account also leaves open the possibility that there may be languages in which all predicates are like English bridge verbs in directly selecting complementizers merged in Force but like Irish in that Force does not trigger movement of Fin. If such a language also has the Fin* property, V+T should be able to freely raise to Fin, giving rise to the absence of root-embedded asymmetries. This may well be the situation in the "symmetric" V2 languages Yiddish and Icelandic; see note 20.

    28. If Force is non-interrogative, Foc may still be [+WH]. This can account for semi-questions and exclamatives like:

(i)   It's amazing how many people were there.
(ii)   We found out who did it.

See note 20 and McCloskey (1992).

29. Following Roberts (2001: 103), Foc* triggers movement to both specifier and head, since the head which moves there has no feature that is capable of licensing the content of Foc, although it can morphologically realize it.

30. Welsh is often described, e.g. by Thomas (1982: 213), as having modal auxiliaries, e.g. *gallu, medru,* both "can," *dylwn,* "should/ought." These verbs are rather like English modals in showing some temporal restrictions compared to regular verbs, in not having direct objects, and, in the case of *dylwn,* in resisting non-finite forms. They are probably best analyzed as defective main verbs. They are quite unlike *bod,* whose principal trait is that it possesses more forms than other verbs, not fewer.

31. Willis (1998: 130f.) shows that, despite the general obligatory XP-fronting in main clauses in Middle Welsh (i.e., the V2 nature of the language at this period), *bot* (the Middle Welsh equivalent of *bod*) systematically blocks XP-fronting. This fact must be connected to the idiosyncrasies of contemporary *bod* discussed here, but it is very hard to see how.

32. King (1993: 138) notes that *mi* can marginally occur as a mild intensifier before present and imperfect forms of *bod*:

(i)   Mi rydw i' n   mynd.
             Prt am I Asp go
             'I *am* going.'   (King's translation)

In terms of the account to be given in the text, we might think that in these cases *mi* can occur in Force, indicating strong assertion. However, *mi* here might be linked to its origin as a 1sg pronoun (see Willis 1998: 225f., 227f., on this development). An anonymous reviewer points out that sequences such as *mi oedd* are found in dialects, a point that clearly requires further analysis. Note that (i) was rejected by speakers of Southern Welsh I tested it with.

33. In more literary varieties, interrogative *a* precedes interrogative forms of the copula:

(i)   A ydych chi' n   mynd?
             Prt are   you Asp go?
             'Are you going?'

I return to this point in 4.1.

34. *Y* is often written before *mae* in examples like (61c). However, I continue to regard this element on a par with the *r-* prefix on the affirmative imperfect forms as part of *bod* in these cases. On this view, it is restricted to occurring before *mae* because the two elements are really a single form *ymae.* It is tempting to place the *y* that cooccurs with present and imperfect *bod* in Force. However, examples like (i) show that this is not possible:

(i)   Mi wn   i mai yn yr ardd   y mae Hefin.
             Prt know I that in the garden Y is   Hefin
             'I know that Hefin is in the garden.'
             (Tallerman 1996: 115)

As we saw earlier, *mai* is in Force here, and so *y* cannot be. Moreover, it follows the focused PP *yn yr ardd* and so is most likely in Fin with *mae.*

35. Rouveret actually handles this differently. As I have mentioned in notes 33 and 34, certain particles do appear with *bod* in this variety. They are, however, impossible in

identificational sentences like those under consideration here, and this is Rouveret's point. In the terms here, the issue becomes a question of the absence of the prefix *r-* on the imperfect forms of *bod* in this context. Presumably, like *a* and *y*, *bod* does not raise from Fin to Foc in focused sentences (the fact that it appears in Fin is enough to guarantee complementary distribution with focus particles, since the focus particles are in Fin as argued in the previous section, and to account for the extra tenses) but does in identificational copular clauses—appearance in Foc is incompatible with initial *r-*; cf. Wh-questions where there is no *r-* and *bod* is plausibly in Foc.

36. The analysis of subject-positions that I will give in 2.1, would have to treat *Siôn* as occupying a position lower than SpecAgrSP in (63a). This does not affect the point that Rouveret's argument establishes here, though.

37. This implies that in these clauses the subject is in a position lower than T. In fact, this would only apply to echo pronouns, as full DPs are not allowed where an *ei*-pronoun precedes *bod*. I will not go into the implications of this here.

38. Interestingly, *bod* can show up in the imperfect exactly where there is extraction of the subject (see Willis 2000: 554–555 for discussion and analysis):

(i)   Pa   lyfrau wyt ti 'n   meddwl oedd yn   addas?
            Which books are you Asp think   was Pred suitable?
            'Which books do you think were suitable?'
            (Willis 2000:554 [53])

(ii)   ??Rwy'n meddwl oedd y hen lyfrau yn   addas.
            Am-I Asp think   was the old books Pred suitable
            'I think that the old books were suitable.'
            (Willis 2000: 555 [56b])

This contrast shows that *oedd* does not raise where extraction takes place. In this sense, the ungrammaticality of (ii) is parallel to (iii) (although the judgment does not seem to be as strong, as [ii] is seen as marginal rather than impossible):

(iii)   a.   *Who did leave?

         b.   *Que sent bon?
                 What smells nice?
                 (see Friedemann 1990)

For a proposal regarding these examples, see 5.1.

39. In this context, it is striking to observe that Cinque (1999) postulates two T-positions, one for Past and one for Future, and that T(Past) is structurally higher than T(Future).

40. Here I'm assuming that the dummy verb *gwneud*, "do," is generated in T and raised to AgrS, like its English counterpart (*pace* Rouveret 1994, chapter 1). I'm also assuming that verbal noun *gweld* (mutated here, hence the absence of initial /g/; see table 2.1 of 2.2.1) is a non-finite verb form, following Borsley (1996) and *pace* Rouveret (1994). In 3.2, I summarize Borsley's arguments. In that section, I will propose a more articulated structure that corresponds to the VP in (82), one that comes closer to Rouveret's (1994) proposal.

41. It is natural to think that the PP *yn yr ardd* satisfies the EPP in (86b), but the marginal possibility of (i) shows that this is not right:

(i)   Mae 'na   yn yr ardd   blant.
                       Is   there in the garden children
                       'There are children in the garden.'

Judgments are divided on (i): some informants prefer it to (86b), while others reject it
entirely. This gives some reason at least to doubt that the PP *yn yr ardd* satisfies the EPP
in (86b). I return to these constructions in 2.3.4.4.

42. These observations led Comrie (1977) to conclude that this construction violates
the Motivated Chomage Law of Relational Grammar, in that it appears to be a case of
"spontaneous demotion." In this, it resembles Cinque's (1988) non-argumental *si* of (i):

(i)   Si mangia gli spaghetti.
                       SI eats   the spaghetti
                       'People eat spaghetti.'

It is likely therefore that the passive construction shown in (87) is an impersonal rather
than a passive (see Roberts 1987 on this distinction). In 3.2.2, I will suggest that Welsh
does not have voice morphology.

Chapter 2

1. Pollock in fact argued that V raises to T in French but crucially proposed that T was
the highest position in the I-domain. Since I have been following Belletti's (1990) proposal
that AgrS is higher than T, I rephrase Pollock's conclusion this way. I do not follow
Chomsky's (1995, 4.10) proposal that there is no AgrS because of (a) my wish to minimally
retain Pollock's empirical results regarding the split-I system, e.g. his account of the
position of French infinitives; and (b) the evidence for AgrS provided by the subject clitics
of Northern Italian dialects; see later. In fact, as emerges later, there are good cross-linguistic
reasons to assume that AgrS divides into at least two components, forming an "agreement
field."

2. King (1993: 3) is explicit about the fact that he is referring to contemporary spoken
Welsh (cf. "A distinction must first be made between the Colloquial [or Spoken] Welsh in
this grammar and Literary Welsh . . . Colloquial Welsh is a first language for native speakers
of Welsh"). Thomas (1982: 215) gives the following paradigm for the dialect he discusses
(thanks to an anonymous reviewer for pointing this out): *weles i*, "I saw"; *welodd ef/hi*, "s/
he saw"; *welso ti/ni/chwi/hwy*, "you(sg)/we/you(pl)/they saw." Although I am not concerned
with dialects here, the fact that such dialects clearly have verb-movement, although they
do not conform to Vikner's generalization, can be handled in terms of the analysis to be
proposed later. These dialects are analogous to a number of Northern Italian dialects
discussed by Poletto (2000) in which the subject-clitic paradigm is reduced to a small
number of distinctions. As we will see later, the crucial factor that triggers verb-movement
in Welsh is the affixal status of subject-agreement morphemes—in other respects, they are
analogous to Northern Italian subject clitics. A syncretized paradigm may trigger movement
just as well as a non-syncretized one, and this must be what is going on in dialects of the
type discussed by Thomas. Clearly, all of this implies that Vikner's generalization does not
hold for subject-clitic languages.

3. A reviewer points out that Thomas (1982: 215) states: "Since the appropriate pronoun
must accompany the finite verb in all but a few grammatically conditioned contexts in the

vernacular, the inflection is redundant." But this does imply that the vernacular is not a null-subject language. To establish this, the status of examples like (88b) and those in note 41 of chapter 1 is crucial. Whatever the situation in the variety Thomas describes, the optionality of *yna* in examples like (88b) indicates that a fundamental part of the usual null-subject phenomenology is attested in the variety under investigation here. That Welsh differs significantly from the null-subject languages that have been most discussed in the literature (Spanish, Standard Italian, Greek, etc.) is not in doubt, however; see later.

4. It has often been noticed that Icelandic is problematic for this generalization, as Icelandic distinguishes five persons in many tenses of many verbs. However, Icelandic is a V2 language, and it seems that this property interferes with the correlation between verb morphology and null subjects, for reasons that are unclear.

I make no proposal regarding East Asian null-argument languages, except to observe that something quite different must be going on as these languages appear to lack agreement systems altogether. See Huang (1984, 1989) and Davis (1998).

5. Spanish and Greek allow VSO orders:

(i)   Comió Juan la   manzana.
              ate   John the apple
              'John ate the apple.'

(ii)   Efaje o Yiannis to milo.
              ate   the John   the apple
              'John ate the apple.'

However, VSO order in these languages is distinct from what is found in Welsh and the other Celtic languages for exactly the reasons being considered in the text: it is not connected with anti-agreement, and the subject can appear in the orders in (7) and (8). See Zubizarreta (1998) for a proposal regarding the Spanish order in (i), Belletti (1999) for a proposal regarding the difference between Italian and Spanish in this respect, and Philippaki-Warburton (1985) on the Greek order in (ii).

6. Many Northern Italian dialects have subject-clitic inversion, similar to the well-known French construction, in root interrogatives and various other "residual V2" environments. The clitics that are involved here are visibly different from those that are found in non-inversion contexts; the paradigm is often different, the forms of the clitic are different, and the interrogative clitics interact with C-elements and, in some dialects, with negation (see Zanuttini 1997 on this last point). The formal difference is illustrated by the following pair from the Cereda dialect (Central Veneto; Poletto 2000, 3.1):

(i)   Cossa fa-lo?
              What does he?
              'What is he doing?'

(ii)   No so   cossa che el fa.
              Not I-know what that he does.
              'I don't know what he's doing.'

All of these differences point to treating the inverted clitics as syntactically quite distinct from the non-inverted ones. Following Poletto (2000, chapter 3), I assume that they are affixes in the C-system. Cf. also Sportiche (1998) on subject-clitic inversion in French.

7. The history of these paradigms supports this proposal. J. Morris-Jones (1913: 332–333) observes that the 3sg *-ith/-iff* form of the non-past tense in (5) derives from the combination of an *-id* ending, ultimately from Indo-European (the primary ending *-ti*), with the initial consonant of the pronoun *fo* (*-id-f* > *it-ff* > *iff*; *-ith* is the variant in the North-Western dialects). Also, the 1pl and 2pl derive from suffixed pronouns. Morris-Jones points out that the expected 2pl ending, given regular sound changes from Indo-European, would be *-ed*. This ending combined with the initial consonant of the pronoun *chwi* (which Morris-Jones refers to as "affixed"), giving the ending *-t-ch* from which the *-t-* was then lost. The 1pl forms incorporated the pronoun *ni* in a similar way on the basis of analogy. Further, it seems that the 1sg and 2sg forms of the present/future of *bod*, "be," have endings that are historically pronouns: in *wy-f*, "am," and *wy-t*, "are"(2sg), only the stem *wy* derives from the relevant Indo-European/Proto-Celtic root. We can also observe that although the 1sg *-f* can be traced back to the Indo-European primary thematic ending *-mi*, it is also relatable to the pronoun *fi*. If plural pronouns were able to attach to verbs and become endings, then we would also expect singular ones to do so, and in this way the pronoun may have "reinforced" the historically derived ending. The 3pl ending *-nt* in Literary Welsh is clearly of Indo-European origin (cf. the Latin form). The colloquial *-n* ending may again have been reinforced by the similarity with the pronoun *nhw*. Finally, although Morris-Jones does not comment on this, the 2sg endings in *-t* are not historically motivated and are clearly relatable to the 2sg pronoun *ti* (cf. also Rowland 1853: 75, n. 1).

8. A reviewer points out that *-dd-* also appears in the 3pl of *i* (*iddyn*, "to them") and in all persons of some prepositions. This in fact supports the idea that *-dd-* functions as a morphological support and lacks person/number features of its own.

9. The historical origin of *-dd* is unclear. See note 7 for remarks on the history of other endings.

10. It is interesting to speculate that Welsh and Irish also differ from the languages in (12) in having verbal nouns (see 3.3, for discussion and analysis of Welsh verbal nouns). One analysis of verbal nouns would treat them as lexically unspecified roots, i.e., neither V nor N (I will in fact adopt a slightly different analysis in 3.3). We could relate the presence of verbal nouns to the Celtic agreement pattern in (13) by speculating as follows: perhaps the lack of verbal agreement is connected to having roots unspecified for categorial features. This idea would be consistent with Marantz's (1997) proposal that lexical elements are category-neutral, their category being determined by the functional material they associate with (thanks to Anna Roussou [p.c.] for this suggestion).

11. Why are there no subject clitics in weak-agreement languages? It is not clear how to answer this question but the observation is well known.

12. Unsurprisingly, similar variation to that observed with verb-agreement shows up in the forms of the agreement endings on prepositions in various varieties. A reviewer points out that (25) could be, in some (unspecified) vernacular: *arna i/ti*, *arno fo*, *arni hi*, *arno ni/chwi/nhw*. See note 2 on syncretic agreement in vernaculars and later for a treatment of the "echo pronouns." Informants for Standard Welsh whom I consulted judged the plural forms as slightly unnatural without the echo pronoun, but not the singular ones; cf. (30).

13. It is reasonable to refer to *plant* in (27a) as a subject, although the evidence given in 1.3, shows that this DP is not in the Specifier immediately subjacent to V but much lower, probably in the canonical object position. This is exactly analogous to referring to *molti* in (28b) as a "postverbal subject" even though the possiblity of *ne*-cliticization shows that it is VP-internal and indeed may well be in the canonical direct-object position (see Belletti and Rizzi 1981, Burzio 1986).

14. According to Stephens (1982: 73–75), Breton shows the same pattern as Welsh in this respect. McCloskey and Hale (1984) discuss two dialects of Irish where the situation appears to be like Welsh.

15. There exists another construction, traditionally known as the "abnormal order," where agreement is required:

(i)   Myfi a **gefais** anrheg.
                me Prt got-1sg present
                'I got a gift.'
                (Tallerman 1996: 98)

This construction is somewhat archaic, having been very productive in Middle and Biblical Welsh but rarely found in the twentieth century. On the one hand, Tallerman argues that this construction is different from the focus construction, in particular in that it does not involve movement but rather a resumption strategy. On the other hand, Willis (1998: 6) argues that this construction was not syntactically distinct from the focus construction in Middle Welsh and that it was in fact a V2 construction.

Tallerman treats the fronted constituent as adjoined to CP; it may be that it occupies Rizzi's (1997) SpecTopP, since (a) it has a topic (as opposed to focus) reading and (b) more than one constituent can be "fronted" in this construction but not in the focus construction. However, Willis (1998: 51f.) analyzes apparent multiple-fronting cases as involving base-generation of adverbs in the C-system, or left dislocation, thus maintaining a general V2 analysis of this construction for Middle Welsh.

16. It might seem that expletives are thus immune from Case requirements, since, as non-arguments, they do not require Case-licensing on the view being developed in the text. Why, then, do we not find expletives in traditionally Caseless positions, such as subject position of infinitives? The simplest answer to this (which again is in line with Chomsky 1995, 2000, 2001) is that the distribution of expletives is entirely conditioned by the EPP, not by Case, and that the EPP does not apply to the subject position of non-finite clauses (recall that we are assuming that there are no pronominal empty categories). The problem with the latter assumption is that expletives are required in the subject position of certain non-finite clauses, viz.:

(i)   For *(there) to be life on Mars . . .   (*for*-infinitives)
(ii)   We believe *(there) to be life on Mars. (ECM)
(iii)   *(There) being life on Mars, . . .   (ACC-*ing* gerunds)

Following recent proposals by Hornstein (1999) and Manzini and Roussou (2000), it is possible to treat both (argument-) control and raising as A-dependencies and assume that the EPP can be satisfied by the tail of an A-dependency. Now, it is known that a filled C blocks control and raising (see Kayne 1991); i.e., a filled C prevents the formation of an A-dependency across the CP-boundary. Arguably, in (i)–(iii) C is filled: this is clear in (i), is the case in (ii) according to Kayne (1981), and holds for (iii) according to Roussou and Roberts (2000) (in whose analysis *-ing* occupies C and is lowered to I in ACC-*ing* gerunds). Hence the only way to satisfy the EPP in these examples is by expletive insertion.

17. The formulation in (39i) deviates in one crucial respect from that given by Rizzi (2000). This is the version argued for in Roberts (2000). The difference between the two formulations is that Rizzi's defines interveners in structural terms; his version of (39i) refers to "structural" type only. See the discussion of Long Head Movement in chapter 4 for a justification of the formulation given here.

18. A further logical possibility is (i):

(i)   *DP$_1$ Pers   DP$_2$ Num   . . .   t$_{DP1}$ t$_{DP2}$

Here two arguments are licensed as Nominative. However, this is ruled out by relativized minimality as well, as can be easily verified.

19. A reviewer objects that DOM is neither necessary nor sufficient for objecthood. But neither is ACC Case, and the claim being made here is that DOM is a phonological reflex of ACC. ACC is doubly dissociated from the notion of direct object, as is well known. Quirky Case-marked objects and objects of passive and unaccusative verbs (like *molti* in [28b]) are objects but not ACC. Subjects of ECM clauses are ACC but not objects.

20. A reviewer points out a number of possible exceptions to this generalization. They are as follows:
(a) adverbs, as in (i):

(i)   Fe welais i nhw **Ddydd** Sul.   (dydd)
            Prt saw   I they Sunday
            'I saw them on Sunday.'

(b) nouns in apposition to proper nouns:

(ii)   Ieuan **druan**   (truan)
            Ieuan poor
            'poor Ieuan'

(c) vocatives
(d) *bod*, "be," following the initial DP in a copular construction:

(iii)   Chi fydd   y   **ddwy** smartia.   (dwy)
            you will-be the two-f. smartest
            'You'll be the two smartest.'

There are three possible ways of dealing with these examples. The first, simplest possibility is to show that they in fact obey (54) despite initial appearances. This may work for (a) if adverbs systematically occupy Specifiers, as proposed by Cinque (1999). The constructions in (b), (c), and (d) are very poorly understood, and so we cannot rule out that the configuration in (54) is relevant.

A second, and less desirable, possibility might be to weaken (54) to core cases, including those that involve Case-licensing. Since none of (a)–(d) involve Case-licensing, the analysis of DOM proposed here is unaffected.

A third solution would be more radical. We could contemplate following Sproat (1985) in treating soft-mutated forms as default forms, with non-soft-mutated forms being triggered by the morphosyntactic environment. We would then claim that lack of soft mutation can be a morphophonological reflex of NOM (and perhaps GEN; see chapter 3). Some support for this idea comes from the fact, noted by Sproat, that nouns inside compounds are mutated (e.g., *llys*, lit. "household" + *mam*, "mother" = *llysfam*, "stepmother"). It is likely that the context in (54) is not relevant word-internally.

21. Under the copy theory of traces, we can in fact think that the copy is mutated and then deletes. The representation of (62) is thus (where underlining indicates the copy relation):

(i)   <u>Pwy</u> a welodd Megan <u>bwy</u>?

The mutated Wh-word *bwy* is deleted. If we stipulate the ordering of PF operations in this way, we also ensure that *L* always attaches to something at PF.

22. The adverbial clausal negation *(d)dim* (see note 5 of chapter 1) undergoes soft mutation in a fashion that looks suspiciously like DOM. However, there are cases where *(d)dim* mutates that are clearly not connected to DOM. We can see this most clearly with unaccusatives and in passives with the order *(d)dim ei*:

(i)   a.   Ddiflanodd   y   dyn ddim.
              disappeared   the man Neg
              'The man didn't disappear.'

       b.   Wnaeth Emrys ddim ei   daro.
              did   Emrys Neg 3sgm   hit
              'Emrys didn't hit him.'

Following the standard analysis of unaccusatives and passives (Burzio 1986, Baker, Johnson, and Roberts 1989), I assume that there is no accusative in (i). Nevertheless, the mutation appears on *(d)dim*. This suggests that the mutation of *(d)dim* is not a case of DOM, i.e., a realization of Accusative Case. Of course, there is in any case no reason to think that an adverbial negative element should be able to receive ACC Case. But *(d)dim* nevertheless appears to show an interesting mutation alternation that deserves comment (and which falls under the generalization in Borsley and Tallerman 1998). In particular, *(d)dim* shows up in existentials and impersonal passives where there is no argumental subject and no overt expletive. The minimal contrast appears in existentials, where an overt expletive-like element *yna*, "there," optionally appears in subject position. Where *yna* appears, *(d)dim* must mutate; where it does not appear, *(d)dim* cannot mutate:

(ii)   a.   Fydd   dim dosbarth wythnos nesa   — no ICM of *dim*
              will-be Neg class   week   next

       b.   Fydd yna ddim   dosbarth wythnos nesa   — ICM of *dim*
              will-be Neg   class   week   next
              'There won't be class next week.'

However, as we saw in note 6 of chapter 1, these are instances of what Borsley and R. Morris Jones (2000) call "quantifier *(d)dim*." Here *(d)dim* forms a DP with *dosbarth* and the first consonant of the DP fails to undergo DOM in (iia) because it is in subject position, while it undergoes DOM in (iib). This is a regular case of DOM applying to a VP-internal element in a locative/existential construction; these constructions are treated in 3.4.4 (see in particular the discussion of [77]). However, the occurrences of *(d)dim* in (i) are instances of adverbial *(d)dim* that we do not need to consider a mutated item. The one environment where adverbial *(d)dim* could show up unmutated would be in the negative versions of existential/locative sentences with the locative PP fronted, i.e., the negation of (86b) of chapter 1, repeated here as (iii):

(iii)   Mae yn yr ardd   blant.
              is   in the garden children
              'There are children in the garden.'

However, there is apparently no grammatical negation of (iii):

(iv) *Does dim yn yr ardd   blant.
      Neg-is neg in the garden children

I conclude that adverbial *(d)dim* is always in fact *ddim*. Synchronically there is no soft mutation here.

The really intriguing question is why *ddim* cannot be followed by an object:

(v)   *Wela' i ddim Gwen eto.
      see-fut I neg Gwen again
      (Borsley and R Morris-Jones 2000: 29)

There is a clear sense in which *(d)dim* is "taking away" the Case that would otherwise appear on the direct object here, which this analysis could capture in terms of locality— *(d)dim* is closer to the mutation trigger than the direct object is, if it occupies a position c-commanded by *v* and c-commanding the direct object.

This phenomenon should perhaps be related to the cross-linguistically common phenomenon of genitive of negation (as analyzed in Russian in Pesetsky 1982). Suppose that ACC-licensing is blocked by negation (for unclear reasons) and that no GEN is available (this is consistent with the proposal for GEN-licensing in chapter 3, [1c]). In that case, the direct object cannot be Case-licensed. Of course, this begs the question of how Negation blocks ACC-licensing. However, this analysis comes at the cost of sacrificing the argument made in 1.1, that the subject must raise from its base position because it precedes *(d)dim*. If the subject is generated in Spec, P, then it will always precede *(d)dim* in any case, and so I leave the question of the restriction in (v) open.

23. Support for this analysis might be gathered from the following paradigm:

(i)   *Fe welwyd o.
      Prt saw-Pass he

(ii) Fe'i   welais o.
      Prt-him saw-1sg he
      'I saw him.'

(iii) Fe welais o.
      Prt saw-1sg he
      'I saw him.'

In all of these examples there is a null subject. The pronoun *o* is ungrammatical in (i) because no ACC is available as the clause is passive, and it is unable to function as a subject echo pronoun as the passive morphology does not have sufficient features to allow *o* to double it (this may follow from Poletto's generalization regarding agreement relations; see 2.1.2). In both (ii) and (iii), which are active clauses, *o* is ACC. The grammaticality of (64a) with an echo pronoun, in contrast to (i), is due to the fact that the pronoun can "echo," i.e., copy agreement features from, the clitic in (64a). Since there is no clitic in (i), this cannot happen. If Case features are also subject to Poletto's generalization, then the clitic must be NOM in (64a).

24. A similar analysis can be maintained where the main clause contains an indirect object, as in (examples from Borsley 1999):

(i)   Gorchmynodd i 'w fab **ddychwelyd** yn brydlon.   (dychwelyd)
             ordered-3sg   to his son return   punctually
             'He ordered his son to return punctually.'

(ii)   Erfyniodd arnaf **fynd** gydag ef bob cam.   (mynd)
             begged-3sg on-1sg go with he every step
             'He begged me to go with him every step.'

(iii)   Mae'n well ganddo   **fynd** adref.   (mynd)
             is   Asp better with-3sgm go   home
             'He prefers to go home.'

These examples pose no specific problem for the analysis of DOM, although of course we have to say that the indirect-object PP is higher than the *v*-position that is responsible for the DOM on the VN of the complement clause.

25. Borsley and Tallerman (1998) propose that finite CPs cannot be mutated; this is a reasonable alternative for (73b). To the extent that finite CPs do not need Case and in fact resist Case according to Stowell (1981), this is expected under my approach, but must be stipulated under theirs. The same observation applies to Borsley's (1999) observation that Prepositions never undergo DOM. Non-finite clauses are also "Case resistant" (see Stowell 1981: 167f.), but, arguably, clauses that contain verbal nouns in Welsh are comparable to English gerunds and as such are not Case-resistant (see Stowell 1981: 148). Clearly this generalization does not extend to the *bod*-clauses of 1.2.3, which I analyzed as finite CPs. The "Case-resistance" generalization would have to apply to formally finite CPs, which *bod*-clauses clearly are not, but (73b) clearly is. In 3.3, I develop the idea that verbal nouns are participial phrases.

26. One might wonder why Burzio's generalization does not apply here, i.e. why there is ACC where there is no external θ-role. It seems that Burzio's generalization applies to argument structures, and copular constructions do not have argument structure. Independent support for this idea comes from the fact that accusative clitics are available in Spanish copular constructions:

(i)   Las   hay en Chile.
             them has in Chile
             'There are them (i.e., mountains) in Chile.'

For more on Burzio's generalization, see 3.2.2.

27. Borsley (1999: 274) discusses one instance of DOM that may be relevant here—namely, DOM with apparently postposed objects in ditransitive constructions with the order IO > DO:

(i)   Rhoddodd Emrys i Megan **ddarlun** o Gwyn. (darlun)
             gave   Emrys to Megan picture of Gwyn
             'Emrys gave a picture of Gwyn to Megan.'

Borsley points out that an analysis of ditransitives along the lines proposed by Larson (1988) can be appealed to here. Something along the lines of what has just been proposed in the text will give the right result, as long as PP is above an occurrence of *v*P. However, it should be noted that my informants showed an overwhelming preference for DO > IO order in double-object constructions, in fact rejecting examples like (i).

Borsley also (1999: 273) points out the following alternation, which involves different possible positions for the Experiencer PP of a psych-predicate:

(ii)   a.   Mae chwant arnaf i **fynd** adref.   (mynd)
        •   is   desire on.1sg I go home
              'I want to go home.'

        b.   Mae chwant mynd adref arnaf i.
              is   desire go   home on.1sg I
              'I want to go home.'

Here, too, it may be that the PP *arnaf i* raises in the same manner as *yn yr ardd* in (71) and triggers DOM (realized on the verbal noun of the lower clause) in the same manner. See 3.2.3, for some further speculative remarks about the relationship between psych-constructions and existential/locative constructions.

28. These principles can be seen as Agree relations in the sense of Chomsky (2000, 2001).

Chapter 3

1. I am making this assumption both for simplicity and in order to maintain parallelism with what I assumed about adverbial APs in 3.1. Giusti (1993, 1994) and Cinque (1994) have proposed that adnominal APs are in Specifier-positions, and Cinque (1999) has proposed the same for adverbial APs. Naturally, such proposals entail further elaboration of the functional structure.

2. Similar considerations hold for *pob*, "every/each."

3. I prefer to use the designation QP rather than NumP (as in Rouveret 1994: 215f., Duffield 1996: 324f.) in order to keep this category distinct from its natural clause-level analogue. See note 16.

4. There are a few further complications here. First, the soft mutation triggered by feminine *un*, "one" (not illustrated earlier), and feminine *y* does not affect /Â/ and /r/. I will leave this aside. Second, the feminine definite article does not trigger mutation on a following numeral: *y tair/*dair gath*, "the three-fem cats-fem." This may be related to the fact that low numerals (up to four) have feminine forms *dwy, tair, pedair*, although it is difficult to see exactly how. Third, as David Willis (p.c.) points out, the definite article triggers mutation on the *masculine* form of "two," *dau: y ddau dyn,* "the two men." I will leave these points aside, although they are problematic for the general issue of mutation as it stands.

5. A reviewer points out that the whole string of adjectives that follows a feminine singular noun shows mutation:

(i)   y   gath fawr ddu   (mawr, du)
               the cat big black
               'the big black cat'

This favors the NP-adjunction analysis of adnominal APs mentioned earlier. Assuming that analysis, we have the structure in (ii) for (i):

(ii)

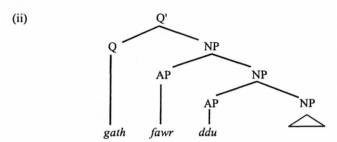

If (16) really refers to the leftmost mutable consonant inside a head-governed XP, then, since segments of maximal projections do not block head-government, we expect the whole string of adjoined APs to mutate. If (16) does not refer to head-government, then the notion "leftmost edge" referred to in (16) has to be sensitive to the segment-category distinction, too; I leave this matter of formulation open.

Note also that it is the feminine article that triggers mutation on N. A feminine Noun in D does not trigger mutation:

(iii)   gwraig dyn/*ddyn 'wife of a man'

Feminine y is thus yL in terms of the convention introduced in 2.3.2. But as (i) and (iv) show, a feminine noun does trigger mutation on AP:

(iv)   cath fawr/*mawr y dyn   'the man's big cat'

It may be that minimality is also relevant for mutation, in that (iii) contains a D closer to *dyn* than the D that triggers mutation.

6. There is one class of exceptions to (18A), pointed out by Rouveret (1994: 216). Nouns modified by prenominal adjectives function as the possessed argument:

(i)   hen gath y wraig
            old cat the woman
            'the woman's old cat'

I treat this as further evidence that prenominal adjectives are adjoined to the noun they modify. Rouveret also observes (p. 223) that numerals can precede possessed nouns:

(ii)   pedair cainc   y   Mabinogi
            four   branch the Mabinogi
            'the four branches of the Mabinogi'

I follow Rouveret's (1994) suggestion that here the numeral is the head noun of a recursive construct-state construction. Note that if this idea can be extended further, the fact that numerals may trigger ICM falls under (16). This proposal comes at the cost of stipulating that numerals, alone among nouns, do not trigger genitive assignment, accounting for the contrast in (iii) (pointed out by an anonymous reviewer):

(iii)   a.   *tri y   llyfrau
                   three the books

        b.   tri o'r   llyfrau
                   three of-the books
                   'three of the books'

Presumably (iiib) is a partitive construction, although I will not speculate about its structure here.

   7. As pointed out by Roberts and Shlonsky (1996: 185–186), *ei*-pronouns differ from their Semitic counterparts in this respect. For example, the Hebrew counterpart of (28b) is:

(i)   beet-ha
                   house her
                   'her house'
                   (Roberts and Shlonsky 1996: 176)

The Hebrew possessive elements are syntactic affixes, like Pers in Welsh. As Roberts and Shlonsky point out, the Hebrew system is more uniform than the Welsh one as regards the morphological properties of the clitic/agreement system. Their essential syntactic properties are the same, however, once this morphological difference is taken into account.

   8. Willis (2000: 544) also gives examples of resumptive pronouns in a PP complement to a VN.

   9. If Prt is to be assimilated to Q, then we might think that left-moved *tout/tutto* in Romance occupies SpecQP. We can then derive some of the variation in participle positions across the Romance languages in terms of the structure in (49), in that *tout* precedes the participle in French and *tutto* follows it in Italian:

(i)   J'ai tout mangé/*mangé tout.
(ii)   Ho *tutto mangiato/mangiato tutto.
                   'I've eaten everything.'

The French participles raise to Prt and the Italian ones on to Agr-Prt (and probably further; see note 12). Participle agreement must appear on French participles by means of an operation analogous to the one that places agreement affixes on unmoved verbs in English. In that case, French Agr-Prt acts like English subject-agreement, Italian Agr-Prt like Welsh subject clitics and Welsh Agr-Prt like Veneto subject-agreement (cf. 2.1). See also note 14.

   10. There is a periphrastic passive in Welsh, formed with the "auxiliary" *cael*, "get":

(i)   Cafodd y dyn ei ladd.
                   got   the man his killing
                   'The man was killed.'

As is clear, the participle here is the VN, with the usual preceding *ei*-pronoun. Intriguingly, an echo pronoun is impossible here:

(ii)   Cafodd y ferch ei gweld (*hi).
                   got   the girl her seeing (she)
                   'The girl was seen.'
                   (Roberts and Shlonsky 1996: 195)

As Roberts and Shlonsky point out, the impossibility of the echo pronoun here is due to the fact that the position the echo pronoun would occupy (SpecVP according to the analysis being proposed here) is filled by the A-trace of the passivized DP *y ferch*. Cf. the impossibility of echo pronouns in extraction from the object of a verbal noun. Here again, *ei* is effectively a case of participle agreement.

In terms of the analysis to be proposed in the next section, it is possible that the *cael*-passive is one case where Asp contains a Kaynian empty P that incorporates to the auxiliary.

This construction is problematic for the proposals in the text in that Voice appears to have a strong feature here, which licenses a by-phrase or implicit argument:

(iii)   Cafodd y dyn ei ladd gan y   plismon.
               got   the man his kill by the policeman
               'The man was killed by the policeman.'

The Kaynian empty P associated with *cael* must clearly be playing a role, but it is not easy to see how.

11. The V-feature is responsible for attracting the participle. It is strong in Italian but not in French; see notes 10 and 14.

12. Kayne suggests that this category is a kind of CP, but I will treat it as AspP. Nevertheless, the formal similarity between structures like (54) and the basically tripartite C-I-V structure of clauses is noticeable.

13. Belletti (1990) and Cinque (1999) provide evidence that participles can raise through a fairly complex functional structure in Italian and some other Romance varieties. I account for this by assuming that "Asp" is probably a cover term for a more complex reality. This does not affect the proposal in the text: the point here is that the overt preposition-like aspectual particles of Welsh correspond to an abstract incorporating Preposition in Romance. These elements appear in the highest Asp-position in Welsh and incorporate with BE in Romance, whatever the structure of the rest of the "aspect field." The lack of incorporation has a clear morphological reflex in the Welsh particles; the presence of incorporation has a reflex in the existence of the Have-auxiliary in Romance. See also note 10.

14. If we adopt this view of the structural status of P, we cannot relate the proposals being made here to Mahajan's proposals regarding Ergative Case-marking. This is a problem if we follow the published version of Kayne (1993) (as I have done in the text), as Mahajan implicitly acknowledges. Since this question does not affect my account of the contrast between Welsh and Romance, I will not comment further here.

Note also that Freeze (1992), on which Kayne (1993) is partly based, observes that no OV language has a locative proform. This is a further point that cannot be captured here but is not germane to the comparison between Welsh and Romance that I am pursuing.

More important, the analysis presented in the text cannot as it stands account for Freeze's observation that verb-initial languages (VSO and VOS) never show a Have-auxiliary. On the account given here, the absence of a Have-auxiliary is an accidental morphological property of P, quite unrelated to V-movement.

15. The order *A Gianni piacciono i soldi*, "To John please the moneys" (i.e., "John likes money") is a possible variant of (64c). In this order, the parallel with the Russian example in (63c) is clearer.

16. There are fairly obvious ways to collapse Num, Q, and Voice, but I will not speculate in this direction here.

Chapter 4

1. As mentioned in 2.3.2, the particles are frequently not pronounced, but their mutation effects remain. This implies that the particles are subject to a low-level PF-deletion rule, and as such are present in the syntax (see also Willis 1998: 3, note 1).

Willis (2000: 551) argues that Colloquial Welsh has a zero-particle that triggers soft mutation.

Willis (1998: 194f.) argues that "true" VSO orders arise fairly suddenly in Early Modern Welsh, treating this as a consequence of the loss of V2. In these examples, the initial V does not undergo soft mutation:

(i) Gellwch wybod yn hysbys am bob peth y fo kyfiownys na wnaf i yn erbyn ych wllys.
   You-can know publicly about every thing Prt be-subjunc just NAD will-do I against your will
   'You may know publicly that, regarding everything that is just, I shall not act against your will.'
   (TWRP, Yr Enaid a'r Corff, 139–141 [MS 16th century]; Willis (1998: 196 [20b])

The mutated form of *gallu*, "to be able," would lack initial /g/ (see table 2.1). In contemporary Welsh root affirmative declaratives, neither a particle nor soft mutation is obligatory. We must conclude that either the particle or the mutation is optional. On the grounds of general consistency, I assume mutation is optional and a particle is always syntactically present.

2. In the negatives of so-called "abnormal sentences" of Biblical Welsh (see note 15 of chapter 2), the negative element *ny* must follow the topicalized constituent:

(i)   Y   dyn ny daeth.
             the man neg came
             'The man didn't come.'

It is not clear what is going on here; see Tallerman (1996: 119) for discussion.

3. The situation is more complex and interesting than these brief comments imply. In particular, *y* appears, along with "resumption" (presence of overt agreement and an optional echo pronoun), in long-distance subject and object extractions (where "long-distance" is defined as crossing two bounding nodes):

(i)   y   dyn yr hoffwn   iddo ddod   — subject of infinitive
        the man prt I-would-like to-3sg come
        'the man who I would like to come'

(ii)   y dynion y dywedodd Wyn y byddant yn darllen y llyfr — subject of finite clause
        the man prt said Wyn prt will-be-3pl Asp read the book
        'the men that Wyn said will read the book'

(iii)   y   dyn y gwelai Wyn ef   — object of finite verb
        the man prt saw   Wyn he
        'the man Wyn saw'

Note that the echo pronoun is obligatory in (iii), where there is no agreement possibility (see 2.2). Moreover, in (iii) it is not the case that two bounding nodes are crossed, so this is not a true instance of long-distance movement. The interesting question then is: why do long-distance extractions behave as indirect extractions (i.e., requiring particle *y* and resumption)? As is well known, Irish allows long-distance "direct" extraction, with the relevant particle (*aL*, leniting *a*—in fact identical to Welsh *a*, which also lenites as I briefly mentioned in 2.2) showing up in all intervening Cs (see McCloskey 1979, 2000, 2001):

(iv)   rud a gheall   tú a dhéanfa
          thing aL promised you aL you-would-do
          'something that you promised you would do'

In Welsh, the exact equivalent of (iv) is grammatical at least for some speakers (*contra* the judgment reported in Rouveret 1994: 398):

(v)   y dynion a wn   i a ddaeth
          the men   Prt know I Prt came-3sg
          'the men that I know came'

If we carry over the analysis of the Irish relative particles proposed by McCloskey (2000), we might be able to treat Welsh *a* as triggered by Move to its Specifier and *y* as triggered in other cases (merge into its specifier or nothing in its specifier). I will not pursue this here, however. See Awbery (1976), Sadler (1988), and Rouveret (1994) on direct and indirect relatives in Literary Welsh. On long-distance extraction in Colloquial Welsh, see Willis (2000).

    4. Strictly speaking, "LVM" is a misnomer. As Schafer (1994) shows, other predicative heads can appear in this construction:

(i)   Sioul eo ar mor.
          calm is the sea
          'The sea is calm.'
          (Schafer 1994: 2)

The analysis I propose later carries over to this type of case.

    5. The auxiliary "have" in Breton is formed from the combination of an agreement proclitic and *bezañ*, "be," as we briefly saw in 3.2. These forms are in complementary distribution with particles, while *bezañ* alone apparently is not. It appears, then, that "have" (or perhaps just the proclitic particle) raises to Fin in Breton in examples like (i):

(i)   Al levr en deus lennet Anna.
          the book 3sg is read   Anna
          'Anna has read the book.'

In examples like (ii) the form *emañ* is exactly cognate with the Welsh *y mae* whose status was briefly discussed in note 35 of chapter 1 (as can be seen from comparing [1] and [14], Welsh *y* corresponds to Breton *e*).

(ii)   Emañ Anna o   lenn al levr.
          is   Anna Asp read the book
          'Anna is reading the book.'

    6. Given the analysis of Welsh participial phrases proposed in chapter 3, and the fact that *o* in (19a) is an aspectual particle like Welsh *yn* and *wedi*, it is likely that the fronted

constituent here is larger than VP, in fact probably AspP. This does not affect the contrast that these examples establish in the text discussion. One could try to claim that, since the fronted category in (19a) and other relevant examples later is bigger than VP, LVM is true VP-fronting of a VP that is obligatorily emptied of everything except the verb. However, it is hard to see why such VP-fronting would be so local and sensitive to properties of C, features of LVM that come out naturally on the analysis being defended here.

For expository simplicity, I continue to call the clearly phrasal category that undergoes fronting in examples like (19a) VP.

7. Breton in fact allows nominal object shift, as Schafer (1994: 37-49) shows (and as already mentioned in note 9 of chapter 1), as in:

(i)   a.   Breman e   wel Maia an treñ.
                    now   prt sees Maia the train
                    'Now Maia sees the train.'

        b.   Breman e   wel an treñ Maia.
                    now   prt sees the train Maia
                    'Now Maia sees the train.'

Schafer shows that Breton object shift has the same properties as object shift in the Scandinavian languages as described by Holmberg (1986), Vikner (1994), and the references given there.

8. Here I revert to the structure with a unitary AgrSP. Since subjects appear very "low" in Breton (see 1.1), it may well be that they do not raise as far as SpecNumP, unlike their Welsh counterparts according to the analysis in 2.1. I continue to leave the question of the position of subjects in Breton open.

9. This classification is extremely close to the structural division between the C-system (operator heads) and the I-system (non-operator heads). However, Rizzi (1997) argues that topics are non-quantificational, but I nevertheless tentatively list Topic under the operator heads as an element in its Specifier forms an A'-type dependency with its trace (which, like typical A'-traces, requires Case and obeys Principle C in GB terms). In many languages Neg is part of the I-system. In the Celtic languages, where Neg is frequently (perhaps always; see the brief discussion in 1.1) part of the C-system, the structural division corresponds more closely to the functional one, although perhaps still not exactly given the *pas*-like negative elements found in Welsh and Breton.

10. Another construction that may be connected to (34) is Scandinavian Stylistic Fronting. This construction is best-known in Icelandic, although it is attested in Faroese (Holmberg 2000), in older stages of Swedish (Platzack 1987), and in Middle English (Trips 2001). Originally discussed by Maling (1990), this construction has given rise to a considerable literature (see the overview in Trips 2001). An Icelandic example is:

(i)   Þaþ fór   að rigna, þegar farið var af   stað.
              it   began to rain   when gone was from place
              (Maling 1990: 78)

Stylistic Fronting shows a number of properties that are highly reminiscent of Breton LVM and that can be analyzed as in the text. First, it is strictly clause-bound, unlike V2 topicalization:

(ii)   *Menn sem lesa reyna að þessar bækur . . .
                        people who read try   to these books . . .
                        (Sigurðsson 1989)

Second, it is subject to an "accessibility hierarchy" that basically states that negation blocks
fronting of VP-internal material, as in (iii):

(iii)   a.   þetta er glæpamaðurinn sem ekki hefur verið dæmdur.
                   this is the-criminal   that not had   been convicted
           b.   *þetta er glæpamaðurinn sem dæmdur hefur ekki verið.
           c.   *þetta er glæpamaðurinn sem verið hefur ekki dæmdur.

This is exactly parallel to (20b), except that the "low" negative element fronts in Icelandic
but not Breton, a fact we can readily attribute to the presence of a negative marker merged
in the C-system in Breton but not in Icelandic. Stylistic Fronting differs from Breton LVM
in that, where there is both a non-finite auxiliary and a non-finite main verb only the main
verb may front. Compare (iv) with (25a, b):

(iv)   a.   Verðbólgan varð   verri en   búist   hafð verið við.
                   inflation   became worse than counted had   been on

           b.   *Verðbólgan varð   verri en   verið hafð búist   við.
                   inflation   became worse than been had counted on
                   (Maling 1990: 82)

The fact that predicative adjectives and particles like *við* in (iv) can be fronted suggests
that Stylistic Fronting does not allow auxiliary material to be fronted. Otherwise the locality
facts are as in Breton.
    However, Stylistic Fronting presents a number of further puzzles. Foremost among
these is the "subject-gap" condition: the construction can only take place where there is a
subject gap. Note however, that since subjects occupy a lower position in Breton than in
Icelandic (see chapter 1), we could perhaps regard this condition as always satisfied in
Breton. It is also plausible that this condition is connected to the EPP, as Holmberg (2000)
has suggested. Furthermore, Stylistic Fronting can apply to DPs and PPs, which is clearly
not the case for the Breton construction. It remains to be seen whether this last property
can be connected to the fact that Icelandic is a true full V2 language, unlike Breton. See
also Holmberg (2000).
    11. These examples, certainly (37a) with a fronted expletive, cannot involve focus.
Recall that Middle Welsh had both the abnormal and the focus construction productively
(if they were distinct; see Willis 1998); see note 15 of chapter 2, Tallerman (1996), and
Willis (1996, 1998) on the abnormal construction.
    12. Cf. the development of the vocalic clitics in many Northern Italian dialects, discussed
in Poletto (2000) and briefly mentioned in 2.1.
    13. Verb-initial clauses are allowed in the V2 Germanic languages in contexts where
they can be interpreted as "lively narrative style," as in:

(i)   [. . .] *Kommt* eine Frau herein und . . .
                        'There comes in a woman, and . . . '

Here I assume that the particular discourse context is connected to a feature in Force, and so Fin is selected by Force just like in residual V2 cases. Some languages appear to mark this feature overtly; cf. Old English *þa*, Old French *si*.

14. There is a question regarding how the preverb and verb are combined in (47a) and separated in (47b). Assuming excorporation from the verb in Fin is not a possibility, the preverb must be able to "skip" the verb in (47b). While it is not completely clear how to account for this, we can at least note that preverbs and verbs do not act as interveners for one another and in this respect parallel verbs and particles in Icelandic Stylistic Inversion (cf. note 9).

15. Poletto (2000, chapter 4) shows that in Rhaeto-Romansch left-dislocation is impossible in declarative V2 clauses but allowed in interrogative clauses with Wh-movement:

(i)   a.   Gonoot va-i a tòaza sya
                    often   go I at home his
                    'I often go to his house.'

      b.   *Gonoot i vad a tòaza sya
                    often   I go to house his

      c.   Gonoot ula va-al pa?
                    often   where goes-he Q
                    'Where does he often go?'

The important thing about these examples in this context is that we can see I-to-C movement in the form of subject-clitic inversion in both cases. The difference between declaratives and interrogatives has to do with the possibilities of XP-fronting rather than head-movement. (In terms of the analysis to be proposed later, we expect that declarative V2 tolerates no further fronting operations, while Wh-movement may in principle tolerate non-operator fronting. See later.)

16. *Bod* in the present and imperfect may appear to be an exception to this, given the analysis proposed in 1.2.3. However, we might think that V1 is possible where special tense-marking results, just as it is possible where special agreement-marking results according to my analysis of absolute agreement forms in Old Irish.

17. Zwart (1993, 1997), following Travis (1984), proposed that subject-initial V2 clauses do not involve the CP-level. Roberts and Roussou (2002) argue against this on the grounds that (i) it involves essentially a Topic Criterion, or topic-feature checking, but topics do not behave in such a way as to justify this idea (they can be iterated, cf. Rizzi 1997; they are never in situ), and (ii) an approach like Zwart's cannot explain why there are no languages with strong Top-features but weak Wh-features, in other words, why we might not find a language of the type in (51).

18. The fact that auxiliaries but not main verbs move into the C-system in residual V2 contexts in English shows that T raises and that V does not move to T in this language, as is well known. It is possible that Fin* in various marked root clauses (induced by selection from Force) is responsible for the appearance of *do* when no other auxiliary is available.

19. V2 is also found in languages with agreement rich enough to license null subjects, at least under certain conditions. The best-known example of this is Old French (Adams 1987, Renzi and Vanelli 1983, Roberts 1993, Thurneysen 1892, Vance 1988, 1997). In such languages, null subjects show up just where we have V2:

(i)   Si firent -   grant joie la nuit.
             so made (they) great joy the night
             'So they made great joy that night.'
             (Clark and Roberts 1993: 320)

We can account for the impossibility of verb-first orders with null subjects at the Fin-level if we assume that there is no *pro* able to appear in SpecFin and satisfy the EPP. Then the EPP will inevitably be violated. However, it remains unclear why null subjects are allowed just when the verb moves to Fin.

20. Note that relativized minimality doesn't predict the strength of the islands created by A-interveners, either. In fact, the correct statement regarding island strength is that certain movement types, notably argument Wh-movement, are exempted in virtue of their inherent properties from sensitivity to interveners in the way defined by relativized minimality.

21. Yiddish in fact allows extraction from embedded V2 clauses, while Icelandic does not. See Vikner (1994: 108f.) for discussion and examples. Besides the obvious observation that this fact indicates that the two systems are different in some way, I have nothing to say about this here.

22. However, in the Agr-system expletive insertion is entirely independent of V-movement to Agr (i.e., of Agr*), as English shows. But, as (56) attests, this is true at the C-level. Clearly more research is needed here.

Chapter 5

1. The difference between the two principles lies in the notion of intervener, MLC referring to narrower classes of features than RM.

2. Arguably, the presence of an intervening agreement field wouldn't change anything, as it wouldn't be able to contain relevant features, as mentioned in 4.2.

3. One might wonder whether there are further intersections among the three feature classes. A feature like Focus might be a good candidate for sensitivity to both interfaces and the computational system. I will not speculate about the intersection of (A) and (B).

Holmberg (2000) proposes a notion of P-feature in his analysis of Stylistic Fronting that is very close to the notion of PFS-feature put forward here. Cf. note 10 of chapter 4 on Stylistic Fronting and Holmberg (2000) for similar proposals regarding the relationship of Stylistic Fronting and Breton LVM. Similar proposals regarding the interaction of phonological features and syntactic movement have also recently been made by Ndayiraije (2000) and Zwart (2001).

4. Probably the most important such case is in deriving the "mirror-image" order of affixes in agglutinative languages as compared to auxiliaries/particles in other languages, discussed and illustrated at length in Cinque (1999, chapter 3).

5. Of course there is much cross-linguistic variation regarding how this can be done. Agglutinating languages allow the process to be iterated, while inflecting languages limit the number of affixes that are allowed per stem. See Cinque (1999, chapter 3) for discussion.

6. This approach can account for the possibility of excorporation of V from *v* discussed in 2.3.4.1 if we simply assume that Incorporation does not apply to purely phonological features but only to morphological ones. This can replace (61) of chapter 2.

7. Zwart (2001: 53) points out that head-movement may be involved in determining the different possible temporal interpretations of the examples in (i):

(i)   a.   I heard that you sang in the Concertgebouw.
      b.   I heard you sing in the Concertgebouw.

As is well known, (ia) allows for the time of hearing and the time of singing to be different, while (ib) requires simultaneity of the two events. Zwart argues that the interpretative restriction in (ib) is due to the fact that it involves restructuring. Restructuring is seen as movement of formal features of the lower verb to the higher verb; this operation is visible at PF in some languages, e.g., Dutch, but not in others, e.g., English. Feature-movement is equivalent to head-movement in Zwart's system, and so head-movement is in fact responsible for the different interpretations here.

8. Friedemann (1990) points out that *que* must be proclitic on a verb in C and that the ungrammaticality of (14b) shows that *sent* is therefore not in C. It is thus presumably in I, following Pollock (1989). Since main verbs can raise to C in French interrogatives, (14a) and (14b) are parallel. Friedemann's argument shows that the ungrammaticality of (14a) is not a peculiarity of English *do*-support. This intuition is exploited in Roussou's (1994) account of (14a). Since I do not adopt Zwart's (1993, 1997) analysis of V2, subject-initial V2 clauses would in fact violate the condition. However, XP-movement in the case of V2 is special, since in a sense there is no Probe, only an EPP-feature. See later.

9. An unfortunate aspect of this approach is that it offers no obvious account for Cheng's (1991) generalizations on cross-linguistic variation in Wh-movement.

10. The same may hold for Pers in weak-agreement languages. Perhaps this position is completely deactivated in these languages (and hence no subject clitics; cf. note 11, chapter 2), and the EPP holds at the Num level in the configuration of (14b). Then Vikner's generalization might concern V-to-Num, as was already mentioned in 2.1.

11. This is a possibility for accounting for null subjects in East Asian languages.

12. I.e., declarative; cf. 4.5.2.

13. Note further that the system of phrase structure from Chomsky (1995, chapter 4), which is also assumed in Chomsky (2001), does not have the notion "head" as a primitive concept, and so head-movement cannot be eliminated independently of XP-movement. According to this system, the nearest correlate to the earlier X'-theoretic notion of head is that of minimal projection, defined as a category with no internal (syntactic) structure. But elements like *who* in *Who did you see* and *John* in *John was arrested* are probably minimal projections, and we must allow them to move. Hence the system proposed here is conceptually superior to an unformulable alternative that lacks head-movement.

References

Acquaviva, Pado (1996) Negation in Irish and the Representation of Monotone Decreasing Quantifiers. In: Borsley, Robert D., and Ian Roberts (eds.) *The Syntax of the Celtic Languages: A Comparative Perspective.* Cambridge: Cambridge University Press. 284–313.

Adams, Marianne (1987) From Old French to the Theory of Pro-drop. *Natural Language and Linguistic Theory* 5: 1–32.

Adger, David (1996) Aspect, Agreement and Measure Phrases in Scottish Gaelic. In: Borsley, Robert D., and Ian Roberts (eds.) *The Syntax of the Celtic Languages. A Comparative Perspective.* Cambridge: Cambridge University Press. 200–223.

Adger, David (2000) Feature Checking Under Adjacency and VSO Clause Structure. In: Borsley, Robert D. (ed.) *Syntax and Semantics XXXII: The Nature and Function of Syntactic Categories.* San Diego: Academic Press. 79–100.

Alexiadou, Artemis, and Elena Anagnostopoulou (1998) Parametrizing Agr: Word-order, V-movement and EPP-checking. *Natural Language and Linguistic Theory* 16.3: 491–539.

Aoun, Joseph (1981) *The Formal Nature of Anaphoric Relations.* PhD Dissertation, MIT.

Aoun, Joseph, Norbert Hornstein, David Lightfoot, and Amy Weinberg (1987) Two Types of Locality. *Linguistic Inquiry* 18: 537–577.

Awbery, Gwenllian (1976) *The Syntax of Welsh: A Transformational Study of the Passive.* Cambridge: Cambridge University Press.

Awbery, Gwenllian (1990) Dialect Syntax: A Neglected Resource for Welsh. In: Hendrick, Randall (ed.) *Syntax and Semantics XXIII: The Syntax of the Modern Celtic Languages.* San Diego: Academic Press. 1–25.

Baker, Mark (1985) The Mirror Principle and Morphosyntactic Explanation. *Linguistic Inquiry* 16: 373–416.

Baker, Mark (1988) *Incorporation: A Theory of Grammatical-Function Changing.* Chicago: Chicago University Press.

Baker, Mark, Kyle Johnson, and Ian Roberts (1989) Passive Arguments Raised. *Linguistic Inquiry* 20: 219–251.

Barss, Andrew (1986) *Chains and Anaphoric Dependence.* PhD Dissertation, MIT.

Belletti, Adriana (1990) *Generalized Verb Movement.* Turin: Rosenberg and Sellier.

Belletti, Adriana (1999) Aspects of the Low IP Area. Talk given at the Cartography Seminar, Pontignano, Italy.

Belletti, Adriana (2000) Participles. To appear in: Van Riemsdijk, Henk, et al. (eds.) *The Syntax Companion.* Dordrecht: Kluwer.

Belletti, Adriana, and Luigi Rizzi (1981) The Syntax of *Ne*: Some Theoretical Implications. *Linguistic Review* 1: 117–154.

Belletti, Adriana, and Luigi Rizzi (1988) Psych Verbs and Theta Theory. *Natural Language and Linguistic Theory* 6: 291–352.

Benincà, Paola (1995) *La Variazione Sintattica.* Bologna: Il Mulino.

Bergin, Osborn (1938) On the Syntax of the Verb in Old Irish. *Ériu* 12: 197–214.

den Besten, Hans (1983) On the Interaction of Root Transformations and Lexical Deletive Rules. In: Abraham, Werner (ed.) *On the Formal Syntax of the Westgermania.* Amsterdam: John Benjamins. 47–138.

den Besten, Hans, and Gerd Webelhuth (1989) Stranding. In: Grewendorf, Günther, and Wolfgang Sternefeld (eds.) *Scrambling and Barriers.* Amsterdam: John Benjamins. 77–92.

Biberauer, Theresa (2003) *Verb Second (V2) in Afrikaans: A Minimalist Investigation of Word Order Variation.* PhD Dissertation, University of Cambridge.

Bobaljik, Jonathan, and Andrew Carnie (1996) A Minimalist Approach to Some Problems of Irish Word Order. In: Borsley, Robert D., and Ian Roberts (eds.) *The Syntax of the Celtic Languages: A Comparative Perspective.* Cambridge: Cambridge University Press. 223–240.

Borer, Hagit (1986) I-subjects. *Linguistic Inquiry* 17: 375–416.

Borsley, Robert D. (1986) Prepositional Complementizers in Welsh. *Journal of Linguistics* 20: 277–302.

Borsley, Robert D. (1992) Celtic Clause Structure. In: Börjars, Kersti, and Nigel Vincent (eds.) *Functional Categories in Complementation* (Eurotyp Working Paper 111, 3) European Science Foundation. 3–21.

Borsley, Robert D. (1993) On So-called Verb-Nouns in Welsh. *Journal of Celtic Linguistics* 2: 35–64.

Borsley, Robert D. (1996) On a Nominal Analysis of Welsh Verb-Nouns. In: Ahlqvist, Anders, and Vera Capková (eds.) *Dán do Oide: Essays in Memory of Conn R. Ó Cléirigh.* Dublin: Institiúid Teangeolaíochta Éireann. 39–47.

Borsley, Robert D. (1999) Mutation and Constituent Structure in Welsh. *Lingua* 109: 267–300.

Borsley, Robert D., and Andreas Kathol (2000) Breton as a V2 Language. *Linguistics* 38: 665–710.

Borsley, Robert D., and Robert Morris-Jones (2000) The Syntax of Welsh Negation. *Transactions of the Philological Society* 98:1, 15–47.

Borsley, Robert D., Maria-Luisa Rivero, and Janig Stephens (1996) Long Head Movement in Breton. In: Borsley, Robert D., and Ian Roberts (eds.) *The Syntax of the Celtic Languages: A Comparative Perspective.* Cambridge: Cambridge University Press. 53–74.

Borsley, Robert D., and Ian Roberts (1996) (eds.) *The Syntax of the Celtic Languages: A Comparative Perspective*. Cambridge: Cambridge University Press.

Borsley, Robert D.. and Janig Stephens (1989) Agreement and the Position of Subjects in Breton. *Natural Language and Linguistic Theory* 7: 407–427.

Borsley, Robert D., and Margaret Tallerman (1998) Phrases and Soft Mutation in Welsh. *Journal of Celtic Linguistics* 5: 1–33.

Brandi, Luciana, and Patricia Cordin (1989) Two Italian Dialects and the Null Subject Parameter. In: Jaeggli, Osvaldo, and Kenneth Safir (eds.) *The Null Subject Parameter*. Dordrecht: Kluwer. 111–142.

Brody, Michael (1999) Mirror Theory: Syntactic Representation in Perfect Syntax. *Linguistic Inquiry* 31: 29–56.

Burzio, Luigi (1986) *Italian Syntax: A Government-Binding Approach*. Dordrecht: Kluwer.

Calder, George (1990) *A Scots Gaelic Grammar*. Glasgow: Gairm Publications.

Cardinaletti, Anna (1990) Es, Pro and Sentential Arguments in German. *Linguistische Berichte* 126: 135–164.

Cardinaletti, Anna (1991) Subject/Object Asymmetries in German, Null-Topic Constructions and the Status of SpecCP. In: Mascaró, Joan and Marina Nespor (eds.) *Grammar in Progress: GLOW Essays for Henk van Riemsdijk*. Dordrecht: Foris. 75–84.

Cardinaletti, Anna, and Ian Roberts (1991) Clause Structure and X-Second. Ms., Universities of Venice and Geneva.

Carney, James (1979) Aspects of Archaic Irish. *Éigse* 17: 417–435.

Carnie, Andrew (1995) *Non-Verbal Predication and Head Movement*. PhD Dissertation, MIT.

Carnie, Andrew, and Eithne Guilfoyle (2000) (eds.) *The Syntax of Verb-Initial Languages*. Oxford/New York: Oxford University Press.

Carnie, Andrew, Elisabeth Pyatt, and Heidi Harley (2000) VSO Order as Raising out of IP? Some Evidence from Old Irish. In: Carnie, Andrew, and Eithne Guilfoyle (eds.) *The Syntax of Verb-Initial Languages*. New York: Oxford University Press. 39–60.

Cavar, Damir, and Christopher Wilder (1992) Long Head Movement? Verb Movement and Cliticization in Croatian. *Arbeitspapier* 7 (Institut für Deutsche Sprache und Literatur II) Johann-Wolfgang -von-Goethe Universität, Frankfurt am Main.

Cheng, Lisa Lai-Shen (1991) *On the Typology of WH Questions*. PhD Dissertation, MIT.

Chomsky, Noam (1957) *Syntactic Structures*. The Hague: Mouton.

Chomsky, Noam (1964) *Current Issues in Linguistic Theory*. The Hague: Mouton.

Chomsky, Noam (1965) *Aspects of the Theory of Syntax*. Cambridge, Mass.: MIT Press.

Chomsky, Noam (1981) *Lectures on Government and Binding*. Dordrecht: Foris.

Chomsky, Noam (1982) *Some Concepts and Consequences of the Theory of Government and Binding*. Cambridge, Mass.: MIT Press.

Chomsky, Noam (1986) *Knowledge of Language: Its Nature, Origin and Use*. New York: Praeger.

Chomsky, Noam (1991) Some Notes on Economy of Derivation and Representation. In: Friedin, Robert (ed.) *Principles and Parameters in Comparative Grammar*. Cambridge, Mass: MIT Press. 417–454.

Chomsky, Noam (1993) A Minimalist Program for Linguistic Theory. In: Hale, Ken, and Samuel Jay Keyser (eds.) *The View from Building 20: Essays in Honor of Sylvain Bromberger*. Cambridge, Mass.: MIT Press. 1–52.

Chomsky, Noam (1995) *The Minimalist Program*. Cambridge, Mass.: MIT Press.

Chomsky, Noam (2000) Minimalist Inquiries: The Framework. In: Martin, Roger, David Michaels, and Juan Uriagereka (eds.) *Step by Step: Essays in Honor of Howard Lasnik*. Cambridge, Mass: MIT Press. 89–155.

Chomsky, Noam (2001) Derivation by Phase. In: Kenstowicz, Michael (ed.) *Ken Hale: A Life in Language*. Cambridge, Mass: MIT Press. 1–52.

Chomsky, Noam, Adriana Belletti, and Luigi Rizzi (2000) *On Language and Nature*. Siena: University of Siena Press.

Chung, Sandra, and James McCloskey (1987) Government, Barriers and Small Clauses in Modern Irish. *Linguistic Inquiry* 18: 173–238.

Cinque, Guglielmo (1988) On *si*-Constructions and the Theory of Arb. *Linguistic Inquiry* 19: 521–581.

Cinque, Guglielmo (1994) On the Evidence for Partial N-Movement in the Romance DP. In: Cinque, Guglielmo, Jean-Yves Pollock, Luigi Rizzi, and Rafaella Zanuttini (eds.) *Paths Towards Universal Grammar: Studies in Honor of Richard S. Kayne*. Georgetown: Georgetown University Press. 85–110.

Cinque, Guglielmo (1999) *Adverbs and Functional Projections*. New York: Oxford University Press.

Clack, Susan (1993) Towards a More Nominal Verb-Noun in Middle Welsh. Talk given at the Linguistics Association of Great Britain Autumn Meeting, University of Wales, Bangor.

Clark, Robin, and Ian Roberts (1993) A Computational Approach to Language Learnability and Language Change. *Linguistic Inquiry* 24: 299–345.

Cocchi, Gloria (1995) *La Selezione dell'Ausiliare*. Padua: Unipress.

Comrie, Bernard (1977) In Defence of Spontaneous Demotion. In: Cole, Peter, and Jerrold Sadock (eds). *Syntax and Semantics VIII: Grammatical Relations*. New York: Academic Press. 25–55.

Cottell, Siobhan (1995) The Representation of Tense in Modern Irish. *GenGenP* 3: 105–124.

Davis, Henry (1998) *Person Splits, ϕ-features and Temporal Architecture*. Paper presented at the 21st GLOW Colloquium, Tilburg.

Déprez, Vivienne, and Ken Hale (1986) Resumptive Pronouns in Irish. *Proceedings of the Harvard Celtic Colloquium* 5: 38–48.

Diesing, Molly (1988) Bare Plurals and the Stage/Individual Contrast. In: Krifka, Manfred (ed.) *Genericity in Natural Language: Proceedings of the 1988 Tübingen Conference*. SNS-Bericht 88–42. Seminar für Natürlich-Sprachliche Systeme, Universität Tübingen. 107–154.

Diesing, Molly (1990) Verb Movement and the Subject Position in Yiddish. *Natural Language and Linguistic Theory* 8: 41–79.

Doherty, Cathal (1996) Clause Structure and the Modern Irish Copula. *Natural Language and Linguistic Theory* 14: 1–46.

Doherty, Cathal (1999) The Syntax of Old Irish Clause Structure. Ms., University College Dublin.

Doherty, Cathal (2000) Residual Verb Second in Early Irish: On the Nature of Bergin's Construction. *Diachronica* 17.1: 5–38.

Donati, Caterina (1996) *Elementi della Sintassi della Comparazione*. PhD Dissertation, University of Florence.

Duffield, Nigel (1995) *Particles and Projections in Irish Syntax*. Dordrecht: Kluwer.

Duffield, Nigel (1996) On Structural Invariance and Lexical Diversity in VSO Languages: Arguments from Irish Noun Phrases. In: Borsley, Robert D., and Ian Roberts (eds.)

The Syntax of the Celtic Languages: A Comparative Perspective. Cambridge: Cambridge University Press. 314–340.

Emonds, Joseph (1978) The Verbal Complex V-V' in French. *Linguistic Inquiry* 9: 151–175.

Emonds, Joseph (1980) Word Order in Generative Grammar. *Journal of Linguistic Research* 1: 33–54.

Fassi-Fehri, Absulkeder (1993) *Issues in the Syntax of Arabic Clauses and Words.* Dordrecht: Kluwer.

Ferraresi, Gisella (1997) *Word Order and Phrase Structure in Gothic.* PhD Dissertation, University of Stuttgart.

Freeze, Ray (1992) Existentials and Other Locatives. *Language* 68: 553–595.

Freeze, Ray, and Carol Georgopoulos (2000) Locus Operandi. In: Carnie, Andrew, and Eithne Guilfoyle (eds.) *The Syntax of Verb-Initial Languages.* New York: Oxford University Press. 163–184.

Friedemann, Marc-Ariel (1990) Le Pronom Interrogatif *Que. Rivista di Grammatica Generativa* 15: 123–139.

Friedemann, Marc-Ariel, and Tali Siloni (1997) Agr_{OBJ} is not $Agr_{PARTICIPLE}$. *Linguistic Review* 14: 69–96.

Fromkin, Victoria et al. (2000) (eds.) *Linguistics: An Introduction to Linguistic Theory.* Oxford: Blackwell.

Giusti, Giuliana (1993) *La Sintassi dei Determinanti.* Padua: Unipress.

Giusti, Giuliana (1994) Heads and Modifiers Across Determiners: Evidence from Rumanian. In: Cinque, Guglielmo and Giuliana Giusti (eds.) *Advances in Rumanian.* Amsterdam: John Benjamins. 103–125.

Giusti, Giuliana (1997) The Categorial Status of Determiners. In: Haegeman, Liliane (ed.) *The New Comparative Syntax.* London: Longman. 95–123.

Guasti, Marie-Theresa, and Luigi Rizzi (2002) Agr and Tense as Distinctive Syntactic Projections: Evidence from Acquisition. In: Cinque, Guglielmo (ed.) *The Functional Structure of DP and IP.* New York: Oxford University Press. 167–194.

Guilfoyle, Eithne (1990) *Functional Categories and Phrase Structure Parameters.* PhD Dissertation, McGill University.

Haegeman, Liliane (1996) Verb Second, the Split CP and Null Subjects in Early Dutch Finite Clauses. *GenGenP* 4.2: 133–175.

Haegeman, Liliane (2001) Antisymmetry and Word Order in West Flemish. *Journal of Comparative Germanic Syntax* 3.3: 207–232.

Haider, Hubert (1997) Precedence Among Predicates. *Journal of Comparative Germanic Linguistics* 1: 3–41.

Hale, Ken (1989) Some Remarks on Agreement and Incorporation. Ms., MIT.

Halle, Morris, and Alec Marantz (1993) Distributed Morphology and the Pieces of Inflection. In: Hale, Ken, and Samuel Jay Keyser (eds.) *The View from Building 20: Essays in Honor of Sylvain Bromberger.* Cambridge, Mass.: MIT Press. 111–176.

Harlow, Steve (1989) The Syntax of Welsh Soft Mutation. *Natural Language and Linguistic Theory* 7: 289–317.

Harlow, Steve (1992) Finiteness and Welsh Sentence Structure. In: Obenauer, H., and A. Zribi-Hertz (eds.) *Structure de la Phrase et Théorie du Liage.* Saint-Denis: Presses Universitaires de Vincennes. 93–119.

Hendrick, Randall (1996) Some Syntactic Effects of Suppletion in the Celtic Copulas. In: Borsley, Robert D., and Ian Roberts (eds.) *The Syntax of the Celtic Languages: A Comparative Perspective.* Cambridge: Cambridge University Press. 75–96.

Heycock, Caroline (1995) Asymmetries in Reconstruction. *Linguistic Inquiry* 26: 547–570.

Holmberg, Anders (1986) *Word Order and Syntactic Features in the Scandinavian Languages and English.* PhD Dissertation, University of Stockholm.

Holmberg, Anders (2000) Scandinavian Stylistic Fronting: How Any Category Can Become an Expletive. *Linguistic Inquiry* 31: 445–484.

Holmberg, Anders, and Christer Platzack (1995) *The Role of Inflection in Scandinavian Syntax.* New York: Oxford University Press.

Hooper, Joan, and Sandra Thompson (1973) On the Applicability of Root Transformations. *Linguistic Inquiry* 4: 465–497.

Hornstein, Norbert (1999) Movement and Control. *Linguistic Inquiry* 30: 69–96.

Huang, C.-T.-James (1984) On the Distribution and Reference of Empty Pronouns. *Linguistic Inquiry* 15: 531–574.

Huang, C.-T.-James (1989) Pro-drop in Chinese: A Generalized Control Theory. In: Jaeggli, Osvaldo, and Kenneth Safir (eds.) *The Null Subject Parameter.* Dordrecht: Kluwer. 185–214.

Huang, C.-T.-James (1993) Reconstruction and the Structure of VP: Some Theoretical Consequences. *Linguistic Inquiry* 24: 103–138.

Jespersen, Otto (1917) *Negation in English and Other Languages.* Copenhagen: Det Kgl. Danske Videnskabernes Selskab. Historisk-filologiske Meddelelser 1: 1–151.

Jonas, Dianne (1996) *Clause Structure and Verb Syntax in Scandinavian and English.* PhD Dissertation, Harvard University.

Kayne, Richard (1972) Subject Inversion in French Interrogatives. In: Casagrande, J., and B. Saciuk (eds.) *Generative Studies in Romance Languages.* Rowley: Newbury House. 70–126.

Kayne, Richard (1981) On Certain Differences Between French and English. *Linguistic Inquiry* 12: 349–371.

Kayne, Richard (1982) Predicates and Arguments, Nouns and Verbs. GLOW Newsletter.

Kayne, Richard (1983) Chains, Categories External to S and French Complex Inversion. *Natural Language and Linguistic Theory* 1: 107–139.

Kayne, Richard (1989) Null Subjects and Clitic Climbing. In: Jaeggli, Osvaldo, and Kenneth Safir (eds.) *The Null Subject Parameter.* Kluwer, Dordrecht. 239–261.

Kayne, Richard (1991) Romance Clitics, Verb Movement and PRO. *Linguistic Inquiry* 22: 647–686.

Kayne, Richard (1993) Towards a Modular Theory of Auxiliary Selection. *Studia Linguistica* 47: 3–31.

Kayne, Richard (1994) *The Antisymmetry of Syntax.* Cambridge, Mass.: MIT Press.

King, Gareth (1993) *Modern Welsh: A Comprehensive Grammar.* London: Routledge.

Koopmann, Hilda, and Dominique Sportiche (1991) The Position of Subjects. *Lingua* 85: 211–258.

Kratzer, Angelika (1994) *On External Arguments.* Occasional Paper 17, University of Massachusetts, Amherst.

Ladusaw, William (1979) *Polarity Sensitivity as Inherent Scope Relations.* PhD Dissertation, University of Texas, Austin.

Laenzlinger, Christopher (1998) *Comparative Studies in Word Order Variation.* Amsterdam: John Benjamins.

Laka, Itziar (1990) *Negation in Syntax: On the Nature of Functional Categories and Projections.* PhD Dissertation, MIT.

Larson, Richard (1988) On the Double Object Construction. *Linguistic Inquiry* 19: 335–391.

Lasnik, Howard (1981) Restricting the Theory of Transformations: A Case Study. In: Hornstein, Norbert, and David Lightfoot (eds.) *Explanation in Linguistics*. London: Longman. 152–173. [Reprinted in: Lasnik, Howard (1989) *Essays on Restrictiveness and Learnability*. Dordrecht: Kluwer. 125–146.]

Ledgeway, Adam (2000) *A Comparative Syntax of the Dialects of Southern Italy: A Minimalist Approach*. Oxford: Blackwell.

Lieber, Rochelle (1980) *On the Organization of the Lexicon*. PhD Dissertation, MIT.

Lieber, Rochelle (1983) New Developments in Autosegmental Phonology: Consonant Mutation. In: *Proceedings of the West Coast Conference on Formal Linguistics II*. 165–175. Stanford: Stanford Linguistics Association.

Longobardi, Giuseppe (1994) Reference and Proper Names. *Linguistic Inquiry* 25: 609–666.

Longobardi, Giuseppe (1996) The Syntax of N-Raising: A Minimalist Theory. Ms., University of Venice.

McCloskey, James (1979) *Transformational Syntax and Model-Theoretic Semantics*. Dordrecht: Kluwer.

McCloskey, James (1990) Resumptive Pronouns, A-bar Binding and Levels of Representation in Irish. In: Hendrick, Randall (ed.) *Syntax and Semantics XXIII: The Syntax of the Modern Celtic Languages*. San Diego: Academic Press. 199–248.

McCloskey, James (1991) Clause Structure, Ellipsis and Proper Government in Irish. *Lingua* 85: 259–302.

McCloskey, James (1992) Adjunction, Selection and Embedded Verb Second. Ms., University of California at Santa Cruz.

McCloskey, James (1996a) On the Scope of Verb-Movement in Irish. *Natural Language and Linguistic Theory* 14: 47–104.

McCloskey, James (1996b) Subjects and Subject Positions in Irish. In: Borsley, Robert D., and Ian Roberts (eds.) *The Syntax of the Celtic Languages: A Comparative Perspective*. Cambridge: Cambridge University Press. 241–283.

McCloskey, James (2000) Resumption, Successive Cyclicity and the Locality of Operations. Ms., University of California at Santa Cruz.

McCloskey, James (2001) On the Morphosyntax of Wh-Movement in Irish. *Journal of Linguistics* 37.1: 67–100.

McCloskey, James, and Ken Hale (1984) On the Syntax of Person-Number Inflection in Modern Irish. *Natural Language and Linguistic Theory* 1: 487–553.

Mahajan, Anoop (1994) Universal Grammar and the Typology of Ergative Languages. Ms., University of California at Los Angeles.

Maling, Joan (1990) Inversion in Embedded Clauses in Modern Icelandic. In: Maling, Joan, and Annie Zaenen (eds.) *Syntax and Semantics XXIV: Modern Icelandic Syntax*. San Diego: Academic Press. 71–91.

Manzini, Maria-Rita (1983) On Control and Control Theory. *Linguistic Inquiry* 14: 421–446.

Manzini, Maria-Rita, and Anna Roussou (2000) A Minimalist Theory of A-movement and Control. *Lingua* 110: 409–447.

Manzini, Maria-Rita, and Leonardo Savoia (forthcoming) *I Dialetti Italiani*. Bologna: Il Mulino.

Marantz, Alec (1984) *On the Nature of Grammatical Relations*. Cambridge, Mass.: MIT Press.

Marantz, Alec (1997) No Escape from Syntax: Don't Try Morphological Analysis in the Privacy of Your Own Lexicon. *University of Pennsylvania Working Papers in Linguistics* 4.2: 201–225.

Mohammad, Mohammad (1988) *The Sentential Structure of Arabic.* PhD Dissertation, University of Southern California.

Morris-Jones, John (1913) *A Welsh Grammar: Phonology and Accidence.* Oxford: Oxford University Press.

Morris-Jones, Robert, and Alan R. Thomas (1977) *The Welsh Language: Studies in Its Syntax and Semantics.* Cardiff: University of Wales Press.

Müller, Gereon (1998) *Incomplete Category Fronting.* Dordrecht: Kluwer.

Müller, Gereon, and Wolfgang Sternefeld (1993) Improper Movement and Unambiguous Binding. *Linguistic Inquiry* 24: 461–507.

Ndayiraije, Juvénal (2000) Strengthening PF. *Linguistic Inquiry* 31: 57–84.

Ó Siadhail, Michael (1989) *Modern Irish.* Cambridge: Cambridge University Press.

Penner, Zvi, and Thomas Bader (1995) *Topics in Swiss German Syntax.* Bern: Peter Lang.

Pesetsky, David (1982) *Paths and Categories.* PhD Dissertation, MIT.

Philippaki-Warburton, Irene (1985) Word Order in Modern Greek. *Transactions of the Philological Society* 2: 113–143.

Platzack, Christer (1987) The Scandinavian Languages and the Null Subject Parameter. *Natural Language and Linguistic Theory* 5: 377–401.

Platzack, Christer (1998) A Visibiltiy Condition for the C-domain. *Working Papers in Scandinavian Syntax* 61: 53–99.

Poletto, Cecilia (2000) *The Higher Functional Field in the Northern Italian Dialects.* New York: Oxford University Press.

Pollock, Jean-Yves (1986) Sur la Syntaxe de EN et le Parametre du Sujet Nul. In: Ronat, Mitsou, and Daniel Couquaux (eds.) *La Grammaire Modulaire.* Paris: Les Editions de Minuit. 211–246.

Pollock, Jean-Yves (1989) Verb Movement, Universal Grammar, and the Structure of IP. *Linguistic Inquiry* 20: 365–424.

Renzi, Lorenzo, and Laura Vanelli (1983) I Pronomi Soggetto in Alcune Varietà Romanze. In: *Studi linguistici in onore di Giovan Battista Pellegrini.* Pisa: Pacini. 121–145.

Ritter, Elisabeth (1988) A Head-Movement Approach to Construct-State Noun Phrases. *Linguistics* 26: 909–929.

Rivero, Maria-Luisa (1991) Patterns of V-raising in Long Head Movement and Negation: Serbo-Croatian versus Slovak. *Linguistic Review* 8: 319–352.

Rivero, Maria-Luisa (1994) The Structure of the Clause and V-movement in the Languages of the Balkans. *Natural Language and Linguistic Theory* 12: 63–120.

Rizzi, Luigi (1982) *Issues in Italian Syntax.* Dordrecht: Foris.

Rizzi, Luigi (1986a) Null Objects in Italian and the Theory of *pro. Linguistic Inquiry* 17: 501–557.

Rizzi, Luigi (1986b) On the Status of Subject Clitics in Romance. In: Jaeggli, Osvaldo, and Carmen Silva-Corvalán (eds.) *Studies in Romance Syntax.* Dordrecht: Foris. 391–419.

Rizzi, Luigi (1987/2000) Three Issues in Roman Dialectology. In: Rizzi, L. *Studies in Universal Grammar and First-Language Acquisition.* Routledge Leading Linguists. London: Routledge. 80–95.

Rizzi, Luigi (1990) *Relativized Minimality.* Cambridge, Mass.: MIT Press.

Rizzi, Luigi (1996) Residual Verb Second and the Wh-Criterion. In: Belletti, Adriana, and Luigi Rizzi (eds.) *Parameters and Functional Heads.* New York: Oxford University Press. 63–90.

Rizzi, Luigi (1997) The Fine Structure of the Left Periphery. In: Haegeman, Liliane (ed.) *Elements of Grammar.* Dordrecht: Kluwer. 281–337.

Rizzi, Luigi (1999) Some Issues in the Theory of Locality. Talk given at the workshop "Linguistic Theory: The State of the Art." Certosa di Pontignano.

Rizzi, Luigi (2000) Relativized Minimality Effects. In: Baltin, Mark, and Chris Collins (eds.) *Handbook of Syntactic Theory.* Oxford: Blackwell. 89–110.

Rizzi, Luigi, and Ian Roberts (1989) Complex Inversion in French. *Probus* 1: 1–39.

Rizzi, Luigi, and Leonardo Savoia (1991) Conditions on /u/ Propagation in Southern Italian Dialects: A Locality Parameter for Phonosyntactic Processes. In: Belletti, Adriana (ed.) *Syntactic Theory and the Dialects of Italy.* Turin: Rosenberg and Sellier. 252–318.

Roberts, Ian (1985) Agreement Parameters and the Development of English Modal Auxiliaries. *Natural Language and Linguistic Theory* 3: 21–57.

Roberts, Ian (1987) *The Representation of Implicit and Dethematized Subjects.* Dordrecht: Foris.

Roberts, Ian (1993) *Verbs and Diachronic Syntax: A Comparative History of English and French.* Dordrecht: Kluwer.

Roberts, Ian (1994) Two Types of Head Movement in Romance. In: Lightfoot, David, and Norbert Hornstein (eds.) *Verb Movement.* Cambridge: Cambridge University Press. 207–242.

Roberts, Ian (1998) The Syntax of Direct Object Mutation in Welsh. *Canadian Journal of Linguistics* 42: 141–168.

Roberts, Ian (1999) Verb Movement and Markedness. In: deGraff, Michel (ed.) *Language Creation and Language Change.* Cambridge, Mass: MIT Press. 287–328.

Roberts, Ian (2000) Head Movement. In: Baltin, Mark, and Chris Collins (eds.) *Handbook of Syntactic Theory.* Oxford: Blackwell. 113–147.

Roberts, Ian (2001) Language Change and Learnability. In: Bertolo, Stefano (ed.) *Language Acquisition and Learnability.* Cambridge: Cambridge University Press. 81–125.

Roberts, Ian, and Anna Roussou (2002) The Extended Projection Principle as a Condition on the Tense Depedency. In: Svenonius, Peter (ed.) *Subjects, Expletives and the EPP.* New York: Oxford University Press. 125–155.

Roberts, Ian, and Ur Shlonsky (1996) Pronominal Enclisis in VSO Languages. In: Borsley, Robert D., and Ian Roberts (eds.) *The Syntax of the Celtic Languages: A Comparative Perspective.* Cambridge: Cambridge University Press. 171–199.

Rohrbacher, Bernhard (1997) *Morphology-Driven Syntax.* Amsterdam: Benjamins.

Rögnvaldsson, Eiríkur, and Höskuldur Thráinsson (1990) On Icelandic Word Order Once More. In: Maling, J., and A. Zaenen (eds.) *Syntax and Semantics XXIV: Modern Icelandic Syntax.* San Diego: Academic Press. 3–40.

Roussou, Anna (1994) *The Syntax of Complementizers.* PhD Dissertation, University College London.

Roussou, Anna (2002) C, T and the Subject: That-t Phenomena Revisited. *Lingua* 112: 13–52.

Roussou, Anna, and Ian Roberts (2000) *Pou*-complements and Acc-*ing* constructions: A Comparative Analysis. In: Agouraki, Yoryia, et al. (eds.) *Proceedings of the Fourth International Conference on Greek Linguistics.* Thessaloniki: University Studio Press. 201–208.

Rouveret, Alain (1991) Functional Categories and Agreement. *Linguistic Review* 8: 353–387.

Rouveret, Alain (1994) *Syntaxe du Gallois: Principes Généraux et Typologie.* Paris: CNRS Editions.

Rouveret, Alain (1996) *Bod* in the Present Tense and in Other Tenses. In: Borsley, Robert D., and Ian Roberts (eds.) *The Syntax of the Celtic Languages: A Comparative Perspective.* Cambridge: Cambridge University Press. 125–171.

Rowland, Thomas (1853) *Rowland's Welsh Grammar.* Wrexham: Hughes and Son.

Sabel, Joachim (1999) On V-to-I Movement in German. Talk given at the University of Stuttgart.

Sadler, Louisa (1988) *Welsh Syntax: A Government-Binding Approach.* London: Croom Helm.

Santorini, Beatrice (1990) *The Generalization of the Verb Second Constraint in the History of Yiddish.* PhD Dissertation, University of Pennsylvania.

Santorini, Beatrice (1994) The Rate of Phrase Structure Change in the History of Yiddish. *Language Variation and Change* 5: 257–283.

Schafer, Robin (1994) *Nonfinite Predicate Initial Construstions in Modern Breton.* PhD Dissertation, University of California, Santa Cruz.

Shlonsky, Ur (2000) The Form of Semitic Noun Phrases: An Antisymmetric, Non N-Movement Account. Ms., University of Geneva.Sigurðsson, Halldor (1989) *Verbal Syntax and Case in Icelandic.* PhD Dissertation, University of Lund.

Siloni, Tali (1997) *Noun Phrases and Nominalizations.* Dordrecht: Kluwer.

Sportiche, Dominique (1998) Subject Clitics in French and Romance Complex Inversion and Clitic Doubling. In: Johnson, Kyle, and Ian Roberts (eds.) *Beyond Principles and Parameters.* Dordrecht: Kluwer. 189–222.

Sproat, Richard (1985) Welsh Syntax and VSO Structure. *Natural Language and Linguistic Theory* 3: 173–216.

Starke, Michal (2000) GROUP: Chains, X-bar, and Islands Are Facets of the Same Phenomenon. Talk given at the 23rd GLOW Colloquium, Victoria/Gasteiz.

Stenson, Nancy (1981) *Studies in Irish Syntax.* Ars Linguistica 8. Tübingen: Gunter Narr Verlag.

Stephens, Janig (1982) *Word Order in Breton.* PhD Dissertation, University College London.

Stowell, Timothy (1981) *The Origins of Phrase Structure.* PhD Dissertation, MIT.

Stowell, Timothy (1989) Raising in Irish and the Projection Principle. *Natural Language and Linguistic Theory* 7: 317–360.

Stump, Geoffrey (1984) Agreement vs. Incorporation in Breton. *Natural Language and Linguistic Theory* 2: 289–348.

Stump, Geoffrey (1989) Further Remarks on Breton Agreement. *Natural Language and Linguistic Theory* 7: 429–471.

Suñer, Margarita (1993) Indirect Questions and the Structure of CP. In: Campos, Hector, and Fernando Martinez-Gil (eds.) *Current Issues in Spanish Linguistics.* Georgetown: Georgetown University Press. 283–312.

Svenonius, Peter (2002) (ed.) *Subjects, Expletives and the EPP.* New York: Oxford University Press.

Tallerman, Margaret (1996) Fronting Constructions in Welsh. In: Borsley, Robert D., and Ian Roberts (eds.) *The Syntax of the Celtic Languages: A Comparative Perspective.* Cambridge: Cambridge University Press. 97–124.

Tallerman, Margaret (1998) On the Uniform Case-licensing of Subjects in Welsh. *Linguistic Review* 15: 69–133.

Tallerman, Margaret (1999) Welsh Soft Mutation and Marked Word Order. In: Darnell, Michael, Edith Moravcsik, Frederick Newmeyer, Michael Noonan, and Kathleen Wheatley (eds.) *Functionalism and Formalism in Linguistics.* Volume 2: *Case Studies.* Amsterdam: John Benjamins. 277–294.

Tallerman, Margaret (2001) A (Very!) Preliminary Look at Unaccusativity in Welsh. Talk given at the 8th Welsh Syntax Seminar, Plas Gregynog.

Thomas, Alan (1982) Change and Decay in Language. In: Crystal, David (ed.) *Linguistic Controversies*. London: Edward Arnold. 209–220.

Thurneysen, Rudolf (1892) Die Stellung des Verbums im Altfranzoesischen. *Zeitschrift für Romanische Philologie* 16, 289–371.

Thurneysen, Rudolf (1946/1980) *A Grammar of Old Irish*. Dublin: Dublin Institute of Advanced Studies.

Travis, Lisa (1984) *Parameters and Effects of Word Order Variation*. PhD Dissertation, MIT.

Trips, Carola (2001) *From OV to VO in Early Middle English*. PhD Dissertation, University of Stuttgart.

Tuttle, Edward (1986) The Spread of ESSE as a Universal Auxiliary in Central Romance. *Medioevo romanzo* 11: 229–287.

Vance, Barbara (1988) *Null Subjects and Syntactic Change*. PhD Dissertation, Cornell University.

Vance, Barbara (1997) *Syntactic Change in Medieval French*. Dordrecht: Kluwer.

Vanelli, Laura, Lorenzo Renzi, and Paola Benincà (1986) Typologie des Pronoms Sujets dans les Langues Romanes. *Actes du XIIe Congrès des Linguistique et Philologie Romanes*. Aix-en-Provence. 163–172.

Vikner, Sten (1994) *Verb Movement and Expletive Subjects in the Germanic Languages*. New York: Oxford University Press.

Vikner, Sten (1997) V-to-I Movement and Inflection for Person in All Tenses. In: Haegeman, Liliane (ed.) *The New Comparative Syntax*. London: Longman. 189–213.

Vincent, Nigel (1982) The Development of the Auxiliaries HABERE and ESSE in Romance. In: Vincent, Nigel, and Martin Harris (eds.) *Studies in the Romance Verb: Essays Offered to Joe Cremona on the Occasion of His 60th Birthday*. London: Croom Helm. 71–96.

Watkins, T. Arwyn (1991) The Function of the Cleft and Non-cleft Constituent Orders in Modern Welsh. In: Fife, James, and Erich Poppe (eds.) *Studies in Brythonic Word Order*. Amsterdam: John Benjamins. 329–351.

Willis, David (1996) *Syntactic Change in Welsh: A Study of the Loss of Verb Second*. PhD Dissertation, University of Oxford.

Willis, David (1997) P-Celtic. Ms., University of Oxford.

Willis, David (1998) *Syntactic Change in Welsh: A Study of the Loss of Verb Second*. Oxford: Clarendon Press.

Willis, David (2000) On the Distribution of Resumptive Pronouns and Wh-Trace in Welsh. *Journal of Linguistics* 36: 531–573.

Wurmbrand, Susanne (1999) *Infinitives*. PhD Dissertation, MIT.

Zanuttini, Rafaella (1991) *Syntactic Properties of Sentential Negation: A Comparative Study of Romance Languages*. PhD Dissertation, University of Pennsylvania.

Zanuttini, Rafaella (1997) *Clause Structure and Negation*. New York: Oxford University Press.

Zubizarreta, Maria-Luisa (1998) *Prosody, Focus and Word Order*. Cambridge, Mass: MIT Press.

Zwart, Jan-Wouter (1993) *Dutch Syntax*. PhD Dissertation, University of Gröningen.

Zwart, Jan-Wouter (1997) *The Morphosyntax of Verb Movement: A Minimalist Approach to the Syntax of Dutch*. Dordrecht: Kluwer.

Zwart, Jan-Wouter (2001) Syntactic and Phonological Verb Movement. *Syntax* 4: 34–62.

Zwicky, Arnold (1984) Welsh Soft Mutation and the Case of Object NPs. In: *Papers from the 20th Regional Meeting of the Chicago Linguistics Society*. 387–402.

Index